The Vegas Diaries

Also by Holly Madison

Down the Rabbit Hole

The Vegas Diaries

Romance, Rolling the Dice, and the Road to Reinvention

HOLLY MADISON

Some of the names and identifying details regarding certain characters have been changed in order to protect privacy. Any resemblance to persons living or dead resulting from changes to names and identifying characteristics is coincidental and unintentional.

HarperCollins books may be purchased for educational, business, or sales promotional use. For information, please e-mail the Special Markets Department at SPsales@harpercollins.com.

A hardcover edition of this book was published in 2016 by Dey Street Books, an imprint of William Morrow Publishers.

FIRST DEY STREET BOOKS PAPERBACK EDITION PUBLISHED 2017.

Library of Congress Cataloging-in-Publication Data has been applied for.

ISBN 978-0-06-245714-1

HB 06.09.2022

To Joe and Mama Irene

AUTHOR'S NOTE

First and foremost, thank you so much for deciding to come along on this journey with me. With *The Vegas Diaries,* my goal is to share with you a period of time that was very important to me and one that turned into the best time in my life up to that point. Chapter one begins in the spring of 2009. I was at my own personal rock bottom: I had just checked out of the Playboy mansion (which I talk about at length in my first book, *Down the Rabbit Hole*) and back into the real world and had gone through two back-to-back, and very public, breakups.

I chose to start over. I had no job, no leads, very few real friends, a mountain of mistakes behind me and a reputation as a reality show bimbo that was going to prove very hard to shake. I picked myself up off the ground, got out of town, and reinvented myself on my own terms.

It's this story of learning to find my confidence and self-sufficiency, set in the wild and crazy world of Las Vegas, that I want to share. Of course, no woman is an island and there are many people I interacted with over the three-year period I cover in this book. Some of them have chosen to live their lives in public view, others have not. It's not my intention to embarrass anyone and I have taken great care to disguise the identities of many of the players who shared this time with me. To that extent, some of the names you will see in the book are real. Others are pseudonyms, in which case identifying details have also been changed. To ease the flow of the narrative and to protect people's privacy, a few of the characters are composites. However, all of the events in the story are based on actual events. All of the stories you will read, how they affected me, and how they made me feel are true. This book is about me and the lessons I learned. People come in and out of our lives. We learn about them and we learn from them. I was fortunate to have all these characters come into my world when they did, because each and every one of them taught me something and contributed to my personal growth.

There comes a time in all of our lives where we have to roll the dice, take a chance, and start over. This was mine. Thank you again for joining me on this wild ride.

The Vegas Diaries

PROLOGUE

"The country here is rich and pleasant, but you must pass through rough and dangerous places before you reach the end of your journey."
—L. Frank Baum, *The Wonderful Wizard of Oz*

February 2002

The velvet curtain raised slowly, teasing the expectant audience, as a collective intake of air seemed to still the room. Inch by inch, a decadent pair of jaw-dropping red six-inch stilettos were revealed, illuminated by a soft spotlight. Attached to these glittering heels were two perfectly toned legs that, as the curtain continued to rise, seemed to go on for miles. Seductively wrapped in silky, sheer stockings, these glamorous, glistening gams existed in a world of their own.

It was my first introduction to the world of burlesque, and I was hooked.

Wrapped in a black vinyl dress that appeared to be painted on, a bouncing blond ball of energy had burst into a Playboy mansion buffet dinner and smacked a flyer in the middle of the table advertising a burlesque show. It was 2002 and a petite beauty named Stacy Burke began frequenting the infamous estate, where I was then living. Stacy was a popular fetish model, and in Los Angeles during that period of time, the fetish scene and the world of burlesque tended to overlap.

"It'll be fun, you really should come!" she repeated after meeting a bit of reluctance from Mr. Hugh Hefner. To say he was a creature of habit would be a wild understatement: He did the exact same things in the exact same order each week—and a Saturday-night cabaret show was not part of the usual agenda. Needless to say, I was surprised when Stacy's charming enthusiasm did the trick: Hef announced that we'd be diverting from our previously scheduled programming in order to attend this adult revue the following weekend.

The show, called *Swank*, was held at the El Rey Theatre—an art deco movie house built on Wilshire Boulevard in the 1930s, which had since been transformed into a live venue.

I wasn't sure what to expect from the show itself. I didn't know much about burlesque at the time and was just grateful that we were doing something that was a departure from our rigid routine.

Our group arrived a few minutes before showtime, and we were led to a VIP table near the stage. Moments after we took our seats, sensuous music started pouring through the speakers, filling the room with a tantalizing, sexy beat. A spotlight hit the center of the velvet curtains, signaling the start of the show.

Each enthralling act, one after the other, topped the last. I was spellbound, my eyes fixated on the seductive performers who seemed to keep the attention of everyone in the room with such graceful ease. There was a woman called Mistress Persephone, with her skin painted blue, performing as a Shiva-style goddess; a blond tassel twirler; and the headliner, an on-the-cusp-of-fame Dita Von Teese. The raven-haired beauty spun around the stage, dancing en pointe—a ruby-red-clad, jewel-box ballerina come to life.

Besides the obvious—the glamour and the sex appeal—there was something else that made this show utterly intoxicating: it felt like art. The skill and craft each entertainer brought to the table was undeniable. The costumes were just homespun enough to say: *I made this. This is my creation.* Every routine was so well-tailored to the individual performer that I had to believe each one was an original number. Every act showcased the artist's individuality. These performers weren't carbon copies of one another, far from it, and they were celebrated for their differences. Sitting around our VIP table was one bottle-blond fembot after the next, clad in some version of the same outlandish bustier, and all slightly dead behind the eyes. In burlesque, a woman could be both sexy *and* unique. In the world I was in, you were compared and judged on your ability to assimilate to a set standard of what made a woman attractive, all the while feeling ever so lucky if you were thrown a token compliment once in a while.

From that night on, burlesque became my obsession. I was desperate to see every show I heard about and read virtually everything I could find on the topic. Not having had any professional dance or stage experience, I didn't imagine taking up the art form myself, but as I learned a long time ago, sometimes fate has a funny way of putting things in your path.

During the second season of the E! reality series *The Girls Next Door*, Hef, the other two girlfriends, and I jetted off on a European press tour. This included a stopover in Paris and a visit to the iconic Crazy Horse, or "Le Crazy," as locals call it.

Located in one of Paris's most fashionable arrondissements, the venue was lit with a simple neon sign that read "Crazy Horse de Paris" above white canopy overhangs. After entering the red-carpeted lobby, we descended the darkened stairway into the self-proclaimed "sanctuary of glamour," an intimate cabaret filled with plush velvet chairs and banquettes swathed in the venue's signature "crazy red" color. As an usher escorted us to our seats, I asked her about the women who performed in the show. I was surprised to learn that every Crazy Horse dancer had to be classically trained in the art, and before even stepping onto the legendary stage, each woman was required to complete another round of rigorous training. This show was not for amateurs.

The lights dimmed and a video lit up across the curtain, showing a scene of the dancers preparing backstage in choreographed chaos. Suddenly the film went dark and the words "God Save Our Bare Skin" splashed across the sparkling curtain, which then lifted to reveal nine of the most flawless women I'd ever seen, wearing bearskins (the tall fur hats made famous by the Buckingham Palace guards) and bondage-inspired costumes that left little to the imagination. To the sound of a military beat, the dancers began stomping, kicking, and saluting their way through Crazy Horse's most iconic routine, showcasing their perfect figures and glowing skin.

The elegant women who graced the Crazy Horse stage didn't seem to be there merely to entertain an audience; rather, they created the illusion that we were their privileged guests, being offered a glimpse behind the luxurious veil of this private world. I was filled with admiration. Next to these gorgeous French burlesque dancers, I couldn't have felt any less appealing. These enchanting creatures were captivating, commanding, and mysterious, brimming with sexuality and sophistication. When the show ended, I jumped to my feet to give a standing ovation.

The usher reappeared to invite us backstage to sign the showroom's legendary guest book and to meet the show's producer. I couldn't stop raving to her about how much I enjoyed the production and how special I thought the entire experience was.

"How tall do the dancers have to be? Do you have a height requirement?" I asked.

"They are generally around five feet and seven inches," she replied in a velvety French accent. I was surprised. The way the tiny stage was framed, the dancers looked like Amazons! I would have guessed they were all at least five-nine.

"How old are the dancers . . . generally?" I continued my line of questioning, eager to find out what it would take for a girl to become one of these performers.

"Usually, as old as twenty-two," she answered.

"Aw, damn, I'm too old then," I said, only half joking.

"No, no, don't be silly," she said, quickly dismissing my resignation. "You could still do it," she continued with a smile. Even though I assumed she was just saying that to be nice, the seed was planted: I wanted to be a performer.

Never mind the fact that I didn't know how or when, or that it was completely incompatible with the short-leash lifestyle I was currently living at the mansion . . . I knew it was going to happen.

My love affair with burlesque was only beginning, but it wasn't just the art form that had enchanted me; it was the people who chose to pursue it. The independent women who used burlesque as an artistic outlet to celebrate their creativity and their femininity on their terms and in their own unique way. Deep down, that was who I wanted to be.

August 2008

"For my second number, I was thinking of doing a routine where I'm wearing nothing but paint and a pair of thigh-high leather boots, painting a giant six-foot canvas with just my body."

I paused, waiting for her reaction to my idea, but I had the distinct feeling that this woman had already heard it all.

"I like it," she encouraged, with a small but kind smile. The producer of the Crazy Horse Paris at the MGM Grand was the same woman whom I had met backstage in Paris a few years earlier. She was a graceful, put-together blond woman in her mid-forties wearing a fitted white T-shirt and a chic black blazer. She crossed one perfectly tailored denim leg over the other to reveal a pair of classic stilettos. She radiated confidence and success simply through the manner in which she conducted herself, and she didn't require obvious designer labels to showcase that.

Her straight shoulder-length hair fell around her face, framing her deep blue-gray eyes and high cheekbones. She looked equal parts European model and boardroom executive. I could easily have been intimidated by this woman, but there was a warmth to her that made me feel comfortable.

"Let's call that number 'Boots' for now, shall we?" She waited for me to nod in approval before turning to the show's choreographer, signaling her to take a note.

Our first meeting, as I was told, was intended to be a "creative discussion" about my possible guest spot with the show's producer, choreographer, and publicist—and I had prepared a list of ideas I thought were both provocative and original.

Weeks earlier, when I was contacted by the Las Vegas branch of the legendary Parisian cabaret, I couldn't believe it! Sure, I had dreamed about being in the production, but I never thought for a minute that they would actually want me to do a guest appearance. When I received the call, it immediately occurred to me that performing in a burlesque show could be a great story line for the next season of *Girls Next Door.*

The series was a huge blessing. Living at the mansion required adhering to a strict set of rules about what the girls could and could not do—but under the auspices of a "plot line for the show," I had been able to do things I wouldn't ordinarily have been able to, such as travel or accept jobs.

Soon, though, worrying about the rules was something that would no longer concern me. In August of 2008, after finally facing the reality that living in Hef's world was not all I wanted out of life, I made the sudden decision to leave him, the mansion, and *Girls Next Door* simultaneously, as quickly as one might pull off a Band-Aid. Naturally, I assumed I would have to abandon my Crazy Horse dream along with it. Why would the production be interested in me if I couldn't offer them some airtime?

"They know I'm not on the TV show anymore?" I asked cautiously when I was contacted to set up a creative meeting with the producers.

The associate kindly reiterated that they were interested in me, not in the reality show.

Eager to get out of L.A. for a bit and escape the tabloid and social scrutiny I was under in the wake of leaving Hef and the show, I happily agreed to fly to Las Vegas for the meeting. I didn't have representation yet and hadn't asked about compensation or what my deal would look like . . . but I really didn't care. They could have paid me nothing and I still would have wanted to do the show. Money was just money; what I wanted was a new project, life experience, and a career.

When we finally took our seats at Wolfgang Puck Bar & Grill inside the MGM Grand, I ordered a meal befitting an aspiring dancer: the chopped vegetable salad. The stylish producer ordered a plate of truffled potato chips with blue cheese sauce for the table, insisting they were absolutely to die for. But when the towering stack of house-made chips arrived, she plucked only one from the top before offering some to the choreographer, who declined. She explained that she was also a dancer in the show and didn't like to eat this close to showtime.

If only I had such restraint, I thought, desperately wanting to gobble up the whole plate of chips. It's not like I devoured handfuls, but I definitely made a dent in the pile.

I took a moment to study the woman sitting across from me. It wasn't just her discipline and manners that had me so enchanted. This woman was a different kind of sexy. She was dressed simply and modestly, covered nearly head to toe, but at the same time exuded such style—the kind that only a Parisian woman can pull off. How could it be that the same ensemble of jeans, white shirt, and black blazer could appear so plain on another woman, but on her it was undeniably polished? Was it the fit? The quality of the garments? Or perhaps just the way she carries herself when wearing them? I wondered if I could ever learn the secrets of how to possess *this* type of glamour.

I looked down at my own outfit: a flouncy black-sequined halter dress that exposed enough cleavage to be considered uncouth by most women, but for me, at the time, was de rigueur. Because the fabric was so light, I thought it was appropriate for daytime, but in reality, the average woman would have worn such a garment only to a nightclub. On my feet was a pair of delicate peep-toe black pumps with three thin, buckled straps running across the width. The women had complimented me on my shoes before we sat down, and that made me glow with pride. Even though it was chilly in the heavily air-conditioned restaurant, I stashed my black hooded jacket underneath the restaurant chair. I couldn't possibly wear a hoodie in front of these ladies! It just seemed so utterly gauche.

"And I *really* want to do 'Laser,' " I blurted out, referring to the "Lay Laser Lay" number that I had seen during my trip to the original outpost of the legendary Parisian cabaret. In the steamy routine, a woman with unbelievably long legs carefully balances herself on a tilted, rotating platform covered with billowing plumes of smoke. Under the light of a vibrant blue laser, the performer takes great care in rolling herself seductively around the revolving stage, looking as if she is climbing over her own body in a fluid dance to a bluesy song. The routine was tightly choreographed and required the flexibility of a gymnast. I was absolutely dazzled.

"Well, you see, that would be difficult," the producer explained, unintentionally bursting my rather large bubble. "Unfortunately, there are regulations here that prevent us from using those types of lasers on stage. And without the laser, the routine looks . . . shall we say, not very pretty?"

"I understand," I continued, crossing my legs and straightening my posture in an attempt to mirror the producer. "But I *love* that number; it's just *so* good! Do you think there is anything we could do to make it happen?"

"We can try, but I must warn you, the routine is quite difficult," she cautioned me.

It can be a blessing to be acutely aware of your limitations, for then you can adjust accordingly. I, for one, had no idea what my limitations were. As far as I knew, all the stars in the sky were ripe for the taking. I saw leaving the mansion as a second chance at life and looked at everything around me with delusionally optimistic eyes. Words of warning fell on deaf ears. I thought I could do *anything* if I worked hard enough, including master a lifetime of dance training in just a few weeks.

Even if we could have somehow managed to find a suitable laser substitute, the routine itself was incredibly demanding—and one that my inexperienced legs would never have been able to pull off. It speaks to the talent and artistry of the dancer I saw perform it that she made it look so effortless. Having an amateur dancer tackle such a feat would have required major changes to the choreography, thereby diluting the entire number. But I was wide-eyed and dangerously determined. Burlesque had become my goal, and I intended to achieve it. For my debut, only the most exciting, most tantalizing number would do!

"Well, Holly," the producer began, her tone warm yet professional, "this has been lovely. We look forward to ironing out all the details. Tell me, would you perhaps be available to spend some time training with our team in Paris?"

My mouth nearly hit the floor. Was she kidding? I was dying to go back to Paris!

"Yes, of course!" I exclaimed, unable to keep the collected composure I was trying so hard to sustain. It felt as if I was running off to join the circus, albeit a circus populated with the world's most beautiful women wearing custom-made Louboutin heels.

As we parted ways, the producer shook my hand and air-kissed each cheek before assuring me that we would be connecting again soon. With her team trailing behind her, she disappeared around the corner, out of the restaurant, and into the buzzing casino. Since my flight back to Los Angeles wasn't for a few hours, I figured I should explore the property and get the lay of the land. After all, I was hoping the resort would be my next place of employment. In an attempt to navigate the casino unnoticed, I threw on my sweat shirt, zipped it up to the top, and pulled the hood over my blindingly blond locks. I walked to where the restaurant's tile met the casino floor and took a light step onto the whimsically patterned red carpet.

At the time, the MGM Grand was the world's largest hotel, clocking in at 380,000 square feet and boasting 6,852 rooms. The casino building alone was as wide as four football fields, and I was standing somewhere near the center. I felt a bit lost, but I didn't care. I was headed nowhere and everywhere.

I passed by the Crazy Horse theater, adorned with a black-and-gold-trimmed facade, a replica of the original at 12 Avenue Georges V. I imagined that the next time I saw the venue, I would be coming straight from the airport, having completed my training in Paris.

Weaving through a maze of blinking slot machines, I nearly collided with a petite cocktail waitress holding a tray of drinks. I wandered past focused blackjack players, bustling crowds engulfing craps tables, and a jovial group of tourists cheering over a game of baccarat. Every corner boasted either a gourmet restaurant promising a once-in-a-lifetime culinary experience or a sleek modern ultra lounge. And just when I thought I'd seen it all, I stumbled upon an enormous rock exhibit, partitioned off with floor-to-ceiling glass walls, that was the resort's Lion Habitat. One of the lions slept peacefully on a rock, one leg dangling over the edge. I meandered a bit more before realizing I was even more lost than when I started.

Casinos aren't meant to be easy to navigate. They are laid out so as to take customers through a confusing maze of distractions and temptations. It's a technique, a trick of the trade. The more time you spend on the casino floor, the more money you are likely to part with. It is in the casinos' best interest to keep players at the tables for as long as possible, which is why there are no clocks, no sense of night or day, and free drinks for anyone who is gambling.

Wandering through the casino, I went unrecognized, as most people were absorbed in their games. It was so unlike Los Angeles, where paparazzi and tabloid culture seemed to have taken over the entire city. With the news of my split with Hef flooding the magazines and blogs, I thought about how nice it would be to come to Vegas for a while. I needed to get away if I was ever going to make a fresh start. Nothing was really holding me to L.A. anymore.

Las Vegas appeared to be a land without judgment. It didn't matter how campy or strange you might be, Vegas seemed like a place where an outsider like me could really thrive. *Living here would be such an adventure,* I thought. Part of me knew I needed to make up for things I had missed in my twenties. I needed to explore who I was, learn to be self-sufficient, and date like a normal person. Instead, I had spent the better part of the last decade adhering to curfews and living someone else's life. I wanted to be free . . . and also finally be able to pursue a career of my own.

The more I thought about it, Las Vegas really did seem like the perfect backdrop for my new world. Ever since I officially announced my departure from *Girls Next Door*, I'd been casually speaking with the network about the possibility of my own spin-off, but because I lacked anything firm on the horizon either professionally or personally (think: new job, new man, or a baby), they weren't sold on the idea. No one could imagine a Holly Madison who wasn't somehow tied to Playboy, even if it was just as a photo editor. *If everything worked out with Crazy Horse, wouldn't my new showgirl life in Sin City be a unique premise for a series?* I thought, already pinning the image to my mental vision board.

Years earlier, I had been hesitant about participating in *Girls Next Door*, but I quickly learned its innate value. It wasn't what I had set out to do with my life, but reality TV was popular at the time and with it came attention and opportunity. If I could continue to do it for a little while, I knew it could buy me some time while I decided what I wanted to do next. Plus, my own television series would offer me a platform that would allow me to reinvent myself in front of viewers who knew me only as

Hef's former girlfriend (a label I was extremely anxious to lose). For some reason it wasn't enough that I reinvent myself *for myself.* I needed to prove it to everyone who said it couldn't be done.

Being known as a Playboy bunny and as someone's ex had created a chip on my shoulder. As much as I tried to ignore it, it was always there, lurking just under the surface. And when you're in Las Vegas and happen upon a rather large chip, you know what they say you should do with it? Bet big. And that's exactly what I planned to do.

I finally arrived at a circular area on the west side of the building that appeared to be the end of the road. On one side of the circle, a set of glass doors led outside to the corner of Las Vegas Boulevard and Tropicana Avenue. On the opposite side was the sports book. To my left was a Rainforest Café, just a few steps from the entrance to the resort's nightclub.

In the center of the area lay a large circular bar resting on an elevated platform just a few steps up off the casino floor. The column in the center reached toward the ceiling and was covered with countless glimmering bottles. It was still too early for a cocktail, but it looked like an inviting place for a soda, at the very least.

"Can I get you something to drink?" a stout bartender asked me, raising his eyebrows as he dried a pint glass.

"I'll have a Diet Coke, please," I said with a smile.

He slid the fizzy drink over to me as I looked up at the giant domed ceiling above the bar. It was plain, had a sort of gray pall, and looked like it had been built as a projection screen of some sort. *That's odd,* I thought.

"You know," the bartender began, attempting to make some friendly bar chatter, "that ceiling you're looking at used to be part of the old *Wizard of Oz* display we had here. It was for the tornado show."

He must have noticed the glimmer in my eye, because he added with an all-knowing smirk, "Actually, this bar sits on top of what used to be the start of the yellow brick road."

"Really?" I asked, genuinely intrigued. I had a soft spot for all things kitsch. "Why'd they get rid of it?"

"The bosses just wanted to get rid of all that kiddie stuff, I suppose." He shrugged, picking up a rag and drying another glass. "When this casino opened in '93, Vegas was trying to make itself a family destination." He laughed to himself. "Guess they figured out the Strip ain't a family kind of place."

"Wow," I said quietly. I was fascinated by these bits of trivia. Las Vegas was barely a hundred years old, but it had such an intriguing history, one that I was eager to know more about.

"Don't be too surprised," the bartender quipped. "Las Vegas is the queen of reinvention: the people, the places . . . heck, even the city itself.

"The *Wizard of Oz* motif had a good run here, but themes, eh, they can't last forever," he continued. "You got to give guests a reason to come back, to see something new. You know?"

He caught my gaze as I nodded in agreement.

"Could I get the check, please?" I asked politely. "I lost track of time and have to get to the airport." I was suddenly anxious to get home; I had a lot to think about.

"Sure thing," he said as he moved to print out my bill. "You know that show the *Folies Bergère*?" he continued casually, referring to the traditional showgirl extravaganza at the Tropicana. "Word is, they're gonna be closin' up shop soon. Longest-running show on the Strip, that was. Fifty years!" he exclaimed, shaking his head.

"Why are they closing?" I asked, my eyes wide with curiosity. This was the business I was about to get into, after all.

" 'Cause it's Vegas," he said with a shrug as he turned to swipe the credit card I had set down in front of him. "It's always 'on to the next.' People want bigger, they want better, they want newer. Like I said . . ." he continued, shaking his head, "Las Vegas is the queen of reinvention."

He turned back toward me, check in hand.

"Good luck," he said, pausing to look down at the receipt, "Miss Madison"—reading my name from the paper—"on wherever your journey takes you."

Chapter 1

"But how about my courage?" asked the Lion, anxiously.

"You have plenty of courage, I am sure," answered Oz. "All you need is confidence in yourself. There is no living thing that is not afraid when it faces danger. True courage is in facing danger when you are afraid, and that kind of courage you have in plenty."

—L. Frank Baum, *The Wonderful Wizard of Oz*

March 2009

Is my laundry molding in the washing machine? I wondered, still not daring to move.

The trip to Paris to train with the Crazy Horse dancers never happened. I didn't run off to join the glamorous French circus, and my dreams of beginning a new life as a showgirl in Las Vegas had fallen flat. Instead, I was sprawled out on a simple black couch in a tiny Santa Monica condo. My muscles were so sore that I couldn't even drag myself the few feet toward the closet that housed my single-unit washer and dryer. As I lifted my head off the cushion, the bright late-afternoon sun poured into my eyes like floodlights. I didn't have any curtains to block it out.

After my initial meetings with Crazy Horse Paris, seven months earlier, I began dating a Las Vegas magician, Criss Angel. Initially I intended for the relationship to be casual, but I quickly (and foolishly) fell much deeper than I meant to.

Within weeks he talked me into moving into his suite at the Luxor to become his much-publicized girlfriend and the relationship quickly took a more controlling turn, resulting in me declining the Crazy Horse Paris opportunity. I knew this was a mistake, and it was then that I realized I had to break it off. I had found myself once again in an all-consuming relationship, similar in many ways to the one I had just left behind.

Every inch of my body hurt. Though I had just taken an hour-long nap, I was still exhausted. I woke up in a panic as the alarm went off on my phone. *What was I supposed to be up for?* I wondered. I had turned my life upside down more than once over the past few months, so sometimes it took a couple of seconds for me to recall where I was and what I was supposed to be doing.

When I remembered that my alarm had been set for a friend's party and not a work obligation, I calmed down.

I was just a few weeks into my first job as a newly single woman. Just five days before its premiere, I had been asked to compete on the eighth season of *Dancing with the Stars*, filling in for an injured contestant. Having the chance to appear on this show was a dream come true! I had been a huge fan of the program for years. There was no question that I had to make it my top priority. I poured myself into the rehearsal schedule, which consisted of grueling eight-hour days, five days a week, with performances the other two days. I felt like I was training for an Olympic competition.

Can I even get on my feet for this party? I asked myself.

When I had returned to my new home earlier that day, I flopped down on the couch for a nap, lacking the energy to even climb the spiral staircase to get to my bed. I had committed to a short snooze, hoping I would feel up to that evening's festivities after a little rest.

My close friend (and former housemate) Bridget Marquardt was hosting a premiere party for her new Travel Channel show *Bridget's Sexiest Beaches*. I had told her that I would come to support her, but I was struggling to gather the strength. My body felt like a punching bag. I spent the next few minutes psyching myself up for the one chore I knew I had to do: moving my car. Earlier, I had forgotten the remote control for my garage door and just parked on the street, but during rush hour it became a tow-away zone, and that was a headache I did not need.

I was really proud of Bridget and wanted to celebrate this moment with her, but I felt like shit. Also . . . the party was happening at the mansion. I wasn't particularly keen on returning to our formerly shared home, even if it was to support a friend.

I bundled myself up in my hoodie, wrapping the hood tightly around my face (hoping to go unnoticed by any of the uninvited paparazzi that had taken up residence outside my apartment), and headed to my car. Before pushing the front door open, I threw on a pair of sunglasses. I was in no condition to be photographed. Quickly I slipped out the door, made the short walk, and climbed into my car. I was already around the corner before any photographers realized I had come out. As soon as the garage door was open just wide enough, I zoomed through and arrived safely to my parking spot without a single photo having been taken. *Victory!* I thought, raising my arms. Just then a pain shot through my side like a bulldozer. I had bruised my ribs in rehearsal that week. I felt like my body was falling apart.

I took my BlackBerry out of my pocket and started typing. I composed a text message to Bridget, apologizing for not being able to make it to her party and congratulating her on her success.

I hesitated before hitting send. Was I *certain* I couldn't make it? I hated the idea of flaking on her, but I knew she'd be surrounded by a ton of well-wishers, including her handsome new boyfriend, and I needed every extra minute of sleep I could find. *Dancing with the Stars* had offered me a lifeline when I needed it most. I couldn't *not* give this opportunity my full focus.

Just a few weeks earlier, I had hit my own personal rock bottom when I left Criss, which was the second of two particularly dramatic back-to-back breakups. After the first breakup, I knew I was in for a period of readjustment. After all, I was stepping out into the real world after spending all of my post-college life in the surreal world of the Playboy mansion. I thought things could only go up when I walked out the door, but my subsequent relationship quickly proved me wrong and I once again found myself picking up the pieces from a relationship that had sapped both my freedom and my self-worth.

Still, my head and my heart were at odds. While it was clear to me (or to my brain, anyway) that getting out of those relationships was the smartest thing I could have done, my heart was still hurting. To add insult to injury, I felt defeated. Immediately after the breakup, I had no job and no leads. It was demoralizing. So I did the only thing I could: I scraped up all my courage and committed myself to starting over . . . again.

But I knew I couldn't operate without a plan. I needed to specifically pinpoint what I wanted for my life before I could go about the business of getting it done. The first thing I had to do was get out from under the shadow of Playboy. I couldn't take myself seriously if for the rest of my life, I trotted around with "former girlfriend" written across my forehead. I was determined to find success on my own. Failure wasn't an option. The day I arrived back in L.A., I began making a list of things that I wanted to achieve.

The first thing I wrote down was "Compete on *Dancing with the Stars*." I had long dreamed of competing on the series. *Dancing* was incredibly popular, so much so that people were clamoring to be contestants. For reality stars and more niche pop-culture personalities, *DWTS*, with its primetime slot, became a platform to reach a wider audience.

Second, I wrote: "Perform in Crazy Horse Paris." I hoped I could reopen the conversation we started a few months earlier and that it wasn't too late to make the guest appearance happen. I still had a fascination with burlesque, and diving into a new project that would require discipline and hard work was just what I needed. For me, the more focus something required, the more determined I became. Learning a challenging art form completely new to me would help give me the self-confidence I needed to feel myself come alive again.

Finally, I added: "Develop my own reality show" to my short list. It makes sense to do what you know—and I knew the "reality" world. *Girls Next Door* had provided me with some great opportunities, and there was no reason to think that a similar show wouldn't do the same. Plus, at the time, having your own reality series was considered a major coup—for personalities and pop-culture fixtures, it was a real sign that you had made it.

Well, when you put your hopes and dreams out into the world, you never know who might be listening. My phone rang the very next morning; it was a producer from *Dancing with the Stars. Holy shit,* I thought. This was beyond eerie! It had been less than twelve hours since I'd written down my goals . . . and now the network was reaching out to me! The producer explained that a contestant slated to compete on the show had been injured and they were searching for a last-minute replacement for their premiere on Monday (which was only five days away). I had interviewed with the producers about being on the program more than once already, but had never been chosen. I was afraid I never would be, as rumor had it that *Dancing* didn't want to commit to having me on the show because they didn't think Middle America would accept me due to my association with Playboy. In hindsight, I think my persistence paid off. They offered me the final spot for season eight, most likely figuring that I was the only person who wanted the chance badly enough to agree to perform on live television with less than a week to prepare. The other contestants had been rehearsing their routines and learning technique for a month; I was given exactly four days. I had my work cut out for me, but this wasn't an opportunity I was going to squander.

I read the text message to Bridget again, then sighed and hit send. Weeks earlier I would have been totally confident strolling into the mansion battered and bruised from rehearsals, wearing sweat pants and a ponytail. However, these days I wasn't exactly popular with the Playboy folks. While typical ex-girlfriend decorum required that the former flames continue to coo over Hef and, in turn, he extended them an open-door policy to the mansion (whether that was for sentimental reasons, damage control, or both, I've never been sure), I was no longer interested in being told how to behave, which meant that my Playboy stock had fallen very low. I was certain that they would have turned me away for something as insignificant as a dress-code violation.

Bailing on a friend was shitty, but I believed it would be best for me to stay as far away from my old life as possible—for everyone involved. I was quickly learning who from that world was a genuine friend and who wasn't. One person I was still close with was the mansion's executive secretary, Mary O'Connor. In fact, I stayed at her house in the Valley whenever I had time to drive out there. She was a loyal friend to Hef, but that didn't stop her from being a good friend to me as well. In fact, I had been insulated from the outside world (and outside people) for so long that Mary was one of the few people I had left. She was also one of my only confidantes, so she understood me and never tried to talk me into coming back to the mansion.

But otherwise, my new life was lonesome, and being lonely was a new feeling. Granted, I had been "alone" in a relationship for years, but being without any of the social swirl I had become accustomed to felt strange. It was uncomfortable to be alone with my own thoughts—I wasn't emotionally ready to process what the last seven years of my life had been about. I was just desperate to move forward. When I exited the television series, along with my life at Playboy, most of my so-called friends took it as a signal to cut ties with me. I no longer had access to the Playboy party invite list and couldn't offer any camera time, so I suppose I no longer served a purpose. It was a rude (but necessary) awakening.

Through the grapevine, I heard Hef was over the moon that I was back from Las Vegas and occasionally staying with Mary. I was certain he viewed my return as a sign of failure, as if I couldn't make it on my own and staying at Mary's was one step closer to my inching my way back behind the gates. The truth was, I just wanted to be surrounded by people who actually cared about me. Mary's warm, cozy home made me feel safe, unlike my modern, empty Santa Monica loft.

Hef and his minions had already made a plan for my future: returning to the mansion for season six of *The Girls Next Door.* I was told it was what the network wanted. It was what the viewers wanted. It was what Hef wanted. But no one seemed to care that it wasn't what *I* wanted.

Not only did I feel like my ex-boyfriend was not so subtly rooting for me to fail, but it seemed as if there was an entire army of people gearing up for what they thought was my inevitable meltdown. When *DWTS* came along, I saw it for what it was: a life raft. Here was a chance to get a ton of exposure (at the time, *DWTS* was one of the most watched shows on television, second only to *American Idol*) and some positive publicity *and* to make good money. But most important, it was an opportunity to start fresh and the first step toward reintroducing myself to a world of people who only thought they knew me.

The stakes were high for me and the pressure was tremendous. During rehearsals, it wasn't always easy for me to hold it together. And at times it was impossible. There were plenty of "bathroom breaks" that were really excuses for me to cry in private when I could no longer hold back the tears. Emotions and memories are fickle beasts. You never know when they're going to pop up, and when you're working your body to the point of exhaustion, it's even easier to let your guard down. Even though my dance partner, Dmitry Chaplin, could not have been more of a gentleman, just being that close physically to a man brought back painful memories. It was hard for me to act "passionate" in the Latin dances that required it. The intense, manipulative, and overly possessive relationships I had been in recently made me feel a tremendous guilt and shame for even *acting* like I was into a guy. It was as if I was afraid of being called a slut simply for dancing with my partner. That's how out of whack I was.

I was facing all my fears at once. All the judgment that I had known was waiting for me the moment I left the mansion (which had, for so long, made me too scared to leave) was now hitting me square in the face. One moment I felt exhilarated by the opportunity to be on *DWTS*. In the next moment I was trembling; terrified that I'd make a fool of myself and prove the naysayers right.

It was a shitty feeling, knowing there were so many people out there waiting for the "spoiled gold digger" and "reality-show bimbo" to fall flat on her face in front of millions of viewers. I wasn't any of those things; I knew it in my heart . . . but that wasn't enough. I needed to prove it to everyone else, too. I know that caring what other people think about you is a huge waste of time, but I was so hurt by all the hate that using it as motivation to better myself was the only way I knew how to deal with it. I would be a success on my own terms. I would make something of myself despite the labels and criticisms. No one was going to tell me what I could and couldn't do. No one else was going to decide for me.

When message boards would fill up with comments like "She can't take these dance rehearsals because she never had to work a day in her life," it only fueled me further. I didn't grow up a spoiled rich girl. Far from it! Like many people, I juggled jobs to make ends meet throughout high school and college. Even after I had made the deal with the devil and moved into the Playboy mansion I hung on to my waitressing job until I was pressured to give it up. I only (barely) kept my sanity because I was able to carve out opportunities to keep busy, whether it was as one of the mansion's tour guides or working my way up to the role of a *Playboy* magazine photo editor. These people spewing hurtful comments from behind the safety of their computer screens had no idea what my life was like, but felt justified in judging it all the same.

Dancing with the Stars was a chance to try and prove myself as something other than "Girlfriend Number 1." It was sink or swim. For the first time in a long time, I felt in charge of my future—and I had great plans for my life.

I jumped out of my car, invigorated, temporarily forgetting how sore my muscles were. I took the elevator back to my condo to get myself into bed early. I had a full day of rehearsals and filming the next day—and I was ready to kick ass.

FIRST I APPLIED THE nude-colored flower-shaped "petal" pasties. Next I placed a stick-on bra cup over each breast. After these were secure, I stepped into the form-fitting two-piece costume covered with swinging beaded fringe and sparkling red Light Siam Swarovski crystals. The costume included a fully padded Victoria's Secret bra sewn into it for an extra level of coverage. In less than sixty minutes I was going on live television in front of millions of viewers to be twirled, tossed, and tangled—and the network was not interested in the possibility of a nip slip. It was modesty by any means necessary, which was, for me, a refreshing change of pace.

I looked in the mirror to inspect my makeup. The show's amazing hair and makeup team had transformed me, giving me red-lipped, Gwen Stefani–inspired makeup and a cascade of straightened platinum extensions. I was thrilled with my appearance! Two weeks prior, I had my first spin in the *Dancing* makeup chair and had been shocked by the amount of makeup they applied. *I look fifty!* I thought with alarm, scared shitless that I would look like a weathered, aged-before-my-time tart on my debut episode. However, I quickly learned that they knew exactly what they were doing. Under the lights, on TV, and in the context of "ballroom," the look worked perfectly. By the time I was in my third week, I looked forward to seeing what the *Dancing* glam team had in store for me. In addition to hair and makeup, contestants were also given a complimentary spray tan each week, then sponged down with additional pigment each day of taping. Finally, a shimmery gold bronzer would be applied after the second layer dried. It sounds excessive, but looked perfect on-camera.

I was in week three of the competition and Dmitry and I were tackling the samba (by far the most difficult dance I learned during my run). My final move of the number essentially had me doing a backbend over my partner's bent leg. Every time we rehearsed the move, I would slam my rib cage into his thigh and it soon began to bruise. The more we rehearsed, the more painful the injury became. And since I didn't have any time to recover, I was exacerbating the injury daily. By now it actually hurt to breathe! There was no time to feel sorry for myself, though. I had dreamed of competing on this show for years, and damn it, I was going to enjoy it!

The evening of the competition, Dmitry and I joined the rest of the contestants in a room behind the stage. I found an empty corner where I could stretch and start warming up. The camaraderie among the dancers and contestants was really something special. Everyone was friendly and supportive of one another. There was no snobbery or meanness.

"Hey, Holly, do you have a Twitter account?" one of the publicists from the show asked as I leaned down, folding myself on top of my legs.

"No, I don't," I answered. "That's the thing that Ashton Kutcher and Demi Moore are doing, right?" I asked, remembering I read a blurb about it in *People* magazine.

"Yeah, everyone's doing it now," the perky PR lady told me, with a sense of forced urgency. "We're asking all the contestants to make an account so they can tweet about the show!"

Twitter had only just become a thing in popular culture. Celebrities were starting to create accounts as a means of connecting with fans and friends. When it first appeared, hashtags weren't hyperlinked, *tweet* wasn't a verb, and no one I knew personally used it.

I agreed to set up an account, posted my first tweet, and then forgot all about it.

I'll never use that again, I thought. How wrong I was!

Just as I put my phone back in my purse, it was our turn to step out under the lights, cameras, and the gaze of the studio audience. Dmitry and I danced our samba, which went by in a fast-paced blur. We stepped back into the holding room after pausing in front of the judges to hear their feedback, feeling exhilarated. All the other contestants were incredibly encouraging, applauding and telling us what a great job we did, even though I knew my technique was sorely lacking (our mediocre scores told me that the judges agreed).

Heading home that night, I was acutely aware that my fate on the show was in limbo. The next day would be that week's elimination episode, and I was frightened that I would be the one to get axed. I went straight to bed, trying to put the fear and anxiety out of my mind.

I hoped for the best, but prepared myself for the worst. During the elimination episode, the contestants and dancers lined up on the ballroom floor. One by one, each couple was declared "safe" and the remaining pool quickly got smaller. I held my breath during each dramatic pause, waiting to hear the outcome. The only thing I could liken it to was being picked last in gym class—but with the entire country watching! From the beginning I was well aware that the odds were never in my favor, but I still hoped to last as long as I could. Each week on *Dancing* brought with it a ton of press attention. The mirror-ball trophy was never going to be mine, I knew that going in. I even expected to be eliminated early . . . but not this early! My goal was to make it at least a third of the way through the competition, which I was so close to doing. I promised myself that if I got just one more week on the show I would make it count.

The elimination came down to two couples: Dmitry and me and Denise Richards and Maksim Chmerkovskiy. The lights turned red and the background music changed to the sound of a loud-thumping heart. No pressure!

I looked down at the floor, anxiety washing over me like a tidal wave, waiting to hear that I was going home.

"Holly and Dmitry . . . you are safe!"

I looked up and let out a huge sigh of relief. I gave Dmitry a big hug; I could tell he was relieved, too. Before I started celebrating, I quickly reminded myself that my safety meant another person's departure. Denise had to be bummed, and I didn't want to rub it in her face, so I kept my expression in check. I turned to Denise and hugged her as well. It couldn't be easy. I know I wasn't looking forward to my turn being eliminated! But I wasn't focusing on that now. I had been given another chance . . . and that's what I needed to concentrate on.

"You looked like you *wanted* to be sent home," my publicist insisted. The show had wrapped, and we decided to grab a drink at a nearby Italian restaurant.

"*Of course* I didn't want to be sent home!" I assured him. "I just didn't want to look like I was gloating."

"I'm not sure that's how it's going to look to the viewers," he quipped, eyebrow raised.

Well, shit, I thought. When it came to most forms of communication, my radar was almost always off. Even my facial expressions communicated the wrong thing. What I assumed was a gracious reaction to my fellow contestant being eliminated probably read more like me not wanting to continue on for another week. For as long as I can remember, I've always been awkward in social situations. Some people are blessed with the ability to navigate these scenarios with ease; I am not one of those people. It was even more reason to get back to rehearsals and work my ass off. Working hard was the best way to show how grateful I was.

"I need to book my next job before *Dancing* is over," I told my publicist. "I'm not going to last much longer, and I need to capitalize off of this publicity while I can." Even with the rigorous rehearsal schedule, I still managed to find time for meetings and auditions. When *DWTS* came to an end—and I never knew which week would be my last—I had to be prepared, racing against the clock to line up my next act. The show provided a much-needed boost to my public profile, while also allowing audiences to see me in a different light. I needed to maximize the momentum. In addition to talking with a few networks about the possibility of my own TV show, I was being considered to headline a major Las Vegas burlesque revue—a dream come true! In fact, this one (called *Peepshow*) was a larger, bigger budget production than *Crazy Horse Paris* and was offering a three-month contract as opposed to a guest appearance that would last just a few weeks. Apparently my run on *DWTS* had inspired this new show's producers to reach out. I dove headfirst into preparing for my audition and figured that if it didn't work out, I would then reach out to *Crazy Horse.* I was careful not to count my chickens before they hatched, as according to industry gossip, a few higher profile names were being considered for this particular project.

Surely they'll want Brooke Burke, I thought. *Everyone loves her.* When I heard Lindsay Lohan was in the running, I was convinced I didn't stand a chance. I couldn't imagine a star with the potential to garner more publicity than Lindsay at that time.

Callbacks for *Peepshow* had me traveling back and forth between Las Vegas and L.A. fairly regularly. *Dancing* was even supportive enough to fly Dmitry and a camera crew out to the desert to allow me to do my rehearsals there before my meetings. During one such trip, I had a hosting engagement scheduled at Privé nightclub. Upon my arrival, the nightclub assigned me a VIP host, a person responsible for making sure everything went smoothly and to take care of anything I might need. Nancy, an energetic twentysomething with a raspy voice and sparkling brown eyes, greeted me at the private Planet Hollywood hotel entrance with a bellhop and keys to my suite.

"Welcome to Vegas!" she beamed. She was tall and thin, with an olive complexion and vivacity to spare. "I'm Nancy."

Nancy wore her hair in a shiny black bob that fringed under her chin. Smoky eyeliner accentuated her almond eyes, and two or three leather bracelets wound up around her wrist to where they met the pushed-up sleeve of a worn motorcycle jacket that was cropped short enough to show off her tiny waist. I thought she was really pretty and had a sexy, Joan Jett vibe about her.

"We're so happy to have you here! How was your flight? Any issues? And the car service? Did everything work out for you? Oh, please, let me . . ." She stuck her phone in her back pocket and lunged toward my suitcase as I tried to collapse the handle down.

"Oh, thanks!" I said as she handed it off to the luggage attendant.

"You like champagne?" she asked. "Of course you do! Who doesn't like champagne? Let's go get some good stuff. My treat."

As a VIP host, Nancy was responsible for keeping me occupied, happy, and entertained. It was the kind of "only in Vegas" career that cropped up to fulfill a need in the hospitality market. Las Vegas nightclubs were cash cows. Over the years, the savviest owners came up with the perfect recipe for maintaining high traffic and relevancy in this tourist-driven desert town: one part celebrity and two parts press, with a dash of sex and a twist of exclusivity. Owners began offering bigger and bigger paydays for celebrities to "host" events at their nightclubs, which drew huge crowds for that specific evening (with high cover charges and even higher bottle-service minimums) and also generated a good amount of media attention. When tourists flocked to Las Vegas for its emerging nightlife scene, they wanted to party at the same places where people like Christina Aguilera and Usher hosted fabulous parties. As these sorts of events became more and more frequent, people recognized that wrangling, managing, and placating some of these celebrities, as well as the big-spending VIPs, was a job in and of itself. Hence Nancy. Her job was to make me feel like I was the queen of Las Vegas for the short duration of my stay there. Anything I could possibly want was only a phone call away, and everything I would need was already accounted for. Nancy's guests never arrived at a restaurant before their table was ready, and they had only the best items on the menu; they never waited for a town car, constantly had a fresh cocktail in hand, and always attended the best parties, seated at the best table. How could I argue with that? So when Nancy asked if I wanted to join her for a show that night before dinner, I accepted immediately. Even though I had been planning on taking a nap in my suite, Nancy's energy gave me a second wind.

When we got to the showroom, I followed Nancy as she bulldozed her way through the crowd and into our seats, trying my best to keep up with her as all eyes were on the two women who were walking in at the last minute. When we finally got to our row, Nancy had already bounced back up to grab drinks from the lobby. Instantly, the stunning redhead with porcelain skin seated next to me caught my eye. She tossed her long auburn mane over her shoulder, revealing a touch of décolletage and dramatic cat-eyed eyeliner. She was wearing leather pants that appeared to be painted on, gorgeous black boots, and a black cashmere sweater that draped perfectly on her slim figure.

She hissed at me from a few seats away.

"Psssst," she half whispered. "Want a cigarette?" She mouthed the words while putting two fingers to her lips to emulate a drag.

"Sorry," I said, smiling. "I don't smoke." *Wait, can you even smoke in here?* I wondered. Something about this woman made me nervous—in a good way. I got the distinct impression that things *happened* when she was around, and I was craving as much *happening* as possible.

Several scenes later, she leaned toward me with a groan. "I'm dying for an excuse to ditch this guy," she whispered, not so subtly gesturing to the clueless-looking man next to her.

"The show's almost over. Maybe you can lose him in the crowd," I suggested. "Are you staying here?"

"Nah," she said, pulling a cigarette out of her purse and lighting it up. "I have a place nearby. I just moved here from Texas," she said, pausing to take a long drag. "I came with him tonight because I thought it would be a good time, but I'm over it."

No sooner had she finished her first inhale, security was headed our way. She squished the butt under her boot and held up her hands as if she were being seized at gunpoint. All I could think about was the cigarette burn scarring the red soles of those $4,000 boots. The guard gave her a stern look before returning to his post.

For some reason, I was fascinated by this woman, despite her having the worst theater etiquette ever. Just like Vegas itself, she had captured my attention.

"I'm Hannah," she whispered, reaching her now-cigarette-free hand toward me.

"Holly," I whispered back, meeting her grasp. "Hey, I'm going to dinner with a few people before this club appearance I'm doing. You want to join us?"

"Sure," she said with a shrug. "Why not?"

After the show, Nancy led us quickly through the crush of people exiting. As predicted, getting out of the showroom was a nightmare, so we easily lost Hannah's companion. With a swipe of a card, Nancy slipped us into a private hallway and out of the madness.

"Well, isn't this nice?" Hannah commented, with a sly smile. Nancy shot Hannah a cutting look—at least I thought she did—as she turned the corner into a brightly lit stairwell, then quickly turned on a radioactive smile as she began her ascent. *Was she annoyed I asked Hannah to join us?* I wondered. *Noooo. Why would Nancy care?* Maybe the madness of the crowd was just putting her on edge.

"Ladies, we're not tourists," Nancy purred, her gravelly voice echoing off the concrete walls. She pushed open a set of heavy doors to the outside. A luxury town car was waiting for us right in front of the exit. *Nancy really did think of everything,* I thought, impressed at the ease with which she navigated this town. *Did she know the secret escape routes from all the buildings?* I wondered, laughing to myself. For most visitors, Vegas could be a tough city to traverse, but Nancy made everything so simple.

Whipping around corners and through stoplights, the car zipped through the back streets of the sprawling MGM Grand property and drove across Harmon Avenue to get to Planet Hollywood's valet entrance.

The newly renovated hotel sparkled like a bright yellow diamond. The glittering Planet Hollywood sign ran across the top of the resort, beckoning to me like a beacon. Ironically, local legend had it that the resort was cursed, haunted, and perhaps even built atop a native burial ground, but to me, it looked like nothing but opportunity. At the time, Planet Hollywood was the most energetic, youthful-feeling resort on the Strip. While many of Vegas's casinos still reeked of stale cigarette smoke that hung underneath the low ceilings and settled onto the clothes and hair of their mainly fifty-plus demographic, Planet Hollywood looked like the vibrant new toy in a box filled with dusty old relics.

The property originated as the Aladdin in 1966, quickly gaining a reputation as one of Vegas's most famed casinos with its giant illuminated golden genie lamp and opulent Arabic décor. When Elvis Presley married Priscilla at the property in 1967, it cemented its status in history as one of Las Vegas's most iconic hotels.

Throughout the following three decades, the property was plagued with a series of criminal investigations, loan defaults, and bankruptcies, leading to the legend of the "curse." But that didn't stop the resort from continuing its expansion, first with a twenty-story hotel tower in 1971, and again in 2000, when the tower was imploded and rebuilt as a 2,500-room, multi-tower hotel. A giant shopping mall was also added to the resort, along with a massive Strip-side facade featuring a faux mountainside and Moorish architecture.

But just as the MGM bartender had warned me, all Vegas novelties eventually grow stale. In 2007, the establishment dropped the Arabic theme, opting for a more modern, contemporary feel, rebranding the resort as Planet Hollywood.

Though the rooms were decorated with pieces of movie memorabilia, such as a hoverboard from *Back to the Future Part II* or Dorothy's dress from *The Wizard of Oz*, the era of theme-heavy hotels had long since passed. Resorts were instead opting to capitalize on creating "luxury experiences" for guests, or, for some lesser quality hotels, "luxury adjacent" motifs. The casino itself boasted a six-story atrium, the entrance to which was lined with sparkling floor-to-ceiling chandelier columns.

Nancy, Hannah, and I walked over the bustling modern casino floor covered in deep reds and shimmering golds and took the escalators up to the mezzanine level, which housed the resort's VIP check-in, nightclub, showroom, and its finest restaurants. Strip House, where we were having dinner, was just a few feet away from Privé, the nightclub where I was hosting. Nancy smiled at the restaurant's hostess and walked straight past her into the dimly lit, velvet-drenched steakhouse. As she led us back to our table, we passed walls covered in vintage boudoir photos and flocked wallpaper. The candlelight bounced off the glass door Nancy opened as she led us into the private dining area. Already there waiting for us were my publicist, my manager, and my friend Angel Porrino. Angel was an adorable, friendly blonde, a Las Vegas native whom I met when she came to Los Angeles for a centerfold audition.

As I introduced Nancy and Hannah to the table, Angel stood up to shake Hannah's hand.

"Oh, my god, you're pregnant!" Hannah exclaimed. "I would have never guessed! You look so tiny! I couldn't see your bump until you stood!"

"Ha-ha, thanks!" Angel laughed in her cute high-pitched voice. "It's nice to meet you."

"So, the other day, I learned a new word," Hannah said, rapidly putting the attention back on herself, "*Blumpkin.* Anyone care to guess what that means?"

"I have a feeling I might not want to know," one of the men at the table responded, jokingly.

He probably didn't. Angel and I (as well as Hannah, apparently), loved gross-out humor, but I had a feeling this word might not go over well with everyone present. Hannah took a seat next to Angel at the far end of the table and leaned in toward her to show her something on her phone. I could tell by the laughter that followed that these two had hit it off right away. I decided that I definitely wanted Hannah as part of my new Vegas family.

"I thought you hated doing club appearances?" Angel asked me, brushing her long, dark blond hair out of her face, innocently unaware that Nancy worked with the venue.

"Usually I do, but I have a feeling tonight will be different," I said with a smile and a reassuring nod toward Nancy, who was now fiercely hanging on every word exchanged. "After all, you guys are here," I added, gesturing around the table.

Club appearances and hosting opportunities were commonplace among public personalities. Everyone from Jude Law to Britney Spears turned a few bucks showing up to a nightclub for a few hours, but for me, there was something soul-crushing about the ones I had done so far. Sure, they paid well, but they also made me feel isolated and adrift. When I left the mansion, I was already feeling very emotionally unstable and unsure of whom I could trust. Flying all over the country by myself, only to sit alongside some nightclub liaison I barely knew, just exacerbated my feelings of loneliness and insecurity. Not to mention, I was surrounded by strange men in random venues, so the thought of even having a single drink felt unsafe to me. During these appearances, you are expected to look like you are partying it up. The best I could do was a bit of dancing while ferociously clutching a Red Bull (too fearful of getting roofied to let it out of my sight for even a moment). While I knew I was fortunate to have the opportunity to make good money for basically doing nothing, my soul craved something with a bit more substance. Luckily, *DWTS* came along, so I had been able to put all hosting engagements on ice for a while.

"So, if you get *Peepshow*, how long do you think you want to live in Vegas?" Angel asked me. She knew I was determined to land the part and was looking forward to my potential move. I didn't have a huge support network, so I was extremely grateful for her encouragement.

"About four years," I blurted out, realizing I hadn't really given it much thought. I had been on survival mode ever since I left the mansion, thinking about what my next few steps would be and how I would stay afloat, not really thinking about a long-term plan.

As Angel nodded her head, I asked myself, *Why four years?* Where had that number come from? Was it a biological clock thing? I was thirty. Had I subconsciously noted that a woman's egg quality drastically drops off at thirty-five, so I should be starting a family and moving on to the next chapter by then? After all, I always knew that I would want a family someday.

Or was it my hunger to recapture some of my lost years? People always reminisce fondly about the social importance of their time in college. People often refer to that time as the best years of their lives, a time when they met their closest friends and made some of their favorite memories. When I was in college, I chose not to socialize, instead concentrating on getting good grades so I could transfer to a better school and keep my scholarships. Even before finishing my education, I moved into the mansion with its bizarre rules and strict parameters. Needless to say, the wild college experience had never been mine. Is that why four years was such an instinctive time frame? I didn't have the answer, but I decided that it sounded (and felt) right. I had four years to get my shit together. It seemed like a fair amount of time to figure out my life, learn to stand on my own two feet, and have a little fun along the way, and Vegas seemed like the perfect place to do that. I needed to find myself in the process, and only after I did that would I allow myself to consider moving back to Los Angeles.

As we were finishing our meal, a towering twenty-five-layer chocolate cake arrived at our table at Nancy's insistence. After a few bites—okay, more like half the cake—I left the restaurant with my guests and hugged Angel good-bye.

"By the way," Nancy asked as Angel walked toward the escalators, "what *is* a blumpkin?"

"I'm gonna let you google that," Angel said with her megawatt smile. "It's pretty gross," she added with a giggle.

Nancy shrugged her shoulders and motioned for us to follow her across the mezzanine. She led our group over to the nightclub's back entrance to begin the evening's festivities.

Once we were settled in our booth, I felt comfortable enough to have a few drinks, for the first time in a long time. For a photo op, the servers carted out a giant cake with "Vote for Holly" scribbled across the top in chocolate frosting, accompanied by a giant chocolate Playboy bunny. Inside, I cringed. I understood that Playboy was my claim to fame, but I was eager to put my bunny past far, far behind me. To outsiders, Hef's and my split was amicable and I seemed to revel in being identified as a "bunny." How could they possibly know any different when they were only sold the sugarcoated fairy-tale version of events?

Quickly I shook it off and enjoyed this fabulous reintroduction to the nightclub scene as we partied at the club into the wee hours. Nancy introduced me to a few acquaintances of hers, some Vegas residents and others regular visitors. One man in particular stood out. Eric was a handsome, impeccably dressed, dark-haired gentleman with piercing brown eyes, who sent me a bottle of Dom after we were introduced. Once we had spent the required two hours at the club, Nancy brought us out for a tour of the casino. At around four A.M. Hannah and I found ourselves at a popular blackjack table in the high-roller lounge. I had a stack of chips in front of me, playing a second hand for the man to my right, when he got a little too comfortable and started rubbing my back. My spine immediately stiffened. Reading my mind, Hannah jumped up from her spot across the table and yanked me away.

"Time to get back to the suite!" she announced, putting on her heaviest Texas drawl complete with a dramatic drunken slur. "And leave these motherfuckers behind!" These guys didn't seem like pushovers, but I think they knew better than to mess with this southern firecracker who looked capable of causing a major scene.

"Thanks for the rescue," I said, yawning as we navigated our way through the crowded casino floor.

Waking up the next morning, I was happy to find myself safely in bed and grateful to Hannah for getting me back to my room. Less than twelve hours after meeting her, she had already proven herself an invaluable wingwoman. I grabbed my phone to text her my thanks when I realized she had already beat me to the punch.

"I am amongst the living!" read the message. It was attached to a photo of Hannah swathed in a fluffy white robe with her wild red hair swirled into a sexy, bedheady nest on top of her head. She was wearing sunglasses and had a Corona in hand. From the looks of it, she was in the courtyard of a luxurious penthouse suite high above the Vegas Strip.

"Where are you?" I replied immediately. I waited for my phone to light up with her response, but nothing. She was clearly off on an adventure.

The next morning, I was back in L.A. and driving to rehearsals when I heard my phone buzz. Hannah had apparently spent the night in Elvis's legendary penthouse suite at the top of the Las Vegas Hilton with Brendan Williams, one of the most notorious billionaire high rollers ever to grace Vegas with his presence.

"Call me," I quickly shot back.

Seconds later my phone buzzed, and before I could even say hello, she was already diving right in.

"You have *no* idea," she began. I could hear her exhaling her cigarette from across the line. "There was this huge party and there were girls everywhere in that suite," she said, drawing out the word *everywhere*. "But he only wanted me." Pause for a drag. "He gave me sixty thousand dollars to gamble with . . . and I won."

"Holy shit!" I shouted.

"The safe in my closet is overflowing with cash," she added nonchalantly. Soon I would learn this was all for Hannah's amusement, because she actually didn't need the money. Hannah's family had plenty of it. "Her" house was actually one of a few that belonged to her parents and wasn't so much a house as it was a compound. This fortress consisted of two giant buildings linked by an underground tunnel, as well as a garage warehouse that held a fleet of cars. The only time I would ever see these vehicles was in Hannah's garage, because she always chose to drive a beat-up Mercedes. She was bold, but not flashy. In some ways, she kept a surprisingly low profile, which was novel to me because I had spent most of my adult life surrounded by L.A. women whose sole mission in their existence was to become famous. Hannah's family would probably have disowned her if she had ended up in the gossip pages or on the entertainment news sites or, God forbid, a reality show. Which was a shame, because she would have been really entertaining.

I HAD RETURNED TO L.A. with one thing on my mind: the Argentine tango. Of all the numbers I learned on *Dancing with the Stars*, this one was by far my favorite. Dmitry and I had a blast practicing the routine, which included an exciting new move where I basically twisted up like a pretzel and flipped out of it into a standing position.

Even though it was the one I loved the most, it was also the number that wound up getting me eliminated. When we finally performed our tango on live TV, I slipped. Literally. At the start of the performance I slid off the barstool we used as part of the dance. I froze for a few brief seconds before jumping back into the number, but that small pause cost us the precious points we needed to advance and we fell to the bottom of the leaderboard. In the end this was an invaluable lesson that every performer needs to learn—the show must go on!

Merely being able to compete on *Dancing with the Stars* at all had been a dream come true; advancing for four weeks into the season was icing on the cake! Considering the fact that I was a last-minute addition, I felt my run on the show was a success—and it was a nice feeling to be proud of myself for a change. As I grabbed my dancing shoes and walked off the lot, I set my sights on my next challenge: lining up a project before returning for the show's season finale. I had eight weeks to pull this off. Luckily, *Dancing*'s popularity meant a sea of press opportunities in the wake of my elimination.

Only a few hours after the show wrapped, I was put on a red-eye to New York to do talk shows and radio broadcasts to promote *DWTS*. The following week, I had a handful of magazine interviews and photo shoots lined up as well. The first was an "at home" feature in my Santa Monica loft, but nothing could have felt less homey.

Perched on a rented piano bench, I adjusted the fifties-style full skirt that covered most of my legs but was cinched tight enough at the waist to flatter my figure (which was smaller than normal due to the last few months of intensive rehearsal). The photographer was snapping away as I put on my best demure smile, trying to exude confidence in my role as a newly single woman.

"Do you really keep this stuff?" someone sneered out of nowhere, dangling a magazine article on the current romantic status of each *Girls Next Door* alum between her thumb and forefinger. I was taken a bit off guard as the woman held the clip far from her body, as if she was carrying a bag filled with dog shit. One of the assistants on the shoot had made herself a little too comfortable in my home. In my head, I wanted to tell her it wasn't appropriate to go through someone else's personal things, but I was taken aback and at the time didn't have the balls to say what I was thinking to this stranger who had just insulted me in my own home.

"Um, yeah," I responded, meekly, pretending to keep my focus on the shoot.

"Ick," she said, with her nose scrunched up. She tossed the clipping back down on my desk. The page consisted of three photos: Kendra Wilkinson and her then-fiancé Hank Baskett; a photo of Bridget and her boyfriend Nick Carpenter; and a picture of me and Criss. The corresponding headlines read like this: "Engaged!" "Still Going Strong!" and "Split!" The latter of course referring to my excruciatingly public failed relationship. It did seem like a strange clipping for me to have around, but at that time, I had just started showing up in magazines and it was still a novelty for me. Even though *The Girls Next Door* had been a hit series for many years, we had been kept carefully sheltered and it wasn't until *after* I left the mansion that anyone ever wrote about me.

Regardless, I was embarrassed that she saw the clipping. I was still suffering from a very broken heart and a pretty bruised ego. Recently, I had told a reporter from *People* magazine that I was "never dating again." After the relationships I had been in, I meant it!

The difference between my life and Bridget's and Kendra's was striking, at least in my opinion. Both of my former housemates had landed other TV shows before the fifth season of *Girls Next Door* had even wrapped. The plan for *GND* season six had been to follow Hef's and my relationship, my work at the studio, and the women that were photographed there. That is, until I had my epiphany and finally left.

On top of snagging TV shows, both of my former castmates also seemed to find themselves in happy relationships with men who wanted them despite the stereotypes that clung to us. It would be easy to assume I was jealous of them, but nothing could have been further from the truth. Their successes gave me hope! Sure, I no longer had the support of Playboy, but I needed to follow my own path and not compare myself to anybody else. There are always consequences for going against the grain, but I was readying myself for the fight.

When the photographer and his assistants wrapped up and left, I went about the business of putting my loft back together. As much as I didn't want to admit it, stress was getting the best of me. As I arranged some coffee-table books, I noticed my hands shaking a little. In less than six months, I had barreled through two dramatic breakups, two moves, and the exciting but rigorous *Dancing with the Stars* schedule.

I looked out my giant windows onto the cloudy "May gray" Los Angeles landscape. Being in L.A. spurred so many memories—often unwanted and not so pleasant. During dance rehearsals, I had lost myself in the work. I was diligent and determined. But at the end of the day, when I was finished, the physical exhaustion left me vulnerable to everything that I wasn't ready to deal with. The finale of *DWTS* was quickly approaching. I knew I needed to keep myself busy until then. I felt like I had to get out of Los Angeles to make a fresh start and get my head screwed back on straight. Honestly, the only time I could remember feeling free lately was during my occasional trips to Las Vegas. I prayed that I would land *Peepshow* so that I would have an excuse to go there. Vegas was calling me home . . . and there was no place like it.

Chapter 2

At once there came running at her from all directions a pack of great wolves. They had long legs and fierce eyes and sharp teeth.
—L. Frank Baum, *The Wonderful Wizard of Oz*

The Eiffel Tower glittered outside my massive floor-to-ceiling windows.

Okay, so it wasn't the *actual* Eiffel Tower, but it would do just fine. The giant metal structure's bright lights reflected across the night sky, awakening the city. Las Vegas came alive after dark, and having always been a night owl myself, I loved that about my new home. Los Angeles was always steadfastly asleep by two A.M. any day of the week.

Landing the part in *Peepshow* had been a dream come true. For weeks, I sat nervously waiting for the phone call. I knew I wasn't the only person they were speaking to and they were deep into auditions with a few other women (some of whom I thought would *for sure* get the part over me), but I embraced the power of positive thinking. I tried to keep myself as visible as possible, doing as much press as I could, in hopes that I would soon get the news I so desperately wanted. And when I finally did, I was absolutely on cloud nine. I couldn't believe that I had actually been chosen! I knew timing had a lot to do with it. Being on *Dancing with the Stars* was such a huge publicity push, and I would be debuting in *Peep* just a month after my season of *Dancing* wrapped.

Peepshow was still new to Las Vegas, but had already established itself as something special, winning rave reviews and the support of the community. The origins of the show go back to 1993, when the show's creator and director, Jerry Mitchell, wanted to do something special to raise money for AIDS research. The disease had heavily affected the Broadway community he was a part of. Along with four other dancers, he put together and performed a sexy show at a New York City nightclub called *Splash*. The event was an instant hit, generating an around-the-block line to get in, a spontaneous second performance, and $8,000 for Broadway Cares/Equity Fights AIDS.

With that success, the show he dubbed *Broadway Bares* became an annual tradition, which would grow bigger, raise more money, and move to successively larger venues. The program attracted Broadway's top talent to lend their time, year after year, both on the stage and behind the scenes.

Each year the production would adopt a new theme, and the eighth year the theme was a naughty take on nursery rhymes. They called that edition *Peep Show*. Eventually Mitchell started workshopping a full-length sexy revue tailor-made to be a permanent Las Vegas show, inspired by the concept of *Broadway Bares*'s burlesque vignettes.

The show was picked up by Planet Hollywood and given an approximately $20 million budget. Broadway's best were brought together to create the lavish costumes, sets, theater design, choreography, original music, and so on. Most of the cast was brought from New York on six-month contracts to open the show. The best of everything was required to create a modern take on the traditional French-inspired spectacles that were brought to Vegas in the 1950s, like the *Lido*, *Folies Bergère*, and *Minsky's Follies*. It was the type of entertainment that had become synonymous with the city but had all but disappeared by 2009. The only such extravaganza that still survived in Vegas was *Jubilee!*, which had been running for an impressive twenty-eight years. As most of the other burlesque shows in town were smaller budget productions in tiny theaters, *Peepshow*'s updated version of a Vegas tradition was welcomed by the community with open arms.

I was completely blown away the first time I saw *Peepshow*. It was such an entertaining, elaborate production. I was totally mesmerized. From the inventive routines, the talented performers, and the sheer quality of every element of the show, it was something special that I wanted to be a part of.

When I was finally offered the *Peepshow* contract, I was ecstatic to see it included a plush two-bedroom high-roller suite at Planet Hollywood to call home, complete with a view of Paris—the hotel, anyway. Before bed, I would curl up on my blue damask sofa and stare out at the dazzling, flashing lights. Whoever had occupied the suite before me had left behind a book about the history of Las Vegas. I devoured it in a single sitting, discovering that the desert city was a sort of phoenix rising from a small spring and managing to survive solely on its residents' ingenuity and determination. Initially, the town site was established as a railroad stop between Salt Lake City and Los Angeles. When the railroad boom failed to last, the residents tried to reinvent the town as an agricultural and mining center, but struggled until the 1930s, when the city became popular during the construction of the nearby Hoover Dam. Not only did the thousands of workers brought in to build the dam flood Las Vegas, but tourists who wanted to catch a glimpse of this "eighth wonder of the world" stopped by the city as well. In anticipation of the dam's completion (and the exodus of workers), the community was prepared. Las Vegas reinvented itself as "the last Western town," with most of the city's casinos hastily adopting the Old West theme. Legalized gambling was now the major draw. In the 1940s, more upscale hotels began appearing on the Strip, turning the city into a true resort destination. While Las Vegas's economy was more secure than ever before, that didn't stop the community from continuing to reinvent itself in order to keep visitors coming back. Resorts began offering amenities and attractions as a means of getting a leg up on the competition, each attempting to outdo the next. Soon these hotels began boasting elaborate concerts, firework shows, and even theme parks built inside the casinos. Las Vegas didn't play by the same set of rules as the rest of the world.

Over a hundred years, many different schemes went boom and bust. But the city never gave up. It just kept reinventing itself. That spoke to me. Las Vegas was not a city born of happenstance; its people made something out of nothing. Being in the middle of my own personal reinvention, I could relate.

I took to hotel living like a fish to water. What wasn't to like? I had a plush suite, twenty-four-hour room service, butler and housekeeping services, and there was always an around-the-clock party happening downstairs. After getting the contract, I packed up my Santa Monica loft, put it on the rental market, and moved to Las Vegas permanently.

However, despite the energy of the casino below brimming with people, my suite felt a little lonely. I had an extra room, so I offered it to one of the few Playmates I kept in touch with, Laura Croft, who was living in Florida at the time. She had told me, just a few months earlier, that she wanted to move to Las Vegas. Before accepting, she had one request. Planet Hollywood had been so generous already, but would they let my new roommate bring her dog? Kindly, the powers that be agreed and Laura was on the next flight to Sin City—with her shih tzu, Farnell, and a suitcase full of whimsical Betsey Johnson dresses. Laura was a button-nose beauty with thick brown hair and an insatiable hunger for all things adventurous. I thought she'd be a perfect addition to this little family I was creating around myself, including Hannah, who was chronically unpredictable; Angel, with her positive spirit and warm, magnetic energy; and Nancy, who I'd stayed in touch with since my hosting gig, and who seemed to know everyone and everything in my new home.

Speaking of knowing the city, in the interest of promoting *Peepshow*,

I began familiarizing myself with the local press circuit. Being out at events all the time wasn't just about having fun and enjoying my freedom; everything had to serve a greater purpose. Why go to a random club to have fun when I could go to an event that could bring me some exposure?

The Las Vegas media scene isn't nearly as cutthroat as that in Los Angeles—or so I thought. There were just a handful of entertainment journalists in town, and if you frequented enough red carpets and photo ops, you'd quickly get to know most of them. While I was still new to the whole PR world, I knew well enough that promotion was key when it came to making a success of whatever project I was involved with. One of my first interviews with a Las Vegan was for a gossip column in one of the city's major newspapers. I had done the interview with its columnist, Jim, while I was rehearsing for the *Dancing* season finale. My press agent had passed along my number for the purpose of doing that interview only. The piece turned out well and was a nice intro into the Vegas market. I wasn't expecting to hear from the reporter again, so I was surprised when he called me on a random weekday afternoon.

"Uh, hi, Holly . . . it's Jim," said the gruff, anxious-sounding man on the phone, "from the paper. We spoke a few weeks ago."

"Oh, hi. How are you?" I said, my voice automatically defaulting to the "polite," man-pleasing, high-pitched tone I was determined to stop using. *I wonder why he's calling me out of the blue?* I asked myself.

"So . . ." he began, trying to sound cheery. I imagined that he was skimming his notes as we spoke. "My friend Cyndi says you were rude to her the other day. What do you have to say about that?"

Huh? I thought. *What the hell is he talking about?*

"Could you please remind me who that is?" I asked, trying to sound as courteous as possible. I barely knew this guy, let alone his friends.

"Cyndi Johnson," he encouraged, hoping to spark my memory. "The reporter for channel nine. She said she interviewed you at the Palms the other day and that you insulted her outfit."

I might have been new to handling press, but this seemed like a ridiculous thing to be calling about. It was clearly asked with the intent of stirring a pot that didn't yet exist. But at the time, I didn't know any better, and, in this particular instance, it was a simple misunderstanding. I couldn't see any harm in clearing it up. I always thought it best to be as straightforward as possible, and, back then, I thought that everyone deserved an answer.

"Oh, no!" I replied, hoping my smile would translate over the phone. "I actually complimented her outfit. Maybe she thought I was being sarcastic or something, but I wasn't. I liked it!"

What was it about my delivery that made her think I was being rude? I wondered, once again having to analyze the way I communicated. I racked my brain, trying to remember just exactly what I had said to that woman. I swore it was something along the lines of "I love your dress! It's a way better choice for this pool party than what I'm wearing." Unseasonably cold winds had been blowing through that day and I had regretted not wearing something warmer. I would have traded my bikini and denim skirt for Cyndi's dress in an instant!

He didn't say anything, so I decided to fill the silence.

"It was so cold that day . . ." I babbled. I explained the events of the Palms pool party that had taken place weeks earlier. "I wore a bikini and a denim skirt and was freezing! She was wearing a cute dress that was *way* more weather appropriate. Oh my god! I really can't believe she thought I was being sarcastic. That's really strange. I meant it sincerely!"

"Well, you know," he whispered into the phone, readying himself to plant the bait, "she used to date Criss Angel."

"Really? She doesn't seem like his type." I blurted out in my surprise, temporarily forgetting that I was speaking to a reporter. Criss, then in his forties, never seemed to date age-appropriate professional women. His roster typically included starlets, go-go dancers, and cocktail waitresses, most of them much younger than him.

"I know, right?" Jim oozed. I snapped back into reality and quickly found a reason to end the call. I didn't think about it again until the next morning when my publicist suggested I take a look at the the local paper. The topic of Jim's weekly entertainment column was none other than my "feud" with veteran Vegas reporter Cyndi Johnson.

"Are you kidding me?" I cried out as Hannah, who had stayed over the night before, pried herself up off the couch. Out of context, my "she doesn't really seem like his type" comment read like I was being bitchy and jealous.

"What are you talking about?" Hannah asked, helping herself to our room service tray, which had been delivered along with the morning paper just a few minutes earlier. I filled her in on my phone call and read her the snarky article as she laughed.

"Anyway, I really didn't mean it as an insult," I continued. "And I *never* expected it to make its way back to this Cyndi person, let alone be *printed* for the entire city to read!"

They say there's no such thing as bad press, but I happen to disagree. This sort of lowbrow attention was muddying the reputation I was trying to build for myself. As soon as the article hit, Cyndi used her own platform as a journalist to put together what I thought was an unflattering and downright mean piece on me for her local entertainment news segment.

With all that bluster, it seemed only natural, somehow, that Donald Trump was the person that brought us together again.

Trump's Miss USA Pageant was being televised from Planet Hollywood and I was asked to be a judge at the last minute. It made sense for the casino to include me, since the pageant would be a network television event, and I was set to be the casino's new headliner. I chose a long leopard-print Roberto Cavalli gown and sparkling chandelier earrings to wear. When I saw the program that included the names of the other judges, I noticed that Cyndi's name was also on the list. She had been a pageant queen at one point herself, so she was a natural choice to judge.

Cyndi was playing double duty as a red carpet reporter for the event as well, and when I saw her on the event's "green carpet," I fearlessly waltzed right up to meet her glare.

"Hi, Cyndi!" I exclaimed, as if I had nothing to fear from her. In reality, I shouldn't have. I never meant to start anything with this woman, so there was no reason for anything but positivity, in my opinion. "I just wanted to clear up any confusion. I never meant to insult your outfit that day at the Palms. I meant what I said as a compliment."

"Well, what do you think of what I'm wearing now?" she asked, gesturing down to her dress and brushing off my apology.

"It looks great!" I replied with a big smile, nervous as to what was coming from her next in front of everyone lining the carpet.

"Oh, good," she purred facetiously, "because I would be soooo disappointed if you didn't like it." There was no mistaking her intentions. Her voice was dripping with undisguised sarcasm.

I smiled, ignoring her undertones, and waited politely for her to thank me for the "interview" and dismiss me. She launched into a few questions, very much along the lines of "What do you *know* about the history of the Miss USA pageant?" and "Have you ever had *any* affiliation with the pageant world yourself?" Her face was grim, as if she were asking me about important world events. Whether she intended it or not, I perceived a subtext: you're not qualified to be a judge, so why are you even here? I saw Jim, the columnist, posted on the carpet nearby, wearing a huge grin on his face. Later that week his column recounted the interaction. Thankfully, he reported that we made peace. After that debacle, I learned to be a bit more prudent when it came to what I said and to whom.

I was diving headfirst into a crash course on how the media can easily spin anything into misconception. Press can work *for* you, but it can just as easily work *against* you. When I was invited for a complimentary manicure at the opening of a new salon in Town Square, I was aware that it was basically a staged photo op. I got a manicure, the photographers got a photo, and the salon got some press—everyone wins! The following week the photo was printed in a weekly celebrity magazine. I was shown looking over my shoulder at the camera, a huge smile on my face while I was getting my nails done. The caption read: "This is what she was used to at the mansion!"

Benign as this may have seemed to whoever wrote it, I found the caption terribly irritating. It implied that I couldn't afford to get my nails done anymore and that this was a rare treat, reminiscent of my days living in Playboy luxury. In reality, I was making more money than I ever had, all on my own. Not to mention, I was completely independent and could get my nails done whenever I liked, without having to worry about being back by curfew, thank you very much! I was proud of myself for landing on my feet even though the odds were against me and I could easily have ended up flat on my face after fleeing the mansion. Was it a bad thing that I wanted everyone to know how well I was doing? I didn't think so. It's a good message—to know that you can stand on your own two feet even if everyone is telling you that you won't be able to.

"This is so frustrating!" I complained to Hannah, passing the magazine over to her as we ate lunch in my suite. "Everyone thinks I'm flat broke. I don't care if they think I have money or not, but I do want everyone to know I'm working! Not to mention happier and better off than I was a year ago!"

"Well, that's what you get." She shrugged, plucking a single potato chip and placing it into her red-lipped mouth, flicking the crumbs off her glossy black nails.

It struck me as an odd thing for her to say.

"What do you mean?" I asked incredulously.

"When you put yourself in the public eye, you are inviting everyone, *including the haters*, to make assumptions about you," she explained. "It's your job to change the conversation if you don't like what they are saying. You have to take control of your own narrative. My dad has to deal with this kind of shit with his business all the time, and it's not always easy." She paused, giving it a bit more thought. "Frankly, I think it's going to be an uphill battle for you because you've been so synonymous with Playboy all these years."

Her phone buzzed, quickly diverting her attention, giving what she said to me a moment to sink in. I wasn't expecting such an informed lecture from Hannah, but you know what? She was a hundred percent right. I was going to have to work my ass off in order to change anyone's mind. My thoughts started to wander back to all the things I wanted to accomplish.

For the next three months, I would be starring in the hottest revue on the Vegas Strip. It was a job I landed on my own—without anyone's help. That was a huge victory for me. It also meant a certain level of security, because for twelve weeks, I had a steady large salary. When I wasn't busy trying to sell a TV show, I spent all my free time doing press and appearing at events. After my three months were up, I wanted *Peepshow* begging me to stay on.

My schedule was about to go from packed to absolutely insane. I knew I wouldn't be able to keep up with it anymore, so I hired Angel as my assistant to help with the day-to-day things that could have easily fallen through the cracks. I became so busy that her help was well worth the money. The flexible schedule was perfect for her, since she had just given birth to her adorable son, Roman. Laura had arrived in town shortly before Roman was born and we had raced to the hospital with bags of Taco Bell (her favorite) in tow for the new mommy. The happiness I felt for Angel and the closeness of our little family of friends helped me feel less alone than I had in a long time.

With the top of my newly purchased convertible down, I cruised down Las Vegas Boulevard feeling the dry desert air on my skin. There would be bumps in the road, of course, but I was *on* the road to becoming the woman I always dreamed of being. At the end of the Strip next to the I-15, a glittering black-and-red billboard shimmered from above: PEEPSHOW STARRING HOLLY MADISON! And there I was, standing twenty feet tall.

Was this really my life? I thought. I couldn't believe how quickly the tide had turned for me and how fortunate I felt. Along with a new job and a new city, I felt like my personal makeover was nearly complete!

My life was finally beginning . . . and I was in for a wild ride.

WITH MY NEW FRIENDS as my partners in crime, I made it a point to maximize my free time, going to as many shows, dinners, and events as we could squeeze in. If I was going to help make *Peepshow* one of the most popular shows on the Strip, I needed to know what we were up against. Nancy suggested we all check out a new nightclub featuring live dancers. She assured us that we wouldn't want to miss her best friend Lindsay, who was performing there that night. I knew that my dancing skills had been sharpened thanks to my time on *DWTS*, but I didn't have nearly the sort of professional training that many of these Vegas showgirls had. I felt intimidated that I'd be compared with them, but I was ready for the challenge and figured I needed to do my research. When I looked around this particular establishment, I saw a few dancers positioned on banquettes around the room. They were dressed in spangled bras and skimpy, cheap-looking boy shorts. One of them listlessly threw around a small, beat-up pair of feather fans. I knew there was better in the city that I had yet to see, but still hoped I could learn something from that night's performances.

After we ordered a round of drinks, Nancy, Hannah, and I dove into a debate about who were the most eligible bachelors in Vegas. Right around the time that we were each taking a stance on whether we would ever date one of the more notorious (and handsome) nightclub promoters in town, Lindsay made her entrance. A hush fell over the restaurant as the longest pair of Wolford-covered legs I'd ever seen stepped one by one onto a platform in the center of the room. This bewitching woman was tall and ballerina thin, with a silky mane of dark blond hair tumbling down her back. Obviously a trained dancer, she performed a slow, sensuous number with the help of a well-tailored men's white dress shirt. Her routine was elegant and clearly took skill—particularly because she performed it in the most towering pair of Brian Atwood platform stilettos I'd ever seen . . . without even so much as a single wobble.

"Now, *that's* a dancer," Hannah whispered to me, gesturing to the lanky beauty. She was right. This woman seemed so untouchable compared with the other performers who had populated the club earlier in the evening. What could she possibly be doing here? When her routine finally concluded, the room erupted into applause and the swan glided off her stage.

As she walked by, Nancy waved to her to come over.

"Your performance was amazing!" I said. "Come sit with us!" I continued, introducing myself to the glamorous creature.

"I'm Lindsay," she said, a cheery smile on her face. "It's so nice to meet you. I can't wait to see your show! I've been seeing the ads for it all over town." She took a seat next to us on the edge of the booth.

"I love your outfit," I said. "Did you put it together yourself?"

"Yes," she said modestly. "We provide our own wardrobe and routines."

"You have such great taste," I remarked, then decided to just be honest and blurted out: "Why are you working here?"

She must have been taken by surprise, as a ladylike laugh escaped her. She shared a brief version of her backstory with us: like me, she was a small-town girl from the Pacific Northwest. She had studied dance all her life, recently moving to Vegas to make a living doing what she loved. She proudly announced that she had just been hired full-time at one of the smaller topless shows in town. She seemed genuinely thrilled, so I tried to keep the surprise from showing on my face. What was this classy broad doing in that show? The one she mentioned was easily the sleaziest one I had seen so far.

I told her that I was starting rehearsals for *Peepshow*, and I was doing a tour around town and had yet to see such a skilled performance as the one she just gave. Lindsay was new to town and clearly passionate about her dreams—something I could relate to. We exchanged numbers and vowed to get together soon.

When I wasn't doing my own personal research for *Peepshow*, I was pounding the pavement to do everything I could to promote it. In order to make the biggest splash possible, I vowed to be seen anywhere and everywhere on behalf of my new project. One of the events I had been invited to was the Playmate of the Year celebration at the Palms. On one hand, attending seemed natural. I had directed Playmate of the Year Ida Ljungqvist's first pictorial back when I worked at the magazine, and Angel and I were eager to go out that weekend. I loved the Palms, but . . . I was still trying so hard to get away from the Playboy brand that I wasn't sure if being seen at this event was the best idea.

Prior to the party, I called Mary to get her advice. I didn't know if Hef was even going and I wanted to find out. I didn't want to go if things were going to be awkward. I knew she'd be honest with me.

"Of course you should come," she said, before lowering her voice and briskly adding, "But Hef says you can't bring your manager."

"I was planning on bringing Angel anyway," I said defensively. I was irritated, because I knew the stipulation meant that he assumed I was dating my manager. There was a strict "no boyfriends" policy for the women at Hef's events, with very few exceptions (the girls needed to appear available, so unless they were dating a celebrity or an athlete who could add some cachet to the event, they were usually out of luck).

Hef wasn't the only person to speculate that I was dating my manager or my publicist. A few other acquaintances had assumed that as well. Somehow a public perception of me had evolved wherein I was unable to carry on a professional working relationship with a person of the opposite sex without sleeping with him. *If I had never been involved with Hugh Hefner, would people still make those assumptions?* The misconception was annoying, to say the least. Mary reminding me of it only fanned the flames. I considered blowing off the event, but I felt challenged somehow, like I needed to show up and let everyone see how great I was doing as a *single* woman.

The night of the event, I stepped onto the red carpet feeling confident. No longer was I dressing to placate someone else's preferences; I looked like myself in an asymmetrical top, a feathered skirt, and tall leather boots. My hair was blown out silky and smooth, curling just past my shoulders, and my makeup was natural, save for a classic black cat-eyed liner.

We walked up to the check-in table, where Playmates were handed cheap adhesive name tags indicating her name and the month and year of her Playmate pictorial. For an event that aspired to be upscale, this touch was very high school reunion. Though I had appeared on four covers, I was never technically a Playmate, so there was no name tag waiting for me. But that's okay. I didn't feel like I needed the introduction.

Angel and I were directed to a table full of Playmates, most of them women I had worked with at the studio. It was nice to catch up. I may not have had the fondest memories of my personal time with *Playboy*, but I had enjoyed my professional time at the studio, or I would not have wanted to come to this event at all. After Ida's presentation, I struck up a conversation with fashion designers David and Phillipe Blond, who graciously offered to dress me for a few upcoming events, which alone made attending the party worthwhile!

And since at the end of the day it was Hef's party, I went over to say a brief hello and thank-you, making a point to acknowledge his three girlfriends. They seemed uncomfortable and distracted. Even the Shannon twins, who were usually so friendly, seemed too exhausted to muster more than halfhearted smiles. *I certainly don't miss that tension,* I thought.

Being thrust back into this scene made my skin crawl. Angel and I wasted no time getting out of there. After my driver dropped Angel off at her home, I was ready to head back to my cozy bed and room service when I felt my phone vibrate.

The name *Rusty Rockets* popped up on my BlackBerry Messenger.

That's random, I thought. Rusty Rockets was Russell Brand's nickname on BBM. The English comedian and I had been "introduced" by a mutual acquaintance weeks earlier. This introduction culminated in us adding each other on BBM, but we hadn't actually messaged each other until this moment.

"He's so *funny*," she had assured me. "You guys would be great together!"

I wasn't really eager to be "together" with anyone, but he came with a glowing reference from a trusted source, so I was a bit intrigued and figured what's the harm in simply exchanging numbers?

He invited me to stop by Tao and join him and a group of people for dinner. I was hesitant. On one hand, I had sworn off romance and was still a bit brokenhearted, so I wasn't really in the mood to meet a guy, even casually. On the other hand, wasn't the best (or at least the most typical) advice for a broken heart to get out, meet new people, have fun, and forget about it? *Maybe that's just what I needed to do.*

"Sure, I'll meet you there," I responded.

Large golden rose-petal-filled tubs lined Tao's entryway, complete with nearly nude bathing beauties lounging inside. I stepped into the cavernous, noisy, and dimly lit restaurant, and after a quick look around, I saw a boisterous giant table smack in the center of the room. That had to be his. Russell was in town filming a movie, *Get Him to the Greek*, and I recognized some of the cast seated at the table. The self-confidence I found on that red carpet less than a few hours earlier had quickly vanished; I was way too intimidated to walk up to that table. I leaned against a column, put my head down, and sent him a message that I was there. From the corner of my eye, I saw him look at his phone and crane his neck toward where I was standing. He pushed back his chair and quickly walked over toward me.

"Hello, there!" he said, bringing me toward him for a hug. He led me to the table, offered the rest of the group a blanket introduction, and sat me in a chair between him and Cassie, the R&B singer, who was sitting next to her then-beau, Diddy. I had to admit that as I looked down the table and recognized some of the other actors, I was kind of blown away. This was as star-studded a crowd as I had ever dined with.

Russell was kind and seemed reasonably down-to-earth. We made small talk about how he was enjoying Vegas and the good times he was having on the set of the film. He was boyishly enthusiastic and witty. My friend had been right: he was funny and easy to talk to. I was definitely happy I decided to go.

He told me that I hadn't been what he expected at all and that when he had first seen me standing there, he'd done a double take. He said I seemed more ladylike than he had imagined, more shy and demure.

"Thanks," I said, trying to keep my smile from breaking out into a huge cheesy grin. Incidentally, that was *just* the kind of thing I liked (and needed) to hear. I was tired of my public image. I felt like everyone assumed I was a cunning, oversexed hot mess, based on what they saw on TV. It didn't matter that I had said only a handful of things to Russell so far, and that he barely knew me. I *needed* to believe that I wasn't crazy and that someone else could see me for who I felt I really was.

"You know, this isn't really me," he said after we finished eating, leaning back in his chair and gesturing around the trendy night spot.

"Me either," I agreed, pleasantly surprised by his admission. I loved Tao, but I did loathe when restaurants got so loud that you could barely hear the person sitting next to you, let alone the person across the table.

He leaned in closer as if he were about to tell me a secret, "I'd much rather just be in bed watching a movie and eating something chocolaty, wouldn't you?"

I couldn't tell if he was being facetious or if he indeed wanted to jump in bed at that moment. He certainly gave off the vibe that anything could be a joke, but I couldn't take the risk. I had been so scared off from guys that *anything* seemed like a dangerous proposition to me at the time. I was hyperaware that the last thing I needed was another notch on my belt, and I certainly wasn't interested in a guy looking for a one-night pump and dump.

"I'm down to get out of here, but I'm going to have to call it a night," I repeated, trying hard to keep a straight face. I felt as if I were a character in an after-school special, staunchly trying to avoid a possible sexual encounter. I finally added: "I've got to get back to my suite. My roommate is expecting me."

"You have a roommate?" he asked quizzically, clearly not expecting my living situation to be so collegiate.

"Yeah," I said, giving him a nervous smile. "Okay, well, I'm going to go . . ."

"Let's share a ride," he said, jumping out of his seat, and motioning toward the charismatic host who was handling this VIP table. "Since we're staying at the same place."

"Okay," I said, grabbing my small black clutch as I stood to leave.

The cute, pullover-wearing host offered to escort us to the back exit. We wove through the hordes of people spilling over from the restaurant's packed bar area. The host pushed open a secret door, hidden in plain sight from the rest of the diners, and we slipped out back and into the alley, where a black SUV was waiting for us.

I directed the driver to the VIP entrance of Planet Hollywood as Russell texted on his BlackBerry while our driver battled the traffic on the Strip. He had already lined up a backup plan for a night on the town, he explained, if I was certain I didn't want to hang out.

"Thanks, but I can't," I insisted, as if my designer outfit was going to turn to rags at the stroke of midnight.

He looked at me and smiled as we pulled up to my destination. Before he could say anything, I jumped out of the car and bounded toward the door as quickly as my over-the-knee boots would carry me. If he meant to give me a good-night kiss or not, I would never know. I wasn't even ready for something as benign as a peck on the lips at that point.

I wasn't lying about the early rehearsals, so I headed up to my room to get some sleep. I smiled as I washed my face and changed into pajamas. In one short night, I had faced a few of my fears (old ones and new) and had had a good time on top of it. I drifted off into a serene sleep, but that feeling of peace was short-lived.

Around eight A.M. my phone started going off.

"Fun night?" my publicist messaged me, along with a link to an online gossip column. I stiffened as I read the headline: "Holly Madison cozies up to Russell Brand in Vegas."

"Uggghhhh," I groaned as I did a Google search, scrolling through the articles and the stock photos of him and me that were pasted side by side. Each headline grew increasingly more salacious, with one insinuating that we were already a couple. Were they insane? We had only just met! The blurbs detailed our dinner together at Tao fairly accurately, but the other part of the circulating story told a completely fictionalized account of us going up to a suite in the Venetian together. According to the report, we were having sex so loudly the people in the room next to us had complained.

"That's not reality, that's a scene from *Forgetting Sarah Marshall*," I grumbled at my phone, continuing to read one ridiculous article. Maybe I wasn't the only one who had trouble separating myself in the public eye from my on-screen persona! I was simultaneously livid and mortified.

It was so frustrating; I felt like I was beating my head against a wall. It didn't matter what I did, people were always going to see me as this bimbo willing to jump into bed with anyone. I was desperately trying to reinvent my image, but I was realizing more and more just what a challenge that was going to be. It seemed like the more I pushed the "single girl" card, the more anxious people were to see me slutting it up.

By lunchtime I'd received a few dozen calls and text messages from people eager for details on my alleged night with Russell. Even one of the cute male dancers from *Peepshow* whom I had been rehearsing with chimed in, congratulating me on finally getting laid. I made some vague comment on social media to dispute the false rumors, but was advised against addressing it directly, as that would just add more fuel to the fire.

I didn't think Russell planted the rumor. He was a big enough celebrity that he didn't need the extra press. Not to mention, tales of his sexual escapades abounded. I highly doubt that he had "plant stories about bagging women" on his agenda. The only thing I could imagine was that someone saw us at the restaurant and figured that when we left at the same time, we *must* have been headed back to screw. I felt confused and upset, but there wasn't much I could do about it. I was never even going to know who planted that rumor.

I received a few messages from Russell that day, but I didn't respond. I was too embarrassed by the entire situation, so I did the only thing I knew how to do and avoided talking about it altogether. After days of my silence he finally sent me a message saying that he hoped I knew he had nothing to do with the rumors. I believed him, but I still couldn't bring myself to respond. When it came to men, I was scared to do anything at all. It was too dangerous to have anything to do with this one; if I should ever be seen with him again it would only encourage the rumors. I removed him from BlackBerry Messenger; I didn't want to be tempted to text him and this way he couldn't reach out to me anymore, either. (Clearly my communication skills needed a bit of work.)

I started to wonder what I could do to make people see that I wasn't the woman the outside world made me out to be. I understood why they thought that way, because for years I'd allowed myself to be portrayed as that person. While I wasn't her, I didn't know how I could possibly prove that. I wasn't looking for sympathy, just the benefit of the doubt. I didn't know how to get out from under this reputation that preceded me. I couldn't very well open up my bedroom door to the public, so I'd have to prove it some other way.

I wasn't the girl next door anymore. I never really was.

I decided that for the next few years, at least, I would have to keep my personal life as far out of the public eye as possible. I had no idea what a challenge that would be.

Chapter 3

Yet Dorothy felt a sort of joyous excitement in defying the storm, and while she held fast to the railing she peered through the gloom and thought she saw the dim form of a man clinging to a mast not far away from her.

—L. Frank Baum, *Ozma of Oz*

Getting up early for church wasn't my typical Sunday routine.

A few days earlier, Angel invited me to go to church with her. I loved spending time with Angel and her family, so I gladly accepted. We invited a bunch of friends to meet us afterward at Simon, the popular brunch spot of the moment. She and I were seated in our booth and had a good amount of time to kill before the rest of our party wandered in.

"They're cute, right?" I whispered to Angel. A few seats away, a group of ink-covered rocker boys who looked to be in their late twenties roared and laughed, as two of the members argued playfully over the retelling of a story. One of the guys, in a worn-out death-metal shirt and blue-streaked hair, began animatedly describing a run-in with a group of girls the night before.

"Totally," she said, not so subtly craning her neck to get a better look. "Should we say something?"

"No!" I gasped, throwing my hands over my mouth. Angel, who was always brimming with confidence, started to rise from her seat with a big cheeky grin on her face. I leaned over the table and waved my hands, gesturing to her to get back into her seat.

I glanced over at the table carefully, and when I was sure they weren't looking at us, decided to stare a little longer. Most of the guys were cute, but one in particular stood out, thanks to the tall Mohawk he sported.

"Hol, come on . . ." Angel encouraged in her cute, I-just-inhaled-helium voice. "That Mohawk guy is cute." I knew she was trying to help and have fun, but she didn't understand how I was feeling.

"Let's just leave it alone, please," I begged, under my breath, praying they hadn't heard her.

"But why?" Her tone was genuine, and I realized she didn't see what was so obvious to me. I didn't want to have to say it out loud, but I didn't seem to have a choice.

"Because they would never be into me," I blurted out. I appreciated that she believed me to have more game than I actually did, but it was a blow to the ego to have to admit it in public.

Angel shot me a look, quick to let me know that my excuse carried no weight with her, but she knew me well enough to let the subject alone for now.

Perhaps if I were a "normal girl," those are the sorts of guys I'd hang out with, but I wasn't. I had only recently turned thirty, but having just come out of a world where any woman over twenty-eight was considered ancient, I felt like I might as well have been a hundred. Plus, my dating history was pretty much public record. Maybe they wouldn't know at first glance, but everyone googles everyone. It was only a matter of time before they figured it out.

These guys would probably think I was gross, I thought. Experience had led me to believe that guys couldn't handle my past.

Luckily, our group started to filter in before Angel could ask me more about it.

"Sorry I'm late," Hannah announced, collapsing into an empty seat and snatching my mimosa to take a swig. "Ooooh, those guys are cute," she said, nodding toward the booth next to us. "That guy with the Mohawk looks so familiar, but I can't place him," she continued, tapping her nails against the table. After a few moments of unsuccessfully trying to place Mohawk man, she turned her attention back to us. "Anyway, I was held up this morning because I had to get an emergency manicure."

She was baiting us. Hannah loved a game of cat and mouse—relishing a good chase—and gingerly picked up a menu, spreading her garishly manicured hand around its edge. Her nails were exceptionally long this time, with obtrusive rhinestones affixed to the red lacquer that seemed in contrast to her usually elevated taste. She waited for someone to ask the question we were all thinking: "Why?"

Hannah was still seeing the billionaire high roller, who had some interesting bedroom fetishes, so she was always good for some scandalous gossip.

"Well, that's quite the manicure." Josh laughed. Josh Strickland was my *Peepshow* costar and had quickly become one of my best friends. We had bonded over being new to the city, our performance schedule, and wanting to live life to the fullest.

"Brendan likes them," Hannah said, flexing her wrist nonchalantly to take a look at her pristinely painted nails. "He asks me to tickle his balls with them and gets off on the rhinestones when I stick my fingers in his ass."

She returned her gaze lazily to the menu—allowing us to fully absorb the punch line. Naturally, we dissolved into various degrees of hysterics. Angel nearly fell on the floor after Josh just about spat a mouth full of water across the table. Even Hannah couldn't resist and joined our chorus of laughter. The idea of this buttoned-up businessman with Hannah's fingers up his ass was just too much.

"It's all right, he's flying me somewhere special on his new jet next weekend," Hannah said with a wink. She loved the combination of upscale mixed with dirty in the same way people like to mix "high" with "low" in their wardrobe. I think a part of her liked knowing people's secrets, too.

"So, Holly, what about Kent?" Josh asked, a smile spreading across his handsome face. Earlier that week, I confided in Josh that I thought one of the dancers in our show, Kent, was cute.

"Josh!" I shouted, playfully tossing my napkin at him. I was embarrassed about my unrequited crush, although it's not like anyone could blame me for having one. Kent was an Adonis: perfectly tanned; disarming smile; muscular but lean; messy dark hair; and a nice-guy personality shrouded in a bit of brooding mystery. He was also openly gay (a fact I let the table in on before the interrogation could commence).

With the cat out of the bag, word started making its way around backstage. I met Kent during my first week of *Peepshow* rehearsals, and I was immediately struck by his good looks. He could have been a model ripped straight off the pages of *GQ* and had a fun, offbeat sense of humor. After he stopped by my dressing room to introduce himself, a gleam in his eye, I commented to one of the dancers on how cute I thought he was.

"Good luck," she scoffed, rolling her eyes and smiling. "He's gay."

"Are you sure?" I questioned, a little disappointed.

"Oh, yeah," she said. "I've known him forever. He just got out of a serious relationship."

For one of my solos, Kent was drafted to teach me the choreography. He was naturally talented, moving with fluidity and grace. It was the sort of skill you were born with, which made him and me an odd fit as teacher and student. He was supremely patient, but so naturally talented that he had trouble breaking down steps in a way that my novice feet could keep up with. Sure, *Dancing with the Stars* had trained me to be able to pick up routines quickly, but my technique was still far from that of a professional dancer. Even though the rehearsals were long, I always looked forward to them.

There was something about Kent that I connected with. Maybe it was that he had a great sense of humor, or the fact that he seemed to be the human embodiment of this new show that I was so in love with . . . or maybe it was that he was kind and friendly and so entirely welcoming.

It was just the sort of thing I needed to distract myself from dealing with that empty pit inside my stomach. Even though a lot of great things were happening in my life, anxiety and self-doubt still lurked just underneath the surface. I was quickly learning that it isn't so easy to shove your past under a rug. Even if it is behind you, it still has the power to haunt you. And if that wasn't enough to keep me up at night, I was considered a "public figure," with every aspect of my life up for debate, analysis, and criticism by thousands of people who had never met me. The Kent distraction was a Band-Aid on a bullet hole, but it was my bullet hole . . . so I could dress it however I wanted.

Even before my first performance, *Peepshow* was seeing a huge surge in advance ticket sales, and we began talking about extending my contract. The producers had originally intended to replace the actor in the role of Bo Peep with a fresh guest star every few months. However, after seeing how well advance ticket sales were doing, they were starting to rethink the plan. But if they kept me on, they had to figure out what to do with the performer they had lined up to replace me: Aubrey O'Day, a pop singer. Would I take three months off and return after Aubrey's run, or would they keep me on and have us co-headline?

I didn't just want to stay with *Peepshow*; I *needed* to stay with *Peepshow.* Not only did I believe in the show, but the pay was amazing, the cast and crew were a delight, and it was the perfect anchor for the four-year period of time I had given myself to come into my own in Las Vegas. The show was my family and my security in my hastily pieced together new life.

I knew that if I had a TV series in place, it would virtually guarantee me an extended run and also serve as a platform for whatever I decided to do next.

After countless meetings, it appeared that a few networks were interested, but no one had yet pulled the trigger. Having spent five seasons on a show, I thought I had a pretty good idea of what made for good reality TV and I knew the colorful cast of characters around me would certainly light up on screen. I was so enthusiastic about selling a series about a single girl making it on her own in Las Vegas, but inevitably got the same question from every network exec: "Do you have a boyfriend?"

"No, that's kind of the whole point," I said. "It's about doing it on my own, but I'm open to the possibility of romance down the road."

"Well, is there anyone you're open to right now?" one particularly abrasive exec asked.

"Right now I have a crush on my costar," I confessed. His eyes lit up, as if he were already crafting the story line in his head. "But he's gay," I added, making it clear that my little infatuation was going nowhere.

"You watch TV, right?" he asked, a hint of annoyance in his voice. I nodded. "Well, every reality show needs a relationship element, so I don't think a series without a romantic interest would work."

So far, my "Single and Fabulous" pitch was flopping. It was discouraging, to say the least. I felt like a show about a single woman doing it on her own sent a much better message for women than the message I had been a part of before. Now I had network executives making me feel like I wasn't interesting enough—that a woman's life in general wasn't interesting enough—without a boyfriend. Even a publicist I interviewed suggested that it was imperative that I "stay relevant," and the easiest way to do that was to start dating another celebrity. I would start dating when I was ready, but in the meantime . . . there was Kent.

When one of the *Peepshow* stagehands asked me if I would like to go on a camping trip and then mentioned that Kent was going, I accepted immediately.

Of course Kent is outdoorsy, I thought. He was basically a living Ken doll.

"Have you ever been canoeing before?" the stagehand asked me next.

"Um, like once or twice at Disneyland," I admitted sheepishly. I grew up fishing with my dad in Alaska, but I had never paddled in a real canoe or kayak. One that wasn't on the safe man-made Disneyfied Rivers of America anyway.

He let out a chuckle. "Well, we're going two to a canoe, so you shouldn't have any trouble. We'll have a full day of activities planned. And be prepared: we'll be canoeing almost all day long, down the Colorado River to Arizona, and then we'll camp out overnight."

"Great," I exclaimed. "I'm in!"

The amount of camping gear I purchased for a twenty-four-hour getaway was slightly embarrassing. I had never been to the Bass Pro Shop before and felt like I needed everything they were selling. I was a bit terrified at the idea of canoeing but euphoric about going on a day trip with Kent. I picked out a camouflage bikini for the excursion. It was my signature blend of sexy and campy (no pun intended). As if my outfit wasn't a total disaster already, I grabbed a pair of hot pink Crocs because I was told we'd be doing a little spelunking along the way and that a wet pair of Converse wouldn't cut it.

Josh, Angel, Lindsay, and I woke up at around five in the morning to drive toward Boulder City, since we'd be launching off near the Hoover Dam. The giant dam, 726 feet high, is located roughly thirty miles southeast of downtown Las Vegas, in Black Canyon. The nearest town, Boulder City, was founded to provide housing for the workers hired to construct the dam.

As we drove, I pulled up some facts on the dam, paraphrasing them aloud for my fellow passengers: "It took ten thousand men to complete the Hoover Dam, over a period of five years. It was actually completed a whole two years ahead of schedule! There was a grand total of one hundred and twelve deaths related to the Hoover Dam project, though, contrary to legend, experts say there aren't any bodies buried in the concrete. Perhaps the creepiest story involves the first ever project-related death: while surveying the canyon on December 20, 1922, a man fell into the Colorado and drowned. Exactly thirteen years later to the day, that man's son was the last person to die on the project when he fell from an intake tower."

"Maybe that's not the best story to tell us right before we spend the night there," Lindsay joked.

When we finally arrived at the legendary dam, I counted about fifteen of us, but I didn't see Kent. People starting coupling off, two to a canoe, and I frantically began scanning the crowd, certain I must have missed him.

"You looking for Kent?" one of the stagehands shouted over the mess of people calling out to one another, trying to avoid tipping over before the journey even began. My crush had become something of a production-wide joke, so it was no surprise that the stagehand knew, too. "He bailed. Came down with something last night. Sorry."

I was instantly deflated. Without Kent's charm to motivate me down the river, I suddenly felt even more ill equipped to handle a canoe than before. I paused for a moment before sluggishly placing my items in my assigned canoe.

The trip went downhill from there. After being nailed by a long-range water rifle and trekking through a muddy, slippery hot spring cave along the way, I was quickly regretting my decision to come. Summers in Vegas can be relentless—and this particular day was forecasted to top out at 110 degrees. Our second stop was a pebble clearing along the side of the river. It looked like a set from *Land of the Lost*, but I was ready for some swimming and a midmorning snack. I needed to occupy my attention to avoid getting sad. *Why didn't Kent text me that he was sick?* I wondered.

"So let's start setting up the tents!" one of the other organizers exclaimed.

"This is where we are camping?" one of the dancers asked, reading all of our minds.

That was the whole thing? I thought. *That's it?* What the hell were we going to do until tomorrow morning? We were maybe two hours into our trip . . . and we were setting up shop already? I hadn't even brought a book with me! I was convinced I'd be spending the whole day battling raging rapids, without a second of spare time!

All morning I watched as one of the cast and one of the crew, who were involved in a "showmance," held hands and stole kisses when they thought no one was looking, laughing at private jokes only they understood.

I had to admit, I was a bit envious. They had each other to occupy their attention, and I had been hoping that Kent would be there to occupy mine. A small part of me hoped that Kent and I would be having a similar sort of adventure together. I knew we were never going to be involved romantically, but I still loved hanging out with him. Watching her giggle as he tenderly tucked a loose strand of hair behind her ear drove home for me the fact that I needed to get my head out of the clouds. I wondered why it was that I felt like I had to constantly have visions of a particular man dancing around in my head. Was I so used to seeking male approval that it had become a habit? What about seeking my own approval?

"I don't think I'm into this whole camping thing," Angel whispered into my ear as she watched one of the crew members attempt to pitch a less-than-sturdy-looking tent.

"Me, either," I agreed. "Should we canoe back?"

Angel got a text from Laura, with a picture of her baby boy cuddled next to a stuffed teddy bear—and I could feel how much she missed him. I, on the other hand, started rapidly texting Hannah to see what she was up to. My stomach started twisting and I nervously wondered what great party was happening tonight that I would be missing out on if I stayed here. *Isn't there a red-carpet event happening tonight?* I wondered, starting to panic just a bit that there was an opportunity to promote the show that I wasn't capitalizing on.

When the head of our props department whizzed up on a speedboat to say hello, Angel and I took it as our cue to escape. She was having separation anxiety, missing Roman. I was just having . . . anxiety.

A funny thing had happened to me since I had seized control of my life. I became *addicted* to controlling it. Sure, my suite was still a mess half the time and I wasn't very disciplined when it came to what I ate, but what I *really* needed to have control over was how I spent my time. If my hours weren't set aside for work or getting precious sleep, I wanted to be having the Time of My Life, on *my* terms and my terms alone. After spending over seven years in all-consuming relationships, constantly making excuses for why I was doing things I really didn't want to do, I realized that living someone else's life was the only adult life I had ever known. When I finally seized my independence, I went in the complete opposite direction. If I ever found myself in a situation that wasn't my ideal scenario, a crushing anxiety would sneak up on me, making my mind race and my heart beat faster. *Don't you have something more productive you could be doing right now?* the little voice in my head would whisper.

That was the other part of the equation. Since I had spent so many years as someone else's accessory, I had to work extra hard to build a life for myself now. I felt almost as if I had awakened from a seven-year coma and desperately craved making up that lost time—both career-wise and socially—on my own terms. Any time someone else tried to tell me what I should do, my instinct was to turn in the exact opposite direction.

My debut in *Peepshow* was rapidly approaching. In so many ways, the character I played, Bo Peep, eerily reflected my real life. The character didn't say much (the show was a musical burlesque revue, so I had lines only in between numbers and during an audience participation bit in the middle of the show), but she was expected to look pretty. I had been terribly introverted my whole life and turned toward a highly sexualized look, perhaps in a subconscious attempt to let my appearance do the talking for me. While it was attention and affection I wanted, the extreme nature of my look perhaps went above and beyond what I was going for, sending the wrong message.

The loose story line of *Peepshow* involves the main character being a busy career woman with no time for love. In the show, Bo Peep falls into a dream world, where more confident women, in the form of grown-up versions of nursery rhyme characters, demonstrate to Bo what it means to be a strong, self-assured woman, comfortable with her sexuality. In the show, Bo Peep finds her man only after she finds her confidence in herself. Though it wasn't a goal I actually wrote down, confidence in myself was perhaps the thing I needed to achieve most during this period of my life.

My first official week starring in *Peepshow* happened to land in the middle of June, during Vegas's busy summer season. There were no "friends and family" performances, so my first night onstage was for a paying audience. To say I was nervous was an understatement! I had a grand total of two live shows before journalists descended on my "press night," where my stage presence would be reviewed and critiqued for the world. I wasn't a talented dancer by any means, so I knew I was going to have to connect with the audience on another level, strictly with personality, enthusiasm, and charm. Luckily, in spite of the nerves that had my dancing feet practically shaking, I got through the show and had an amazing time doing it. As I stood at the end of the middle runway after the final number, covered in rhinestones and white feathers, I was handed bouquet after bouquet of red roses. The audience was on their feet in a standing ovation. I couldn't believe it! I grinned at my costars on either side of me, my friend Josh and another Broadway singer, Shoshana Bean. I felt like a *Ziegfeld Follies* star from long ago.

My first few weeks in *Peepshow* went by in a joyous blur. I bonded with the cast, quickly growing attached to the group. It was easy to forget that most of them, including Kent, would be heading back to New York in only a matter of months. Or maybe I was just in denial, because I wasn't ready to lose this new, albeit makeshift, family. I always arrived backstage two hours before showtime to have a snack and start my hair and makeup (which I insisted on doing myself). The cast would constantly socialize during the day and backstage before the show, and usually hung out at a restaurant or nightclub afterward, too.

Sometimes we would attend one of the pool parties in town, but we quickly learned to save those outings for our days off. Being out in the stifling heat and blistering sun all day (particularly if you've had a cocktail) could easily wipe you out before a performance. July Fourth was always one of the biggest days for poolside celebrations, but since we had a show that night, we didn't go out to celebrate in the typical Vegas fashion. Between performances, I was suffering from a bit of Fear of Missing Out Syndrome, due to opting out of the Independence Day festivities, when one of the dancers shouted, "The fireworks are starting!" A stampede of cast and crew made a mad dash to the back service entrance behind the stage that led out onto a large balcony with a view of the Strip.

"Don't go back there barefoot!" the stage manager called after me. I grabbed my flesh-toned satin heels and placed them back on my feet. I pushed my way out the door just in time to see an enormous red burst light up the sky. I noticed Kent standing off to the side and squeezed my way through the crowd toward him. Napoleon, a little blond mutt Laura had helped me pick out from a pet adoption fair, bounded out behind me. He jumped on Kent, wagging his tail and barking. He loved Kent as much as I did. The display lasted just a few minutes, with a dramatic climax of giant red, white, and blue blooms exploding across the sky. Slowly people began to trickle back inside, but Kent waited alongside me, despite the heat, watching the smoke billow and curl.

"Are you excited to be going back?" I asked him, my eyes readjusting to the darkness. Along with most of the New York transplants, Kent would soon be heading home. They had fulfilled their Vegas contracts and would be replaced with a new cast of locals. I knew this was coming, but that didn't make it easier to see any of them go . . . especially Kent. Ever since the camping debacle, I hadn't been as starry-eyed and dreamy when it came to him, but I still really enjoyed his company.

"Yeah," he began, scratching Napoleon behind his ears.

"I wish you could stay!" I interrupted. "It won't be the same without you."

"I wish I could, too, but there aren't the kinds of opportunities I'm looking for here," he said. I knew that Broadway was his passion. He continued: "I only signed on for a few months, so now it's time to find something else." After a pause, he added, "It's not the best place to meet guys, either."

I agreed. I hadn't been there very long, but I already knew how small a city Vegas could be. Plus, being a party city, the odds were already stacked against you. Most of the local guys I knew worked in nightlife, living like a bunch of perennial Peter Pans with their pick of the women circling through the revolving doors, so you could forget having an easy time finding anything serious.

"I'll miss you," I said. And I meant it. Despite the heat, I didn't make a move toward the door. I wanted to enjoy my last few moments alone with Kent. He was moving on toward the life that was right for him and I was happy to have him as a friend, which we all know is better than a roll in the hay, anyway.

"I'll miss you, too," he said, leaning over to give me a hug. After he pulled away, we stood there for another minute, before he shot me that million-dollar smile. "Come on, doll, we got a show to do."

I turned back around and did what I do best—buried myself in work. I was steady in my resolve that there wasn't any time for romance in my life . . . or so I thought.

Chapter 4

"But, I don't understand," said Dorothy, in bewilderment. "How was it that you appeared to me as a great Head?"

"That was one of my tricks," answered Oz. "Step this way, please, and I will tell you all about it."

—L. Frank Baum, *The Wonderful Wizard of Oz*

"I'm going to give you one more chance, and then I'm going to have to kick you out of here," warned a stern-faced woman with a name tag that read "Suzie."

"Okay, sorry," Nancy grumbled. The former nightclub host was celebrating her new job as an assistant to Eric J. Parkington, a handsome investment banker who split his time between New York and Las Vegas (the same one, incidentally, who had sent me a bottle of Dom at the Privé appearance). At the Peppermill (a Las Vegas landmark that's equal parts coffee shop and seventies-style lounge), each table is topped with a small shaker of multicolored sugar crystals, intended for coffee, but which Nancy had decided to use as her own makeshift confetti. When a shower of sugar landed in Hannah's iced tea, the situation escalated into a full-on sucrose war.

"I'm on a diet, bitch!" Hannah joked as she grabbed the sugar from the next table and started dumping it down Nancy's shirt. Flying sugar rainbows somehow didn't seem out of place in this twenty-four-hour establishment. After all, we were sitting under mirrored ceilings in booths outlined in strips of neon, surrounded by synthetic cherry blossom trees. The loud peals of laughter coming from our table had attracted the attention of the entire diner, including Suzie, the manager on duty.

"You guys need to calm down," she said firmly, "and enough with the sugar."

She grabbed the shakers off the table and disappeared behind one of the many artificial trees that populated the restaurant's interior.

Nancy wasn't the only one sharing good news. I had been thrilled to learn that E! had finally decided to order a pilot for the Vegas-based reality show I wanted to do. Even though I had been told that television shows set in Sin City simply didn't translate, it appeared that someone somehow had changed their mind.

"They're going to send a production team out next month to film a pilot," I told Hannah between bites of my salad. Nancy had gone to the restroom to try and get the sugar out of her bra, and I had been dying to tell Hannah, but didn't want to overshadow Nancy's news. "I have to start making decisions about who should be on it."

I was testing the waters. Hannah was made for TV, but she never seemed interested in the spotlight—which is how I knew she was a real friend. At every press event or red-carpet club appearance, Hannah would sneak around the sea of cameras, dip into a bathroom, and meet us at our table a few minutes later. Unlike L.A., paparazzi weren't lurking around every corner, so Hannah was easily able to fly under the radar.

"Yeah . . . decisions," she yawned, with the sort of monotone inflection that said it all. A short pause hung in the air before I shot her a smile and turned back to my salad.

We appeared to have the conversation without having to say anything—my favorite part about any good friendship. Hannah had zero interest and I was totally okay with that. It almost made me like her more. But her good looks, outgoing nature, and willingness to discuss anything and everything, no matter how personal, would have been great for the show, so I had to at least feel her out.

"I'm sure you'll figure it out." She dangled her fork loosely in her hand and pointed it around the restaurant. "Lots of options around here."

Nancy returned from the restroom, and as if on cue, Lindsay bounded into the neon-lit diner.

"Sorry I'm late," she breathed, ducking under one of the ersatz cherry trees and collapsing onto the booth's blue-and-purple-striped upholstery. "I just drove in from L.A."

"Rough night last night?" I asked, laughing. Being a burlesque dancer, Lindsay prided herself in appearing "put together" at all times. She always had the most perfectly styled, retro outfits and impeccable hair and makeup. But at that particular moment, she looked totally *undone*. She appeared to be wearing last night's makeup, which was so smeared I wondered if she had bothered to look in the mirror without her cat-eye sunglasses on.

"I mean, it was . . ." she started, but abruptly stopped when she spotted a waitress. "Hi, can I please have a mimosa? Light on the juice."

"I guess that answers that," Hannah scoffed.

"Remember that guy?" Lindsay prompted, looking back and forth between Hannah and me. "The actor from that show?"

When Lindsay had moved from Washington State a few years earlier, her first stop on the way to Vegas was L.A. During her time there, she booked a handful of music video gigs, during one of which she met an extremely popular TV actor who had become well known across the country for his work on a popular cable series, and almost equally as well known among the women in L.A. as a player and major asshole.

"Oh no," I said, fearing what I already knew happened. "You didn't?"

An attractive girl with a killer figure, Lindsay turned most heads when she walked into a room. So when she got to L.A., it was only a matter of time before she experienced the thrill of her "first celebrity."

"I did," she said meekly, scrunching her nose and slumping down in her chair.

"Was it at least good this time?" Hannah blurted out.

There is something about the idea of "celebrity" that causes logical, clearheaded people to become total lunatics. Maybe it's because, next to the almighty dollar, fame is the prize most revered in our culture. And Lindsay fell hard: hook, line, and sinker. I couldn't blame her. What young girl didn't grow up daydreaming over the heartthrobs on the cover of *Tiger Beat*? Or have walls covered in pictures of Leonardo DiCaprio, or whomever the idol of the moment was?

So as if on command, Lindsay turned into putty when this actor expressed interest in her. After all, she was a mere mortal and he was a *celebrity*. As an adult, you think you'd be impervious to that kind of thing, but it's surprising how easy it can be to swoon in the face of fame—even if he or she is far from your usual type. He and Lindsay hung out a few times and he wined and dined her, but it was abundantly clear that he wasn't interested in anything serious (which she already knew, but everyone thinks, *What if I'm the one to break the spell?*). Which is why she'd occasionally fall back into his trap.

"Not really," Lindsay admitted. "Honestly, though, I'm done with him." She took a swig of mimosa before adding: "For good."

She went on to explain that he had reached out to her a few days earlier asking if she would come to L.A. He was stuck filming and couldn't leave town, but was eager to see her again. He even offered to buy her a plane ticket, which she took as a good sign, but she insisted that she drive. (She already knew what would become my favorite dating rule: Have your own getaway car!)

"I don't even know how it came up," she said, exasperated. "But for some reason I told him that I'd never actually seen any of his movies.

"I could tell that annoyed him a little, but whatever, I haven't! Plus, wasn't I supposed to play it cool? I didn't want to be a fan girl." She took another swig from her flute. "So anyway, I'm on my way out the door and he tells me he has something for me. I'm not kidding you. I'm about to leave and he hands me a shoebox full of DVDs and says, 'Here are all my movies so you can get familiar with my work.' "

"No!" Hannah and I shouted in unison.

"Oh, I know somebody who hooked up with him," Nancy began, under her breath, stopping after Hannah gave her a dirty look saying, *Shut the fuck up.*

"Ugh . . . why was I even attracted to him?" Lindsay wondered aloud, oblivious to Nancy's and Hannah's exchange. "He's not even hot. I would have never gone out with him ordinarily. It grosses me out."

"That's just it. It isn't an ordinary circumstance," I said, setting down my iced tea with conviction. I had witnessed this same tired story a dozen times over. "Even if he's not your type, when you are fresh off the bus, you think it's super flattering. Right? Like, he could probably have any girl he wants and he's pursuing *you*. Talk about a massive ego boost!

"The same thing happened to me right when I moved to L.A.," I continued. "I've met lots of celebrities over the years . . . but you always remember your first."

My first celebrity "encounter" happened only a few months after I moved to L.A. I had never even seen so much as a local newscaster in person, so the idea of an *actual* celebrity seemed completely foreign to me. If you live outside Los Angeles, it's easy to cast this shroud of otherworldliness on famous people. Simply put, they didn't exist in the same world as us common folk, so it never seemed imaginable that I'd bump into one on the street. You doodle his name on your school notebook; you don't spot him strolling into your neighborhood bar.

So when a member of a pop group at the height of his career entered the restaurant I was working at in Santa Monica, I found myself surprisingly easy prey.

"Hey, can I get a table for three, please?" asked the chiseled blond with blue eyes and hair pulled back into a rough ponytail. I didn't even recognize him. I was just oblivious. Of course, I had heard his group's name a hundred times and had heard their songs (you'd have to be living under a rock not to), but I never paid enough attention to any of those boy bands to know one member from the other. I had always listened to rock, not pop. My proverbial notebooks would have been covered in "Mrs. Kurt Cobain."

"Sure," I said, gesturing for them to follow me toward a table outside my already packed section. With a smile, I handed them each a menu and told them to enjoy their lunch.

Moments later, my coworker Kira scurried up to me and through a fit of nervous giggles said, "He wants *you* to wait on him!"

"Who?" I asked, already forgetting the table I had just sat.

"You're kidding, right?" she asked, looking aghast. She must have decided that I was kidding and added, "I want the tip, though!"

"Okkkaayy," I said, looking around and realizing the table I had just sat was the only occupied one in her section. I just figured she thought the guy was cute or something. He definitely was conventionally good-looking, but he certainly wasn't my type. He had a young Fabio vibe, so I had a hard time taking him seriously.

As I skated over toward the table (yes, I was a roller-skating waitress), I noticed all the servers were pausing between tables, whispering and not so subtly sneaking glances at the young man who looked as though he had just jumped from the cover of a Harlequin novel.

Wait, I thought. *Who is this guy? An Abercrombie model or something?*

"What can I get you guys to drink? How about a beer?" I offered, even though it was still well before noon. As a Hooters waitress, upselling was the first thing we were taught. If we weren't too busy, it was suggested that we sit down and chat with customers, particularly the women and children. After all, Hooters was supposed to be a "family restaurant," despite its tongue-in-cheek name. I'd happily try to upsell this table, but

I wasn't sitting down and fawning all over this guy. He had asked for me specifically, so I had to be as professional as possible, so as not to give him the wrong idea. I'd be cheerful but distant.

As I put in the trio's chicken wing order, I wondered about this fellow. Sure, he was good-looking, but this was L.A. Lots of people are good-looking. He was confident in a way that most people weren't, like he *knew* he was somehow special, but without being a dick. It was a relaxed confidence—as if he knew it was only a matter of time until he got what he wanted.

Over the course of their meal, this guy slowly started to grow on me. I had to admit, there was something about him. Usually guys as good-looking as him weren't as *nice* as he was. Or maybe I was just impressed by the crowd of oh-so-casual gawkers lurking to catch a glimpse of young Fabio.

When the time came to play his trump card, he did so with expert skill. He had years of experience under his belt and knew how to pull the "don't you know who I am?" thing with actual aplomb.

"What's your name?" he asked, sticking out his hand.

"Holly," I said, confidently reaching to shake his.

"Nice to meet you," he said before introducing himself in return.

I took note and glided back to the hostess stand so I could ask everyone who the hell this guy was. I had a name, but as I said, I wouldn't have even known one boy band from another, so what he told me didn't ring any bells.

A group of girls were anxiously waiting for me to return to join in on their gossip session.

"Do you know who that guy is?" I asked, subtly motioning toward the table. Before I could even share his first name with the girls, they all exploded. Kira said that the man I was talking to was a member of one of the most famous groups on the planet.

"Duh," another girl said to me, rolling her eyes. "And he likes *you*! Get his number!"

I didn't have to. The next time I skated back to check on his table, he made the next move.

"Hey, would you like to go out on a date with me this weekend?" he asked point-blank. Immediately I was taken aback, but paused before regurgitating the standard "No, thank you," I'd perfected for the more assertive customers. Most guys who approached me were prone to just offering to "hang out," so there was something flattering about being asked out on a proper date.

Ordinarily, I would never have been interested in this guy. In fact, between school and work, I didn't really have the time to date, period. But I had to admit, I was starting to buy into the hype around him. This wasn't just a guy; this was an *adventure*. I was still young and naïve enough to think that if someone had what it took to become famous, there must be something special about him, right? I hadn't been in town but a few months, so the idea of being around a celebrity was still a novelty to me. And aren't new adventures one of the things I had been searching for, after all?

Just his wandering into the restaurant where I worked was worth a call home. Imagine all the fuss an actual date would create? Most of the folks who stopped into the Santa Monica eatery were tourists, not pop stars. I thought this was just the kind of story my family and friends back home were expecting to hear, so why not?

"Okay," I agreed, with just a hint of reluctance. He handed me his phone and asked that I plug in my number. Without saying another word, I turned to skate away. It would have been even more awkward if I lingered. When he got up to leave, I saw a small swarm of fans approach him for photos, with which he politely complied and flashed his white, toothy pop star grin.

"Oh my god, he got your number! Are you guys gonna go out?" Kira squealed, grabbing the check folder to see how much she just landed. "Wow, he must *really* like you."

"I don't know," I shrugged, trying my best to sound unenthusiastic.

Five minutes ago I didn't know who this guy was. I didn't want to act all giddy now. On the inside I was totally drinking the Kool-Aid, but I didn't want any of them to know that. "I guess I'm supposed to see him this weekend. We'll see."

Half a dozen servers huddled around me—even the manager seemed impressed! I had to admit, I was enjoying all this attention. This guy was a pop idol who was adored by millions, and he had eyes for *me.* As lame as the whole thing sounds, it did kind of make me feel special.

Not long after he called and invited me bowling, which I thought was cute. So far this whole courtship felt traditional and sweet. Isn't a bowling date something straight out of a fifties sitcom? Maybe he'd give me his varsity sweater, too. I think he could sense I was a little hesitant and suggested that maybe I'd be more comfortable if we each brought a friend and we could make it a double date. I jumped at the chance; having a friend along for the ride would make things way less awkward. I invited an acquaintance, who couldn't wait to get a glimpse of this household name in the flesh.

When she and I arrived at the Westside bowling alley, it looked completely closed. Not a single car was in the parking lot.

"Shit," I said.

"Are we in the right place?" she asked me.

"This is where he told me to meet him," I said. Just as I took out my phone to call him, a huge black SUV came barreling into the abandoned parking lot. The back door opened and he came spilling out of the car with his friend, who, I would later learn, just happened to be another member of his group.

"I think it's closed," I said, pointing toward the dimly lit doors.

"It is," he said, a huge grin spreading across his face. "To everyone but us."

He threw his arm around my shoulders, exuding his brand of charming confidence, and led me inside the empty bowling alley. A stocky older man introduced himself as the manager; he handed us each brand-new shoes, set up our lane, and even offered us drinks from the bar. Besides him and the security detail, it was just the four of us on what had to be the most expensive first date I'd ever been on. After an hour or so, we had successfully proven ourselves to all be terrible bowlers and the guys suggested we go to the Santa Monica pier for some rides and carnival games. Since my friend and I were working the late shift that night, and the pier was so near the restaurant, we agreed to go.

It wasn't long before a handful of screaming girls were following us around. I laughed to myself. Here I was, an ordinary girl with a thick mop of strawberry blond hair and a puffy white Gap coat. These crazed fans were probably wondering who the hell I was while at the same time wishing they were in my place. We bounced from game to game as he proved he was one of those guys with luck on his side, slaying each carnival game as if it was nothing. He handed me the giant plush pink teddy bear he won and planted a kiss on my cheek. My friend and I took this as our cue. We thanked them for the fun night and promised to be in touch.

"We have a couple of shows scheduled, but I'll be back soon," he said, pulling me into a big hug. I practically skipped off the pier and down the Third Street Promenade. Despite my initial reluctance, I was actually starting to like this guy. At twenty-one years old, who could blame me? It was all so surreal!

As the days turned into a week, I didn't hear from him.

"He's busy," I told my roommate when she asked about him. She rolled her eyes and dropped it. He finally called the following week. Just like I expected, he blamed his chaotic schedule for being out of touch since our date, but said he was really looking forward to seeing me the next weekend if I was free. He was less engaging than I'd hoped he would be, but I chalked it up to jet lag. *Hey,* I thought. *Maybe he's just not a phone person. I'm certainly not!*

And so our relationship went (if you can even call it a relationship). He would string me along just enough to keep me interested, then disappear. Each conversation was less exciting than the one before, but I was eager to try and recapture the magic of our first date. By that point, I was sort of invested. Not emotionally—it was more of a pride thing. Word had traveled fast, and it seemed like everyone I knew was aware of my celebrity suitor, and it would be a bruise to my ego if I had to tell everyone he blew me off.

When he told me he was coming back to L.A. and suggested we go out, I agreed.

"Why?" my roommate asked after overhearing the phone call. "He's just going to let you down again."

"He is not," I argued, defending my decision. "He's a nice guy!"

"Ughhhh," she said, stamping her foot. "Holly! He is *not* nice. He flakes on your phone calls, he doesn't fly you out to see him, and he makes promises he doesn't keep!"

She was right. I knew that deep down, but I told myself that things might be different in person. He was skilled in the art of smoothing things over, flattering me with his compliments. But this was all a part of his game—his carnival game, where winning me over again and again was the prize. *Was* this all a game to him? The novelty was starting to fade and I was beginning to feel foolish every time someone at work asked me about my celebrity "boyfriend." I felt like I had to see him one more time. Maybe we would capture lightning in a bottle or maybe I would decide he wasn't worth my time, but I needed one last date to know how I really felt, and perhaps to save just a little bit of face.

"Just come over," he pleaded. He was back in Los Angeles for a concert and invited me to meet up at the hotel where he was staying in the South Bay, which is about twenty minutes south of Santa Monica and even farther from downtown (where he was performing the following evening).

"Why are you staying all the way down there?" I asked, dodging the invite.

"Will you please drive down and meet me?" he pressed. "I'm trying to fly under the radar. Fans would find my hotel if I stayed right next to the venue."

Per usual, he said all the right things, and I begrudgingly accepted. Driving down the 405 in my dinged-up old car, I knew this was going to be it: either we were going to have an amazing night together or it was going to fizzle out and be over. I knocked on the door to his hotel room and he answered the door in a velour tracksuit.

"Would you like a glass of wine?" he offered as I stepped into the hotel suite. I had only ever stayed in tiny hotel rooms before, so the suite really impressed me. I was in awe that it came complete with a living room, a bar, and an entryway in addition to a bedroom! I nodded politely and thanked him when he handed me the glass.

"You want to see my new video?" he asked. I noticed just a glint of boyish excitement in his eyes. "I just got a copy."

I wasn't really into his music, so I would have rather just hung out, talked, and enjoyed each other's company. But what could I say? I nodded my head again.

He wandered into the bedroom and popped his DVD into the player. I followed and perched myself on the corner of the bed. He immediately began rattling on: commenting and narrating each segment as if he were a real-life version of *Pop Up Video*. When it was finally over, he called his assistant and asked him to order "the usual."

Even though this was clearly going south quickly, I was still eager to give it one last try. Never mind the fact that he didn't even bother to ask me if I wanted anything when he ordered "the usual." I just thought that maybe if we were forced to have a conversation, then *maybe* there would still be something there.

For about twenty minutes, we talked music. He never asked me what bands I was interested in, instead just rotated through his own collection while I chimed in if it was someone I actually knew about. When I made a comment about one particular artist I liked, a sour look appeared on his face.

"I like him, too, but he did a song with the *other* band," he said, screwing up his face in exaggerated disgust and making a point to avoid uttering the name of the rival boy band, as if they were Lord Voldemort. "It hasn't been released yet."

"Who's the *other* band?" I asked.

Begrudgingly he let the syllables fall from his mouth, with a slight annoyance that I hadn't already known that there was beef between these two supergroups. I got the impression he assumed I was a fan of his, even though I had never tried to fake knowing anything about him, his band, or their music. *Maybe he assumes every young woman is a fan?* I wondered. *Or maybe he thinks the only women who would want to go out with him are fans?* Either way, I registered the whole situation as kind of sad.

Just about as sad as you only being interested in this guy because he is a celebrity, a little voice in my head piped up. Immediately I felt gross and wished I could get as far away from there as I could. Despite being starstruck, I knew that this was not a person I wanted to spend any more time with. But how could I get out of this without being totally awkward? I was starting to feel anxious when I tried to think about what my next move would be.

Suddenly I heard a knock at the door.

"I'll get it," I exclaimed, nearly falling off the bed. I thought it was the thoughtful thing to do, answering the door for him. Not to mention, I was antsy and looking for a distraction, no matter how fleeting, from our awkward conversation.

One of his assistants stood alone at the door. He held a plastic drugstore bag out toward me, reached inside, and set it on the entry table, a knowing look in his eye. I was surprised not to see any dinner, so I thanked him absent-mindedly.

The bag sat there, open. I could see inside it. I expected to see protein bars or shaving cream or some other mundane essentials. Instead, the bag contained nothing but an industrial-sized tube of K-Y Jelly.

"Ummmm," I mused loudly, still standing in the suite's foyer. "Actually, I think I'd better be going. I have class early in the morning."

"Oh, come on, just stay!" he half shouted from the bedroom. "I'll make sure you get a wake-up call."

"No, I have to go." I grabbed the purse I had left in the entryway and bolted. He tried to call out after me, but I wouldn't even turn around.

"I spoke to him only once after that," I told my friends while I set my credit card on the check the waitress had brought to our table. "It was over the phone. He called me as if nothing was wrong, but I basically told him that I felt like he treated me like a groupie and that I was over it. Luckily, I had been at home with my roommate when he called. Something about having her there made me feel like I could actually say what I felt. Usually I'm not that together when it comes to guys—even more so back then. I either ghost on them without a word of explanation or end up getting walked all over," I admitted as I stirred the ice around in my otherwise empty glass.

Obviously, that wasn't the last time I would be interested in a guy in large part because of his fame. I still had a lesson to learn. Famous people aren't special or different from anyone else. In fact, what you see on TV is most often *not* what you get.

"I still cannot believe you dated *him*!" Lindsay said, which made me wonder if she somehow missed the moral of the story.

"Lindsay, he was a tool!" I exclaimed, tossing my napkin at her.

"I know, but I loved him when I was growing up," she said, starry-eyed with nostalgia.

"And you're really wondering how you fell back in bed with the dick bag in L.A.?" Hannah asked her.

"You're so right." Lindsay laughed.

WHEN IT CAME TO romance, I had yet to dip my toe in the Vegas dating pool, unless you count my dine-and-dash with Russell Brand. Nancy had tried to convince me to give one of her friends a chance, but no one she suggested seemed like a good fit. She swore Eric, her new boss, was sick of his girlfriend and wanted to go out with me, but I wasn't about to go out with someone who was still attached.

One afternoon Nancy finally suggested someone who did sound interesting.

I had just signed on for another three months in *Peepshow*, and to celebrate, the casino rolled out some customized slot machines with my picture on them, as well as some blackjack tables emblazoned with my name and likeness. Nancy had come over to Planet Hollywood to hang out while I was photographed with the machines and tables now gracing the casino. As I positioned myself on one of the tables, carefully arranging a hand of cards in a perfect fan for the photo, we talked about her plans for the night. She bent over to artfully place some chips next to me, then leaned back against a chair, and purposefully dropped the name of a comedian I was a fan of.

"Are you kidding? I loved his latest special!" I exclaimed. "I caught it on TV the other day. It was so funny!"

"No way! I didn't know you knew who he was!" Nancy practically shouted over the noisy casino. "He *loves* you!"

This comedian had a huge cult following. People really related to his raw but down-to-earth humor. He was tall, tan, and muscular, but for me, it was more about his sense of humor than his looks. His comedy seemed to hit that perfect balance of self-deprecation and confidence, all while he himself came across as totally approachable. He had likability down to a science.

"I didn't even know you watched it," Nancy repeated, smiling. "He's friends with my boss. I met him earlier today. He is out here to take meetings for a potential stand-up residency. We were talking, and when I mentioned we were friends, he told me he wants to go out tonight and was hoping I would bring you along."

"Totally!" I blurted out. It had been a while since I had been on a date, and he seemed like the perfect guy to break the ice with because I felt like I already knew what he would be like based on what I had seen on TV. Now, this was incredibly stupid of me, because I of all people should have known how a TV show can misrepresent someone's personality! It would appear I still had a lot to learn.

Nancy was waiting for me outside the theater after that night's performance, looking amazing in one of her signature black-on-black ensembles, her shiny black bob swinging just under her chin. I called downstairs and arranged for a driver to meet us outside Planet Hollywood's secret VIP entrance in one of the casino's fleet of black SUVs.

When we arrived at the Wynn, one of the nightclub's managers met us at the South entrance. The manager, a slim, tan blond dressed in a perfectly tailored suit, whisked us through the entrance and ushered us past the long line snaking into Tryst. We were brought past the red tufted walls of the entryway and into the club as the room opened up to reveal a majestic ninety-foot-tall waterfall, lit in shades of red. We arrived at a booth, where Eric stood with the tall, gorgeous brunette girlfriend he was supposedly sick of. The comedian wove his way through the crowded area and sidled up next to me at the table.

"Doug," he shouted in my ear with a goofy grin before jokingly pursing his lips like a duck and squinting his eyes, playing the part of the "ultra douche." I immediately started laughing; it was an exaggerated but pretty spot-on impression of so many of the guys who tried so hard to be cool.

For the next few hours we attempted to have a conversation, yelling over the loud music. He was skilled at delivering a punch line (which I expected, of course). I was laughing nonstop and having a really great time. As the alcohol started to take its hold, he got a little more comfortable and pulled a coin out of his pocket.

"Heads, we're making out tonight," he said through a half-sloshed smile that I registered as mildly charming, only because I had consumed a few glasses of champagne myself. "Tails, we're not."

I laughed and raised my eyebrows as if to feign shock at his presumption. I couldn't decide if the line was so horrible it made me not want to make out with him or if I should have a sense of humor about it. Hey, at least it was something I hadn't heard before.

Lady Luck saved him the embarrassment when the coin landed squarely on tails. I shrugged my shoulders as if to say: Oh well, better luck next time.

Eager to put his luxurious accommodations to good use, he invited us all back to his villa at the MGM Grand's Mansion for an after party. I was digging in my purse to grab some cash to tip our server when he reached over and blocked me from paying.

I looked at him, expecting a punch line to drop—he had to be joking around, right? But he said nothing at first, just looked back at me with a furrowed brow, as if I had seriously insulted him.

"What?" I asked, genuinely confused.

"The *man* should always pay," he demanded, shooting me a dirty look.

"Well, I can handle myself," I snapped back haughtily. I was finally at a place in my life where I was independent, and being able to pay my own way was a serious source of pride for me. I couldn't imagine why he was being so rude about this, but I decided it wasn't worth getting in a pissing contest with him and let the situation dissolve. Regardless, his behavior was a pretty decisive strike against him.

The group of us walked out together and piled into cars to make our way over to the after party. Four of us crammed into the Rolls-Royce waiting for Doug and we were on our way, laughing and joking for the fifteen-minute ride. We pulled up to the hidden-from-view, invite-only, high-roller villas and stepped out into the glass-covered atrium of the Tuscan compound that is the MGM Mansion. It was a perfect 70-something degrees inside the courtyard, though I knew it was well over 95 in the rest of the city. A large fountain muffled the chatter of the rest of our group, who were taking it all in. The Mansion is pretty well hidden—I think Doug and I were the only ones in the car who had seen it before. Even though I was familiar with it, I was still craning my neck to take in the luxe scenery along with everyone else.

Doug led us into his villa, down the hall toward his indoor pool. Nancy and I made ourselves at home, grabbing drinks and taking a seat on two of the rattan lounge chairs next to the pool as we waited for the other guests to arrive. First, everyone who had been at our table trickled in. A few minutes later, the rest of the local nightlife crowd started arriving. As soon as they did, we had some excellent people-watching. Some of the guests dove into the pool fully clothed, others without a stitch. There seemed to be no in between. When our host for the evening decided to get in on the action, he ended up throwing a woman in the pool and spraying everyone (including me) with champagne.

"Fuck!" I yelped, "that shit stings!" The champagne had hit me right in the eye, and it wasn't mixing well with my contact lens.

"Oh, come on! Don't tell me you're afraid of a little champagne!" Doug teased, throwing his muscular arm over my shoulder.

"I'm going to excuse myself," I said grumpily, pushing his arm off my shoulder. "I need to go find a restroom," I said to Nancy, who then got up to follow me.

"Oh, come on!" Doug yelled after me. "Have a little fun!"

Nancy and I walked out of the pool chamber and down the hall, searching for the powder room.

"Looking for the restroom?" a smooth, deep voice asked us as we walked by the villa's cavernous living room, still patting ourselves down with the towels we had grabbed on the way out.

I looked over to see Mr. Eric J. Parkington holding court with his model girlfriend and a handful of other people. He had an eyebrow raised at us and wore an amused smile on his face.

"I'll show you where they are, since Nancy doesn't seem to know where she's going," he said, winking at his new assistant as he got up from the couch. I caught a flash of the deep blue silk that lined the inside of his suit jacket. *Who dresses like that?* I wondered. He always looked so flawless.

Eric lightly placed his hand on the back of my arm and pointed us toward the powder room by the entryway, his eyes sparkling and searching my face as if he were looking for an answer to a question he never asked. *Why can't someone like this guy be single?* I wondered. I couldn't help but compare him to Doug. Sure, they were both good-looking, successful, and roughly the same age, but their styles and manners couldn't have been more different. While Doug was turning out to be a tool, Eric was soft-spoken, well-dressed, mannerly, and mysterious. It was the Jersey Shore versus James Bond . . . and Daniel Craig trumps The Situation every single time.

"He totally likes you," Nancy said after he had walked out of earshot. "You should hit that."

"No!" I laughed, wondering if Nancy had a secret crush on her boss. "He has a girlfriend. Besides, he's not my type," I protested.

Do I even have a type? I asked myself. The handful of people I had dated in my life were all so different and would most definitely fall into their own categories. Eric was just so clean-cut and conventionally handsome, dashing in a Don Draper sort of way, and to say my past dating choices were usually a little more offbeat would be an understatement.

After Nancy and I had cleaned ourselves up, I said good night to Doug. He insisted we keep in touch, and we did, but very casually. I wasn't particularly interested in him anymore, especially after my unexpected champagne shower. It's funny, though, because you would think in order to find success as a comedian in Hollywood, you'd need to be pretty quick on the uptake . . . and Doug didn't seem to be getting the hint.

A few weeks later, my friends and I were back at the Peppermill. Halfway through our first round of margaritas, Nancy's phone buzzed and she almost giddily announced that Doug was back in town and would be joining us. Hannah hit my leg underneath the table, and I gave her a "what the fuck" look while taking a sip from my drink. The evening was about to turn awkward.

A few minutes later, he arrived, inserting himself in our conversation.

"He really likes you!" Nancy whispered to me after Doug had joined in our conversation.

"I think he just likes my boobs," I whispered back. He seemed to have a problem looking into my eyes when I spoke to him.

A friend of Doug's was having a party at Lavo, and he suggested we check it out. Not ready for the night to end, we agreed to give it a chance.

Our group joined a table of some of the comedian's friends, but my friends and I stuck close together. Hannah casually plucked an olive out of her martini glass, and with a glimmer in her eye and a wicked smile on her face, leaned in toward Josh and me: "So how's Aubrey?"

"Fine, so far," I replied. "I haven't really got to know her yet, but she seems to know her part pretty well already."

After the producers officially extended my *Peepshow* contract, it was decided that Aubrey O'Day and I would co-headline for the next three months. Aubrey would be taking over the part of Peep Diva, and I would keep my role as Bo Peep.

"Are you afraid she'll steal the show from you?" Lindsay asked point-blank, locking her eyes on mine over her cocktail glass. As a dancer, she knew firsthand how much backstage drama could resemble something out of *Showgirls*.

"Not really," I said, shrugging. A deal was currently being negotiated for me to sign back on as the solo headliner after Aubrey's scheduled departure in December, but it was still confidential.

Anxiety drove much of my life, but when it came to my career I was actually in a place where I finally felt somewhat secure. I didn't foresee any marble-throwing moments in Aubrey's or my future.

Doug cut into our conversation, asking what we thought of his friend's latest business scheme. Before any of us could answer, the event's photographer approached our table and motioned for Doug and me to lean in for a picture together. Right as I opened my mouth to politely and quietly say, "No, thanks," Doug threw his hand up in the air and shook it vigorously as if to say "no fucking way." He then shouted over the music, "No way, man, I can't do that."

His reaction made me feel surprisingly small. After the whole Russell fiasco, I was trying to avoid being linked to men in the press, but for some reason I couldn't help but feel rejected, anyway. Doug was so rude to the photographer and quick to shoot him down in such an aggressively loud manner. Not only was his rudeness a turnoff, his behavior made me wonder if he was embarrassed to be seen with me. Couldn't he have just said to me, "Do you mind if we skip it this time?" No, he had to overreact so dramatically in front of so many people—it was belittling, to say the least.

Always my knight in shining armor, Josh sensed my hurt and immediately reprimanded the comedian . . . who was becoming increasingly *less* funny.

"Excuse me, you don't turn down a photo with a lady," Josh said sternly, with his signature animated charm. He shot Doug a final withering look before going back to his conversation with Hannah.

"Oh, shit, I'm sorry!" Doug recoiled. He scrunched up his face apologetically. "Now I feel bad. Should I go get that photographer?"

"No, it's okay," I replied with a forced smile, and took a sip from my drink. "I didn't want to take the picture either."

It wasn't whether we took the picture that bothered me. What had put me off was the way he turned down the photo. It was clear to me that this person who had seemed like the self-deprecating, funny "good guy" on TV was kind of the opposite in real life. Doug had offered to drive me back home, so I decided to use the drive as an opportunity to close up shop as gracefully as possible.

The drive back to Planet Hollywood took about thirty minutes, despite being only blocks away. As we inched our way down the Strip, he tried to make small talk. Behind the wheel of his neon-colored sports car, he roared the engine at each green light only to come to a screeching halt a block later at the next red light. Stop and go, stop and go. I couldn't even focus on what he was saying. All I could think about was my stomach heaving up and down as we crawled through the neon jungle. I'd had a few too many margaritas that night.

When we finally turned on a cross-street, the road opened up and he accelerated at a blind rate. As he did this, I felt my stomach lurch up my throat with overwhelming force.

"Pull over!" I shouted, the words exploding out of my mouth before I quickly sealed my lips together to hold anything else from exiting.

His eyes nearly popped out of his head, but he swerved quickly to the side of the street. I pushed the door open and vomited. We sat there for a few minutes, my head in my hands as I made sure I was totally done.

We pulled into the hotel's valet fifteen minutes later without exchanging another word. I gave some sort of halfhearted apology about not being able to hold my liquor and thanked him for the ride. We didn't speak again for a long time. Honestly, I don't think either of us was what the other expected. Having particular expectations about a person because of what you read in magazines or see on TV isn't at all realistic. I knew that I wasn't the person people had seen on TV over the past five years, so I wonder why I had expected this guy to be exactly who *he* seemed to be.

I should have seen it coming a mile away. In fact, we kind of mirrored each other. When Nancy told me, "He loves you!" I should have asked, *Why? He doesn't even know me.* Did he "love" me because of the way I looked? Because I was on billboards all over town? Because he liked me from *The Girls Next Door*?

None of those reasons were good ones, nor was the reason I thought *he* would be fun to go out with: I thought I knew what his personality would be like because I watched him on television. I knew from my own experience on TV, as well as my prior experience in dating celebrities, that what you see in the public forum is, more often than not, *not* what you get in private. The unlikely, thrilling coincidence that the star of the *one* TV special I happened to enjoy was interested in me had made me forget all I had learned.

I was determined to be as cautious as possible next time I dated anyone, famous or not.

Chapter 5

"How about my heart?" asked the Tin Woodman.

"Why, as for that," answered Oz, "I think you are wrong to want a heart. It makes most people unhappy."

—L. Frank Baum, *The Wonderful Wizard of Oz*

"Do you guys want to go house hunting with me next week?" I asked Josh and Hannah without looking up from my phone. I shifted my weight on the barstool, trying to get comfortable in my white pencil skirt, tightly cinched Blonds corset, and Miu Miu heels.

"You don't like livin' in the hotel no more?" Josh asked in an exaggerated version of his South Carolinian accent, raising an eyebrow at me over his glass of pinot. We were sitting at the Strip House bar, all dressed up for that night's special post-show event.

"It would just be nice to have a house," I said, finally looking up from my BlackBerry. "You know, decorate . . . pick out my own furniture, have something to call my own. I love the suite, but I can't live there forever."

"Where's Aubrey?" Hannah purred, looking around for my new red-headed costar. It was the night of Aubrey's premiere party, held at the sumptuous steakhouse next to the show's theater, but strangely enough, she hadn't shown up.

"I dunno." I shrugged, taking a moment to thank the bartender for the cocktail he set in front of me. "She was outside the theater doing press with me after the show," I continued. "She didn't act like anything was wrong . . . Maybe it has something to do with those leaked photos." That evening's show had started uncharacteristically late because every single person in the audience was required to check their phones at the door before entering the theater. A day earlier, photos of Aubrey in her first performance had been leaked, which were then compared mercilessly online with her polished promo shots. She called in sick that night, choosing instead to post a video with her shirt off. It amounted to a swirl of blog publicity for *Peepshow*, but it wasn't the sort of press the show was used to. I didn't know if the whole thing was a cleverly orchestrated publicity stunt on her end or a genuine leak, but my only option was to stay out of it. I had enough drama of my own to deal with!

"I'm not too worried," I added. "I'm sure she'll show up eventually." I was too distracted to give it much thought, scrolling through real estate listings on my phone, trying to find "the one" in the housing market.

With *Peepshow* on autopilot, I was feeling antsy to keep moving forward. There was always the next project, the next goal. I needed to constantly be in action, with not a moment to waste. I started thinking about how nice it would be to put down roots and invest some money in a home. I also started thinking how nice it would be to have a boyfriend. Eight months had passed since my last serious relationship had ended, and I was starting to crave that extra element in my life.

The few guys who had hit me up recently seemed more interested in getting to know the girl on the billboard than in getting to know me. Where in Las Vegas could I find a guy capable of having a serious relationship? I was starting to understand what I was told was the Las Vegas woman's motto: "I only date out of state."

The next day I stopped by Lindsay's apartment to pick her up for lunch when I noticed something unusual among her typical mess of ostrich-feather boas and stray stilettos. It wasn't strange to see books among Lindsay's messes, but they were mostly thrillers or popular fiction.

"Lindsay, what is this?" I asked, holding up the misfit paperback I had just discovered.

"Huh?" she crowed, peeking her head out of her bedroom. "Oh, that's the 'Bitch Book.' Want to borrow it?"

"The 'Bitch Book'?" I repeated, leaning back on her chaise longue and flipping to the table of contents in *Why Men Love Bitches*.

"One of my friends from back home was telling me to read it. It's all about getting a guy to commit," Lindsay shouted over her hair dryer. "Supposedly it works!"

"I hope you're not trying this on your L.A. douche nozzle," I yelled. This sounded like a recipe for disaster.

"No way," she scoffed, strolling into the living room and twisting her hair into a partially dried bun on top of her head. "I'm so over him. That book is about self-respect. I'm tired of being a doormat and always getting my heart broken."

I looked at her incredulously. How could a book magically fix a lifetime of self-inflicted bad-boy addiction? Lindsay was beautiful, talented, and kind, but her lack of confidence didn't reflect that. So many of the choices she made, from the jobs she took to the men she dated, seemed to indicate a dearth of self-esteem.

"You should read it, too," she announced, throwing a very pointed look my way. I casually thumbed through and paused on the last page: *The bitch has a strong will and faith in herself . . . the most attractive quality of all is dignity.*

I had to admit, the advice didn't sound half as cheesy as I would have guessed.

"Okay, maybe I'll look at it when you are done," I conceded, setting the book back down on her mirrored coffee table. After all, her sales pitch did make it sound kind of appealing.

Since my dating experience was severely limited, or at least highly unusual, I was desperate for guidance. The two relationships I had in my twenties could easily be described as *tragic*. Both times I had rushed into the relationships without really knowing the person or what I was getting myself into. I couldn't risk making those mistakes again. When it comes to dating, we're told to *always* use protection—and that's what I planned to do . . . in more ways than one.

It took me less than a day to tear through the "Bitch Book," and I was addicted. The idea that you could take control of your love life appealed to me. I took other recommendations from friends like *The Rules* and *He's Just Not That Into You*. I've always been a voracious reader, and I figured that if I was going to date, I needed to date smart. I thought following a protocol might help me make better choices when it came to love. Though some of the *Rules* sounded a bit repulsive—such as "Don't Stare at Men or Talk Too Much," "How to Act on Dates 1–3," and my personal favorite "Don't Discuss the Rules with Your Therapist"—for the most part, these books seemed to point the reader toward a standoffish, hard-to-get vibe, and that was definitely where I wanted to go. I was done jumping into relationships headfirst, committing myself fully, and then regretting it. The next time I started seeing someone, I was going to go slow, with eyes wide open. And if I needed something as cheesy as a dating book to help me do it, so be it.

HANNAH AND I WERE drying ourselves off after braving a makeshift indoor Slip'N Slide when she nodded to a dude standing by the bar a few feet in front of us and whispered, "Do you know who that is?"

I shook my head. He looked familiar, but I couldn't quite place him. There were plenty of famous people populating the private party in one of the Palms's largest (10,000 square feet, that is) high-roller suites, which included a full-sized indoor basketball court. In fact, the party was thrown entirely for the purpose of one rock star wanting to get "candidly" photographed partying with the scantily clad women currently dancing around him.

I turned my attention back to Hannah and gave her a look that said, *Well, who is he?*

"That's Jeffrey Decker," Hannah continued. "He's a music video director. We saw him in the booth next to us at Simon brunch a few months ago and I couldn't place who he was. He had a Mohawk back then."

Jeffrey's dark hair was now cropped short, but he was indeed the cute guy with the Mohawk I had taken notice of. She gave me a devilish half grin, slowly licked her finger, leaned toward him and stuck it right in his left ear and twisted. This didn't surprise me whatsoever, but I was definitely expecting a "What the fuck?" reaction from this guy (which I wouldn't have blamed him for at all). But to his credit, after jerking his head back, Jeffrey looked over his shoulder, his eyes landing on Hannah, then me, and just smiled . . . a big, magnetic smile.

Instinctively I smiled back, and instantly he got cuter. We caught each other's gaze a few times throughout the party, and eventually he came over to introduce himself. Because I'm so incredibly awkward when it comes to making small talk, I said hello, then promptly turned to order a drink.

Jeffrey stuck close to his crew, including a guy named Drew, a casino host at one of the resorts I frequented. One Grey Goose and soda later, Hannah announced that the party was dead and demanded we leave.

A few days later, I was surprised to get a text from Drew: "Good to see you the other night. My friend Jeffrey Decker asked for your number. Do you care if I give it to him?"

I explained to Drew that I didn't really know Jeffrey beyond our brief introduction and I worried that if he had my number, it might be weird. Plus, the thought of having to talk to a random guy was crippling. I wondered what Jeffrey's motivations were. My self-esteem was so low that I figured any guy who was so anxious to get to know me had to have an ulterior motive.

Recognizing my hesitation, Drew assured me that Jeffrey was a "*really* nice guy" and that I should give him a chance. Eventually I agreed (I had yet to learn that guys will work just as hard to get their friends laid as they will to get themselves laid). Jeffrey did seem friendly and I liked the fact that he didn't balk at Hannah's brashness. *What the hell,* I thought. The only way to meet someone was to put myself out there. I'm pretty sure my soul mate wasn't going to just arrive one day on the room-service cart.

A few days later, my phone buzzed to alert me of a new text message from a number I didn't recognize.

"Hi, Holly, this is Jeffrey. Drew gave me your number. I hope you don't mind :)"

What do I say back? I thought. At least he had been the one to reach out first, which according to *The Rules*, was the perfect first step. Rule 2 was "Don't Talk to a Man First." Check! When it came to responding, the relationship experts would surely encourage me to play it cool, friendly, and just a touch disinterested. I tried to keep it casual by telling him that Drew had asked me beforehand, so it was no big deal.

He said that it was so nice meeting me and that he hoped we'd run into each other again. I knew that how I responded was critical: he might be looking for me to drop a clue as to whether I'd agree to go out with him if he'd ask. I didn't want to give him what he was looking for, so I offered a jokey non-answer about how he was just looking for someone to give him another "Wet Willy."

"Ha! That was the first one I'd had in a long time. Maybe I'll see you around!"

I knew I needed to let the conversation hang, so I put my phone away. After all, Rule 7 is "Always End Everything First." I wanted to do a bit of research about this guy before deciding whether to continue talking with him. I saw that he started following me on Twitter, so I followed him back. After looking at his profile page, I was a little disappointed because he didn't seem to have much of a sense of humor, judging by his tweets, anyway. I hoped that disconnect wouldn't be the same in real life! I decided to dig deeper. I'm the first one to tell people that you can't believe half the shit that's on the Internet, but true or not, I was curious to at least see what was out there. The first thing that came up was his dating history. My heart sank when I realized Jeffrey had been linked to a laundry list of models and TV personalities. No wonder Hannah had known who he was! Ordinarily a director would stay behind the scenes, but based on the tabloid fascination with the women he dated, this guy was recognizable. I was bummed. Jeffrey wasn't sounding like much of a promising option after all. If he went out of his way to date such women, I figured he must be a fame whore.

"He must be really lame because he dates only famous girls or models," I ranted to Hannah and Laura, both of whom were deeply immersed in other business. "It's kind of a turn off. And do I really want to be just another notch on his belt? No thank you."

"Mm-hmm," mumbled Laura, in a faux offering of support as she studiously flipped through a magazine. Hannah stayed quiet, burying herself in whatever text conversation she was having. My girlfriends (especially these two) rarely shied away from voicing their opinions, so I knew something was up.

It dawned on me that I sounded like a hypocrite.

"Okay, fine," I acquiesced. "I know what you're thinking. I don't want to be judged for my dating history either." I plopped down on the couch next to Laura and added: "I get it. Who am I to judge Jeffrey? Anyone who looked at who I dated would get the wrong idea for sure."

I went on. "I should cut him a break and not take everything I read online so seriously. Maybe he is a good guy, but just got involved with the wrong people. Maybe he had really liked the women he dated for who they were deep down? Who knows?

"If he hits me up again, I'll definitely keep talking to him," I announced. Both Hannah and Laura were looking at me with poorly concealed smirks before Hannah started giggling.

"You just fully had a conversation with yourself," Hannah snorted.

I didn't hear anything from or about Jeffrey again until Hannah and I attended an early afternoon pool party at the Wynn the next day.

"Doesn't her hair look fake?" I heard a female voice sneer behind me. We had grabbed some appetizers and were perched around one of the high-top tables surrounding the glittering pool. I glanced over my shoulder to see a woman sneering and pointing at me.

It was true, I was wearing a fall to accentuate my own hair. I didn't care. I liked the way it looked, so I ignored the catty trophy wife behind me. *You try keeping my schedule and finding the time to keep your hair looking perfect.*

Just as the lady behind me was chipping away at my self-confidence, I happened to lock eyes with one of the most gorgeous women in the room. I'm not usually competitive (I've spent a lot of time sharing the spotlight), but I couldn't help feeling a little bit janky when I noticed this particular girl and her perfectly put-together signature look. She reminded me of all the corners I cut when I threw myself together that morning. *What I wouldn't give for an extra hour a day for a professional blow-out,* I thought wistfully. This girl looked like she lived in a blow-dry bar.

She strutted toward me as if on a runway. Her name was Andi and she was a local model. She had a soft, wavy, chocolate-brown mane that tumbled down just past her shoulders, heavy-lidded hazel cat eyes, bronze skin, and perfect, pouty lips that never quite seemed to close. Shorter than the average model, Andi made up for it by oozing sex appeal. Every guy I knew had either dated her or was desperate to.

"How've you been, honey?" she purred, sliding into the seat next to me and tapping me playfully on the arm. Andi was always in perma-flirt mode with anyone she met, male or female. Soft touches, light hair flips, sleepy eyelids, kitten voice . . . this woman was *always* on. No wonder all the guys chased after her!

I had met her a few times at various events. The model population in Vegas is pretty small, and she was one of the premier talents and therefore a familiar face to anyone who spent a fair amount of time in the city, looking at billboards or perusing local magazines. She was friendly, but we weren't close by any means. Andi was a guys' girl and didn't seem to have too many female friends. Hannah, who couldn't stand Andi, excused herself almost immediately from the table.

"I'm hosting a little party at Rehab next weekend, if you want to come," she said. "I'm really hoping some guy there will catch my eye. I'm having zero luck in the love business—especially with this last guy I was seeing."

"I'm not having much luck either," I confessed, deciding to join her little pity party for the sake of conversation, and told her the story about me losing my lunch outside the fancy car of the last guy I had sort of dated.

"Who have you been seeing?" I asked, trying to keep the conversation going.

She looked me straight in the eyes and with her full glitter-glossed lips said, "Jeffrey Decker."

Fuck, I thought. Having spent most of my life trying to avoid awkward confrontations at all costs, I had been finding myself in a shit ton of them recently.

"Oh," I said, almost choking on the lobster slider I had been eating. "Yeah, I just met him recently. He seems, um, nice." It was lame, I knew it, but I didn't know what else to say. I wasn't going to lie and act as if I had never talked to him, but I wasn't even sure if I was interested in him romantically, so there was really nothing else to say.

"Are you guys still together?" I asked. Jeffrey hadn't mentioned having a girlfriend.

"Not really." She pouted, looking down at her lap and picking at the beaded edge of her Haute Hippie skirt. "He's great, but a little too busy with work to focus on a relationship."

"That sucks," I said, trying my best to sound sympathetic. I wondered if she had heard somehow that Jeffrey and I were talking and tracked me down on purpose . . . to claim her turf, piss on the trees, and remind me of a presumed "girl code" that might exist between us. Generally, I think girl code (aka staying far, far away from any guys your friends have dated) is a good idea, but I didn't feel like it applied in this situation. I barely knew Andi. And, no offense, but to stay away from every guy Andi had dated would narrow the dating pool quite drastically.

Jeffrey texted me the following week to let me know that he was set to work on an indie film for the rest of the month. The movie was being shot on location in Australia, and he was heading down under immediately. Jet-lagged and lacking any friends around to distract him, he often wound up diving into long, thoughtful text conversations with me. We were in communication constantly over the next few weeks. For an extreme introvert like me, this is definitely the most comfortable way to get to know someone. We discussed music, movies, travel, food . . . you name it. Being a night owl myself, I'd begun spending hours each night on the phone texting with Jeffrey. We had quickly developed our own rapport: private jokes, stupid nicknames, and sharing secrets. In the span of a month, it was as if we'd become close friends. He knew when I'd have a big meeting, and I'd be sure to ask him about a particularly grueling day on set.

I have to say, the hardest dating book rules for me to follow were numbers 5 and 6: "Don't Call Him and Rarely Return His Calls" and "Always End the Calls First." I translated "calls" to mean "texts." After all, *The Rules* was originally published in 1995. I was enjoying my text-message marathons with Jeffrey so much that I wanted to hit him up all the time. Had I not exercised any restraint, he would have been the recipient of my entire stream-of-consciousness narrative.

He kept saying that we had to get together when he got back to the States, but we never got around to actually locking down a date. I was kind of scared to actually have a face-to-face with him for a change. It was almost as if I wanted the fantasy of a boyfriend rather than an actual boyfriend. I loved having a text message bestie, but was I even physically attracted to him? This remained to be seen.

The next time I was back in L.A., I opted to go to a party at a new Hollywood club with two of the *Peepshow* dancers who also happened to be in town for the day. I hadn't been out in L.A. in ages, so I figured it could be fun, but also, having plans gave me an excuse not to even *think* about texting Jeffrey.

The "hot party" turned out to be a promotional event complete with a gifting suite and a sea of photographers waiting to catch each guest posing next to every product. I instantly began to feel claustrophobic. From the aggressive photographers to the sponsors pushing everyone for photo ops, this felt more like a press engagement than a low-key night out. Usually I was all for press, but that night I hadn't been prepared. It was too loud and hectic to even enjoy my friends' company. I needed to get out of there—and fast. My anxiety was taking over and I could practically feel the walls of the club closing in on me. My mind started racing and it felt as if my pulse sped up.

I told my two buddies that I wasn't feeling so well and was going to head back to the hotel. After we said good-bye, I made my way toward the back exit. It took me about ten minutes to navigate through the pulsating crowd. I reached down to unclasp the skull on my tiny Alexander McQueen clutch and pulled out my phone to call a cab when I noticed I had left my cash and credit cards in my hotel room. *Damn it,* I thought. *How could I be that scatterbrained?*

As I sat there running through my options, wondering who would be desperate enough to pick me up in the back alley of a nightclub, I felt my phone vibrate in my hand.

It was Jeffrey: "Hey! What's up?"

"Hi," I responded instinctively before deciding to add, "I'm in town!"

"Awesome," he shot back almost immediately. "Wanna meet up?"

"Sure, but you'll have to come get me," I texted. "I'm actually stranded and I left my wallet in my hotel room."

"Ha-ha. I'll come rescue you."

I gave him the name of the club and thanked him for being so flexible.

He replied: "No problem. Just give me a few minutes. Should I meet you out back?"

"Perfect," I responded. I loved that he suggested that—and I loved even more that he didn't make me ask. It's kind of an embarrassing thing to have to explain. "Oh, hey, can you pick me up out back so photographers won't see me get into your car? You know, because I'm *such* a big deal." Maybe he wasn't the publicity whore that I pegged him for.

As I waited for him to roll up, I actually felt excited . . . I was crushing on this guy harder than I thought. Fifteen minutes later, my phone buzzed.

"I'm out back."

How the hell did he get here so fast? I wondered. I slipped out the back door and into his idling black Tahoe. When I dropped myself into the passenger seat, I could feel my heartbeat pick up. He was cuter than I remembered.

"Hey, thanks for picking me up," I said breathlessly as I pulled the heavy SUV door shut. "That party just wasn't for me."

"I'm not really down with that scene either," he said, shifting the car into drive. His dark-tinted windows shielded us from the bright camera lights that were flashing around the corner. "You wanna check out a movie? There's a theater near my place that's never busy."

"Sure," I replied as I settled in for the short drive to the theater. I was nervous, but our conversation flowed surprisingly smoothly, thanks to the fact that we had spent about a month texting while he was in Oz.

After the movie, we discussed the soundtrack while strolling back to the parking garage. As we reached the pay station, I stopped myself from offering to pay, remembering I didn't have any money in my purse anyway. The lack of funds made it easy to stick to the rules I was so determined to adhere to, as Rule 4 advised against "going dutch" on a date. Perhaps the outdated verbiage should have given me a clue that I could skip this rule. I awkwardly shifted my weight from my right foot to my left as he inserted his credit card. Not offering to pay didn't feel good. I didn't feel like I was being me. *It's just six dollars,* I tried to reassure myself.

As we walked over to his car he said, "So, do you want to go anywhere else? I don't know about you, but I would definitely like to keep this night going. I don't want it to end."

In a world of guys who act like they are too cool to care, that was quite an endearing statement.

I smiled and said, "I'd love to, but I have to be up really early tomorrow to get back to Vegas." It was true, my schedule was packed. But it was also Rule 11: "End the Date First."

As he pulled up outside my hotel, I said good-bye and basically did a duck-and-roll out of the car, designed to avoid any possible attempt at a good-night kiss, which I sure as hell wasn't going to do in front of the main entrance of the Beverly Hills Hotel under the eyes of whomever might be milling about. Not to mention, it played into Rule 14, "No More Than Casual Kissing on the First Date." *Consider me a step ahead of the game,* I thought. *No kissing* at all *on the first date.*

Racing off as if I were Cinderella leaving the ball must have piqued his interest, because his texts and phone calls were now twice as frequent, imploring me to give him a good day to come to Vegas and visit me (Rule 4: "Don't Meet Him Halfway"). Even though his charms were sneaking up on me, I was more occupied than ever with my career, so it was easy to stick to all this advice I had gleaned from books. Also, with the relationship being somewhat long distance, it was virtually impossible to break Rule 15, "Don't Rush into Sex," or to be a Stage 5 Clinger even if I wanted to be.

I rushed to meet my friends at Lavo after that evening's show to celebrate my latest good news. Earlier that day, I had received the phone call I had been hoping for: E! loved the pilot we had just filmed and had picked an airdate! As soon as I hung up the phone, I ran into Laura's room to tell her and had been in a blur of happiness ever since. There was something about having a definitive airdate that made the whole possibility of being back on TV seem real.

"You're glowing." Hannah beamed. "It actually looks like you've been getting laid. I'm happy for you."

I laughed. "No, but Jeffrey *does* want to come out to visit."

"So why isn't he?" Hannah asked, peering at me from behind her phone. Now that I was looking at her properly, I noticed she was dressed all in black, as she had been the first time I met her. Her hair was pulled back into a chignon and her nails were short, black, and shiny. She pressed me: "What are you afraid of? You've been talking to him and talking about him for months now."

"Let's talk about you," I said, changing the subject. "Your nails are back to normal." I stated as I looked at her manicure, unable to mask the amusement in my voice. "What happened with Brendan?"

She rolled her eyes and held up her hands as if to say "Don't even ask."

"Don't change the subject," Lindsay playfully reprimanded. "Just tell Jeffrey to come! I want to meet him."

"I don't know," I grumbled, reaching for a decadent gourmet fried Oreo. "I will say this; he's much more interesting than I thought he would be."

What *was* I afraid of? Obviously I'd made some major fumbles in my love life (and in the public eye, no less), so of course I was cautious. But Vegas was my oasis, my little isle of safety, free from the paparazzi, and I still had some time before the reality cameras became omnipresent, capturing all of my spare time. If there was a moment to take a risk and put my heart back on the table, this was it. They say, "What happens in Vegas stays in Vegas." Maybe in this case that slogan would actually apply. I decided then and there that Jeffrey visiting me in Vegas would be just the thing.

The first few times he came to visit, it was casual. We spent most of our time together under the scrutiny of all my friends, who had to vet him first. Everyone agreed that he seemed *really nice*. Eventually he became a Vegas regular, despite constantly reminding me that it was his least favorite city.

It wasn't long before Jeffrey became suitemate number three during his visits. Despite being obsessive-compulsive when it came to cleanliness and dog hair, he befriended Laura's pup and even attempted to befriend Napoleon, in spite of the fact that the dog peed on Jeffrey's clothes the first time he stayed over. (Napoleon has always had better radar than me.)

Laura was always polite to him, not to mention supportive of our relationship since it made me happy, but I could sense Jeffrey wasn't her favorite person in the world. That lack of a sense of humor that I had noticed on Twitter carried over into real life, unfortunately. Not only were his jokes not funny, he seemed to have an odd prudishness when it came to humor. Laura and I laughed at all things raunchy, which would make Jeffrey blush like a Victorian lady in a drawing room. Sometimes he even made a disapproving comment when Laura or I would comment on something we thought was funny. He quickly became known on Laura's side of the suite as the Fun Police.

But I didn't care. I was so thrilled to have a sweet guy flying out to see me that I could deal with the disconnect when it came to humor. *After all, nobody's perfect,* I reminded myself.

Among Jeffrey's stranger habits was going down to the casino for ten minutes or so every day.

"What is he doing every time he goes downstairs?" I wondered aloud, petting Napoleon while Laura put a few healthy items away in our small kitchen. "Do you think he's, like, calling another girl or something?"

"He's taking a shit." Laura jokingly condescended to point out, as if it were the most obvious thing in the world.

"Ohhhhhhh . . ." I said, finally putting two and two together. *Not a bad strategy,* I thought. After all, who wants to drop a deuce at your date's house?

The next time *I* had to go, I was in the clear. I had said good-bye to Jeffrey as he headed out the bedroom door on his way to meet some friends at the Palazzo . . . just in time! I zipped to the bathroom, sat on the toilet, and LET IT GO. Without getting too graphic, I'll just say things were loud. Really loud. For more than a few seconds.

I sat there contemplating what was on my to-do list that day.

"I'll be back up later tonight!" Jeffrey yelled and a door shut behind him.

I froze. What . . . the . . . hell had just happened? I thought he was gone! As if the situation weren't humiliating enough, I had left the bathroom door WIDE open, for maximum aural consumption. I leaned forward and put my head in my hands. I was at once petrified and alive with humiliation. At least he had been gentlemanly enough to not mention it . . . or would it have been better had he just put it out there and made a joke out of it? *No way,* I thought, *he is probably too grossed out. The only way to handle this now is just act like it never happened.*

That embarrassing moment aside, Jeffrey's visits were generally delightful. He treated me well and was exceptionally well mannered (a long-lost art form for most men). In fact he was turning out to be so much more of a catch than I expected. I couldn't believe I was admitting this to myself, but he really did seem like a genuinely nice guy. *Who actually ever lives up to that reputation?* I wondered. And isn't that what I was looking for? What most women are looking for? How many times have you heard someone say, "I just wish I could meet a *nice guy*!" It seemed I just might have found one.

"I want you to meet my family," Jeffrey said, dropping the comment like a bomb.

"What?" I asked, nearly choking on my coffee. I was leaning up against the granite countertop in the kitchen of his stark, modern Westwood apartment. On this specific trip I vacated my usual Beverly Hills Hotel residency and agreed to spend time with Jeffrey on his turf. I let down my guard for one moment and he drops *this* on me? Meeting someone's parents was a huge step, and I'd rarely heard of it happening this early in the game. We had been seeing each other for only a month. I don't know what I expected when I first met this guy, but it wasn't this. He was quickly becoming too good to be true. Even his friends couldn't stop gushing to me about how Jeffrey was always saying how much he liked me, how I was so different from other girls he had met, how special I was. It really made me feel good. And since I was hearing it secondhand, he had to mean it, right?

"Grab your stuff," he said. "I'm going to change your flight. We'll drive down to my parents' in Orange County and you can fly out of John Wayne."

I triple-checked to make sure I had packed every last item I brought in my overnight bag (Rule 22: "Don't Live With a Man or Leave Things in His Apartment") and we were on our way! He took me to lunch at his parents' beautiful beachside home. His parents, his sister, and her kids were all there. Normally, this would have turned my socially awkward self into a bundle of anxiety. Interacting with new people who I feared would be sizing me up and passing judgment scared me. But it wasn't like that at all. His entire family was engaging and kind. Our conversations felt natural and lively, and I felt like they really liked me. This was such a huge step, and going so smoothly—on top of it being so sudden and out of the blue. He doted on his nieces and nephews and wouldn't stop talking about how he couldn't wait to be a dad—it was really sweet. *This guy is the real deal,* I thought. He didn't seem afraid of commitment and was even opening up about his wants and desires. I couldn't believe I was saying this about the serial modelizer I had so quickly written off, but he seemed to check all the boxes.

I was done with the bad boys. It was finally time to give the nice guy a chance.

For the next month we had a perfect little courtship. On one of his weekly visits, we walked into Koi, the sushi restaurant around the corner from the *Peepshow* theater, for a late lunch. My pilot was set to air on E! that night and Planet Hollywood was having a private screening in one of their lounges before that evening's *Peepshow.*

"We apologize, the private booth isn't available tonight," the hostess said, tossing her long, silky hair over her shoulder and grabbing two menus.

"That's okay!" I replied cheerfully, "We don't need it. A corner booth would be fine!" I wondered who was in the private booth, kept away from prying eyes by metal beaded curtains. Last time it was taken, I had spotted Maria Shriver. As we followed the hostess through the restaurant to the back corner, we passed Robin Leach, who was at the hotel for the premiere party so he could cover it for his column in the *Las Vegas Sun.*

"Hello, Holly," he greeted me before adding insinuatingly, "and helloooo, Jeffrey." The tone in his voice suggested they had met before.

After we were out of earshot, Jeffrey shot me an annoyed look and muttered: "I didn't know *he* was going to be here."

"It's cool," I said flippantly. "I know him. He won't write about us. He's cool about that kind of stuff."

We took our seats and ordered our usuals. Our conversation wandered on to whether or not we thought Vegas would be a good place to raise kids (a topic he brought up). I was still kind of soured on L.A., and only the negative things about the city were at the forefront of my mind, so I was making an argument for Vegas.

"Besides, the few people I know who grew up here seem really well adjusted," I added, unwrapping my chopsticks as the waiter set down a plate of dragon rolls for me and sashimi for Jeffrey.

"I don't know." He hesitated. "Someone I used to date was born and raised here, and she was *crazy.*"

When he said crazy, I pictured a knife-wielding psychopath.

"Who was it? Anyone I know? How was she crazy?" I asked eagerly, ready for the scandalous scoop.

"You might. She was this model chick named Andi," he replied. I nodded, awaiting his anecdote. Andi seemed perfectly sane to me, but, like I said earlier, I didn't know her *that* well.

"Yeah, we were out to dinner one night and she got all gangsta on me and was like 'Are we serious with each other or not? I need to know because this needs to be locked down,' " he recalled, doing his best impression of her voice and wagging his finger around in an attempt to imitate her.

"Huh, well, she always seemed normal to me," I said, shrugging and reaching over to take a drink of water. *Damn,* I thought, *if that was his definition of crazy, I guess I won't be bringing up* our *status any time soon.*

Not that I need to, I thought. I already knew where we stood. Jeffrey had introduced me to his family, talked all about how he wanted to have kids, traveled to Vegas constantly to see me, and bragged incessantly to his friends about me. I had nothing to worry about.

After sushi, we were walking out toward the escalators that would take us down to the screening when he put his hand on my back and said, "I think I'm gonna let you do this one solo. I promised Drew I would link up with him when I was out here this time. I'll see you after the show, though, right?"

He leaned forward to give me a quick kiss.

"Sure," I mumbled after our lips parted, in a thinly veiled attempt at being nonchalant (because "bitches men love" keep a "slightly aloof demeanor"). Inside, though, I was devastated and kind of dumbfounded. What was with the sudden one-eighty? Jeffrey had seemed so supportive of my career and the new television series. This was a huge moment for me. To add insult to injury, we hadn't even discussed this ahead of time. It had been dropped on me like a bomb minutes before I had to go greet everyone at my screening. I quickly justified his reaction by decided that running into Robin must have freaked him out.

Sure, supporting me during one of my big moments should have trumped his own issues, but things had been going so well that I wasn't going to write this relationship off because of one slipup.

I pushed what had just happened to the corner of my mind where I kept all my unwanted thoughts and put on the biggest smile I could find. I'd deal with it later; I couldn't let a guy ruin my premiere night.

But this would prove a little difficult as I remembered that all of my closest friends knew that Jeffrey was in town. I burned with embarrassment at the thought of having to make feeble excuses for him while my lack of a poker face gave me away. I knew that everyone expected him to be there. Not because I had said he would be, but because that's what boyfriends do—support their girlfriends during their big moments.

Despite the excuse he had given me, I had my own suspicion as to why I thought he didn't want to be there. It hit me that maybe I wasn't the only one avoiding publicity. Maybe he didn't want to be seen with me, at least not publicly. He had no problem introducing me to his family and showing me off to his friends, but did he want to be known publicly as "Holly Madison's boyfriend"? Probably not. Or at least that's what I imagined. And that hurt.

I took a deep breath, put the smile back on my face, and descended the escalator.

"Where's Jeffrey?" Josh asked as I walked in.

"Oh, he promised one of his friends he was going to meet up with him while he was out here," I tossed out, knowing how flaky this sounded—that he would rather hang out with a bro than support his girlfriend on her big night. "No big deal," I added, trying to swipe it away like it was nothing. I am pretty sure that my disappointment showed through on my face, though. A few more people asked me about it, but no one pressed the issue. They weren't buying my forced attempt at being casual about the matter, so they dropped it.

Maybe this is a one-time thing, I thought to myself. I'd just have to file this away as strike one in case he ever tries to pull something similar again. *Maybe he just doesn't understand what a big milestone this is for me.*

I decided not to bring his behavior up to Jeffrey, despite how upset it had made me and that it practically ruined what should have been my big night. I just wanted to forget that it had ever happened, not to mention, I didn't want to run the risk of coming across as "crazy" for having feelings. If I chilled out and let things go back to normal, our relationship would continue to grow . . . I was sure of it.

In fact, I couldn't wait for the upcoming New Year. *Peepshow* was going on hiatus for the entire month of January to add a few elaborate new numbers to spice up the show. The production was a smash and we needed to give audiences a reason to come again. And because I was now the official face of the show with a new yearlong contract, audiences expected to see more of me onstage and I was more than happy to oblige.

I figured that when I wasn't busy with *Peepshow* rehearsals, I'd be spending more quality time with Jeffrey. When I gave him the good news about my month off, my dreams were quickly dashed. He informed me that he was scheduled to spend most of the beginning of the year out of the country, working on a project. I tried to convince myself that it wasn't all bad. After all, our long-distance text messaging was how I ended up falling for him to begin with, so maybe absence would make us grow closer.

It didn't turn out that way, though. I began hearing from him less and less. At first I thought I was just being sensitive and figured he must be busy on set, but I could get away with telling myself this for only so long. I thought he had really cared for me, so what changed? I couldn't let this guy make me feel like shit. He sought *me* out, not the other way around. . . .

I knew I couldn't sit around twiddling my thumbs, waiting to see what would happen when he came back home. Can you say *He's Just Not That Into You*? I wasn't going to try and fight the situation or attempt to change his mind (Rule 18: "Don't Expect a Man to Change or Try and Change Him"). I needed to pull the plug before he had a chance to do it to me.

I decided to preface the breakup with a little test, because deep down, I was still hoping he would pass. I had negotiated a week off for a vacation later in the year, choosing one of the last weeks of September because it was a slower week in Vegas, right after summer tourism died down. I decided that if I told Jeffrey about the vacation and he didn't jump at the chance to plan a trip with me, I would break it off.

The next time he texted, I told him I was in a great mood because I had just signed my contract for that year and it included the weeklong vacation in September.

"That's really awesome! You deserve it!" he replied.

There was no "let's go somewhere together" or "you better be spending it with me!" or anything like that. Okay, now I *really* didn't feel bad about dumping him.

"I've been thinking," I texted him. "We haven't really been talking as much lately and I think it would be better if we stopped seeing each other. It's going to be a really busy year for the both of us and I don't see it working out."

He sent back a row of sad emojis, and our conversation continued, with his supposedly regretful words about how he wished it could have worked out, but there wasn't any begging me to come back or any attempts at trying to change my mind. Before I went to bed that night, to eliminate the temptation of ever texting him again in one of my weaker (or drunker) moments, I deleted his number, email address, and previous text conversations from my phone, reminding myself of Rule 2: "Don't Talk to a Man First."

"These flowers are beautiful," Hannah said the next morning, flicking the giant bouquet of white lilies on my dining table with a lacquered black nail. "Is Aubrey performing tonight?" she asked, that mischievous twinkle in her eyes.

"No." I chuckled. "Her last show was two weeks ago. You know that, Hannah."

"Oh, really? I hadn't noticed," Hannah drawled. "Give Laura a New Year's kiss for me. I've decided I'm going to Aspen."

The flowers were a congratulatory bouquet from the producers of the pilot for *Holly's World*. When E! had presented it as a special earlier that month, it had done well in the ratings, prompting the network to order a full season! I was so thrilled to have this opportunity, but there was barely time to negotiate, let alone celebrate. Figuring out my agreement was a bit sticky, since I was in essence dealing with two very different masters. The network was one; the production company in charge of actually making the show was another.

The deal was amazing in a lot of ways. I was advised to hold out for a "created by" credit, but production wouldn't grant me that, which I thought was odd because the idea for the show *was* my own. It's not like someone else came along and said "Hey, I want to do a show about you as a showgirl in Vegas; let me cast you in a live production, put you up in a hotel, and introduce you to a group of people I'll cast as your friends." No, this was my life that I had created on my own. Not only that, but it was the same idea I had been pitching around for the better part of the year, one that the very same production company had turned its nose up at initially.

Sure, I had grown a lot since I left the mansion a year and a half earlier, but I still had a long way to go when it came to building up my self-esteem. There was still the part of me that thought I had to cut corners, forgo pay, or settle for less than I was worth because I felt like I wasn't good enough.

In the end, that's what I would do when it came to this credit, because, as was typical, I was in a hurry. I knew how fortunate I was to have this opportunity with E! and I wanted to strike while the iron was hot. I didn't need stalled negotiations holding this project up for months or longer. Who knows, the network could lose interest by then. It had been almost a year since my last episode of *GND* had aired, and a year can seem like a decade by Hollywood standards. I knew I had to get back on TV in order to make *Peepshow* as relevant and popular as I wanted it to be.

I shoved my concerns under the rug, focused on all the positives, and signed the contract. I was flying high due to finally landing this TV show, and having the hiatus from *Peepshow* just as we would begin shooting was perfect timing. We planned to spend the month filming the first few episodes, which included a trip to the Riviera Maya in Mexico for a calendar shoot. I couldn't even remember the last time I went on a beach vacation—and it couldn't have come at a better moment!

Walking into the El Dorado Royale Resort surpassed my expectations. The resort stretched down the white sand beach as far as the eye could see. Everything you could have asked for was on the property: pool after pool (with fountains and rivers), bar after bar (including an open-air lounge with wooden swings and a martini bar), and restaurant after restaurant (from formal dining to a casual poolside palapa). We were taken in a golf cart to our casitas, absorbing the tropical wonderland. I spied an adorable iguana darting across one of the lush green lawns and just knew this trip was going to be magical. It didn't disappoint. Each of our casitas had its own private pool and each bedroom a romantic, billowing white canopy bed. We spent the next few days shooting photographs for a calendar and filming whatever drama happened to explode in our wake. Luckily, we quickly got all the content we needed and were left with some free time on the final day of the trip to enjoy the resort. The cast, some of the crew, and I headed to one of the beach bars for a drink on our final afternoon. As we made our way over, Angel asked me what was on my mind. I'd been slightly distracted over the last few days and it hadn't escaped her notice.

"It's the whole Jeffrey thing," I confessed, "I don't get why I still can't stop thinking about him. It's like, *I* dumped *him*! So why do I still care?"

My friends knew just what to ask: *Do you really miss him? Do you actually want him back?* They already knew the answers, but they put it in perfect perspective for me.

"Not really . . ." I cringed. I was embarrassed to admit how I really felt. I didn't necessarily want him back, but it was as if I was feeling slighted because *he* didn't want *me* back. The egotism of it!

"When he didn't go to my screening," I explained, "that was, like, the beginning of the end for me. It was just so disappointing because I thought he was this genuinely nice guy."

"So if you don't really miss him, why are you so bummed about it?" one of our producers asked.

"Because I feel like *I* just got dumped. Even though I'm the one who broke up with him, I feel like that's what he wanted." I sighed. "Like he was just pulling away and blowing me off until I pulled the trigger, because he was too much of a coward to do it himself. It's like this is a reverse dump. I just don't get it. I thought he really liked me, and I thought I was moving slowly and doing everything right, but he lost interest so suddenly."

My bikini-clad support system quickly reminded me how I used to say that Jeffrey had no sense of humor. They pointed out that he didn't like Vegas and that Napoleon didn't even like him.

"That's true," I conceded, stirring my piña colada. "How come it's so easy to forget about those things that weren't working when you're scrambling to pick your ego up off the floor?"

It was almost as if I was so eager to check "boyfriend" off the list of things I wanted in my life that I focused only on the positive aspects of Jeffrey, instead of being a little more discerning. I should have truly taken the time to decide if he was right for me or if I was even passionate about him before letting myself become emotionally attached. I began to realize that I approached Jeffrey the same way that I approached shopping for a house. I was ready to jump at the first okay option instead of waiting for the perfect gem to come along.

"Maybe I just need some time to myself," I thought aloud.

"You'll find somebody better," the bartender cut in. "In the meantime, can I get anyone another drink?"

"Yes!" we all answered in unison.

As I curled up on the plane to try and catch a nap on the way back to Vegas, I thought about how truly ridiculous my relationship with Jeffrey seemed in hindsight. I had approached it with a method. I had done everything right, followed all the advice to a T, and Jeffrey *still* lost interest in me. Not only that, but I hadn't felt like I was truly being myself while I was following all this protocol. It's not like any book could ever tell me how to find the one who is right for me, anyway.

OF COURSE, AFTER YOU break up with someone, so much comes to light. As it turned out, some time later, on the set of a music video, Lindsay met a gorgeous model who couldn't stop complaining about her ex. The ex turned out to be Jeffrey Decker.

"She ended up getting tossed to the side a few months after they met," Lindsay shared with me. "She was really blindsided by it because she swore he was *really* into her. She would always say that he came really fast when they had sex because he was so turned on by her, that he talked about having kids in front of her a lot and always just seemed like such a *nice guy*. She was devastated when he moved on to someone else."

It appeared Jeffrey had a formula. Even his bedroom shtick sounded familiar! Yuck.

Ironically I had tried to work my "*Rules* magic" on this guy while he seemed to be doing the same thing with me . . . and it had worked like a charm! It was as if he had picked up a manual telling him exactly what the "typical woman" wants: to feel special in bed; to finally find a guy who values her, who can't stop talking her up to all his friends, who loves kids and talks about starting a family. The whole time I had been trying to turn myself into one of those "bitches" that men "love," my target seemed to have been fooling me with his own set of Man Rules. All that time I was convinced that the dating books were actually working for me and that I was the one holding the reins, he appeared to have been playing me.

As if dating wasn't tricky enough, I was about to find out how much more complicated it could be when you add a reality show to the equation.

Chapter 6

"In this country everyone must pay for everything he gets."
—L. Frank Baum, *The Wonderful Wizard of Oz*

"I don't know . . . I don't really like these two," I said, pointing at one image before clicking on a second one on my laptop screen. *Peepshow* had just reopened after a six-week hiatus and the first performance back had been photographed for promotional purposes. I was given the shots to approve before they went off to be published in our new programs. The first photo in question was from the new spider-web number that had been added to the show. In the picture, I was facing the camera straight on, wearing a baby-blue chemise and boy shorts set. My midsection, which peeked out from under my cropped chemise, looked a little too wide for my taste. What had happened to my hard-won hourglass figure? Clearly my *Dancing with the Stars* physique wasn't going to last without any maintenance.

"Okay, strike that one off the list!" Angel declared, making a notation on one of the countless Planet Hollywood notepads that littered my dining table.

"And look at this one!" I exclaimed. "I totally have a gut!" I pointed at a photo of me standing sideways, wearing the same outfit. "I'll have to suck it in when I'm onstage tonight."

"Stop it! You look amazing!" reassured Angel, giving me her best "you have to be kidding me" look.

"Thanks." I sighed. "There's always going to be a few bad pictures in every set, right?"

I didn't give it too much thought after that. But the reality was, I was eating really badly. I thought I was making healthy choices and indulging only every once in a while . . . but living like Eloise at the Plaza with unlimited free-of-charge room service—not to mention trying every restaurant in town—had made it really easy for me to treat myself. My typical lunch included what I *thought* was a healthy choice: a grilled chicken sandwich with Swiss cheese and avocado. Sure, it came with a side of fries, but since I only ever ate a few of them, they didn't count, right? Meanwhile, that heavy sandwich would put me in a food coma each day, and an hour-long midday nap was either had or sorely missed, depending on my schedule.

When doing interviews, I'd often get asked how I stayed in shape and would always quip that I was "onstage dancing every night! *Peepshow* is my workout!" I think I actually started to believe that sound bite, but in reality I had become so accustomed to my nightly routine that it was hardly a workout anymore. It was safe to say I didn't even break a sweat.

Immediately, I resolved not only to be more conscious of how I held myself onstage but also to go on a diet or start an exercise routine. However, those resolutions quickly fell to the bottom of my ever-growing to-do list. After I finished going through the photos, I asked Angel if she wanted to come check out the new house I had just purchased.

"Yeah! I can't wait to pick out my room," she said cheerfully, gathering her things and following me down to valet. I had invited Angel and her son Roman to live with me in my new home. She was almost twenty-one and I assumed she would be anxious to get out of her parents' place. I always hated the idea of living alone, so it seemed like an ideal arrangement. Not to mention, it made her spot on the show more secure. One savvy network exec would always ask *why* I was friends with the people I wanted on my show. She wasn't questioning my choice in companions, but rather approaching it from a viewer's perspective: What justified this person's constant presence in my life? Josh was my costar, Laura was my roommate, and Angel was my assistant . . . but somehow "assistant" never seemed like a good enough answer for the executives. Having her as a roommate seemed like a good answer to that question.

The valet swooped around the corner with my pink Porsche, and Angel and I jumped in, put the top down, and made the journey twenty minutes south to the suburb of Southern Highlands. My new house was lovely, but it was surprisingly cookie-cutter for my taste. I would have loved something older and more unique, with an interesting history, but options were limited. In the early 2000s, Las Vegas saw an influx of new residents, which produced row upon row of Spanish or Tuscan tract houses, all nearly identical. I had thus in essence chosen to live in the desert's answer to Stepford. There were still a few neighborhoods that had unique homes with a bit of history, but those houses rarely came up for sale . . . and I didn't have that kind of patience. Instead of waiting for "the one" to appear on the market, I was determined to make the purchase quickly for the sake of achieving my goal.

"When do you want to be settled in by?" Angel asked, pulling her hair into a ponytail as the wind whipped it around.

"Actually, I'm not sure," I replied, watching the lights of the Strip go by in a blur of LED and neon as we flew by on the freeway. "I'm still going to be spending a lot of time in the suite, so I'll play it by ear. I only just started ordering furniture."

No one ever asked me why I was so anxious to buy a house so quickly. In fact I never even asked myself. It was just another goal I had set, another one I was manically determined to check off my list. The goal-checking had become an addiction, one that took my mind off of my past and my problems with it.

We went through the guard gate and rolled into the driveway. My house didn't look much different from the others that surrounded it. It was a four-bedroom Spanish-style home with a screening room in the basement. I loved the natural rock pool with the water slide, Jacuzzi, and palapa hut in the back, as well as the curving princess staircase in the home's entryway. The property's biggest downside, as I would later learn, was the isolation I would experience out in suburbia, feeling far from the excitement and energy of the Strip, but like I had with Jeffrey, I hadn't focused on the features that weren't right for me. In the beginning, I focused only on what I did like, eager to get the purchase done as quickly as possible.

I unlocked the door, turned on the chandelier in the entryway, and led Angel through the house, our heels clicking on the travertine floors. After she saw all the rooms and chose neighboring guest rooms for herself and her son, we went back downstairs to tour the kitchen.

"Do you know what we're going to be filming this month?" Angel asked me as she took a seat at the kitchen island.

"Good question!" I said, grabbing two Perriers out of the fridge. "I asked the last time I was in L.A. and nothing was set in stone, but I did suggest we shoot a blind-date episode. So I might need you to set me up."

Now that Jeffrey was out of the picture, I was starting the rest of the season without a boyfriend. While the series was never sold with the idea that I would have an on-screen love interest, I wasn't opposed to discussing my love life and establishing, for viewers, where I stood . . . which, at that moment, was absolutely nowhere. I had suggested the idea of a blind-date episode and the producers loved it. I promised we would find a good candidate for the episode.

The following week, Angel and Josh scoured *Vegas* magazine's Most Eligible Bachelors list for a suitable suitor. Josh was on the list himself and suggested they browse the other candidates. They wanted to find someone young, good-looking, full of energy, and of course willing to be on the show. Finally they landed on Ricardo Laguna, a handsome, olive-skinned, professional BMX rider.

On the day of our "date" Ricardo came to pick me up at my brand-new, sparsely furnished home. My mom had come to town to see my new place, so she and my friends sat Ricardo in the hot seat and grilled him for a few minutes before he and I left for Pole Position Raceway to race go-karts. This was my kind of first date: all action, no talking! When we finally did sit down to have a bite to eat, our conversation was stunted. As one can imagine, it's not easy to get to know someone when there are cameras hovering over your shoulders. A producer prompted Ricardo to ask me something like "so where do you see this relationship going?" which is of course a bit of a stretch question for a first date, and it made me laugh. Even though, in my mind, the date was all in good fun for the show and not a "real" date, that outing was my first clue that meeting men on-camera wasn't going to be easy.

MY LOVE AFFAIR WITH Las Vegas aside, it was still necessary for me to be back in L.A. every Wednesday for business. Whether it was meetings, press, or photo shoots, there was always something that needed to be done. On more than one of those Wednesdays, I was caught getting coffee with Benji Madden, the guitar player from Good Charlotte.

The unwanted side effect of meeting for coffee in L.A. isn't over-caffeination, it's the high probability of photographers seeing you exit together. I was convinced, for a time, that half the people I would see "working on their next screenplay" at the 'bucks were really spies reporting every entrance and exit of anyone remotely recognizable to the blogarazzi. From there, a romantic narrative inevitably gets created by the press. Ordinarily, this particular situation wouldn't have been that annoying to me. Sure, the press linked us together, but the talk had been pretty innocent. There wasn't the sexual innuendo that had been layered on my alleged connection to Russell Brand almost a year earlier. It seemed like pretty harmless stuff.

What *did* complicate things was the fact that I was at that time shooting a reality TV show. The audience, the producers, and the network had the expectation that I would be honest and thorough when it came to opening my life up to the cameras. And for the most part, I was. I wasn't afraid to discuss any issues I had or break down in tears or appear in a skimpy bikini. But when it came to another person's life, someone who wasn't a cast member—well, *that* was a different story.

Besides the fact that I wasn't going to bamboozle anyone into being on my show, I didn't really think rushing someone I dated on-screen would be good for my love life. I wanted the producers to put themselves in my shoes. If you met a guy you were interested in, would you drop "hey, do you mind filming for my reality show?" on him on the first date? Probably not. And what kind of a guy would say yes to something like that right away? Women get the brunt of the "gold digger/opportunist" L.A. stereotypes, but it's really not fair. There are plenty of guys out there trolling for the same thing. I could name several guys who were "famous" chiefly for dating a woman (or women—some of these guys were serial!) who had her own reality show. This was the *last* type of person I wanted to attract!

But I didn't want to scare away the good guys, either. Asking a guy too early could send him running for the hills. While the opportunity to appear on a reality series might sound like the chance of a lifetime to some, there are plenty of people who don't think it's so cool. It may not fit in with their career or brand, or they may be genuinely too shy to be on camera.

I didn't feel like I was cheating the audience or anyone else by not asking a specific date to be on the show. Besides, in my ongoing quest to establish myself as a single woman, I didn't feel the need to have a man on this first season of *Holly's World*. Doing a blind-date episode was a different story. It provided an opportunity for me to show the audience what my life as a single person was like. The episode even ended with my mom and me having a heart-to-heart at the Peppermill, where I confided in her that I wanted to have a family, but for now I was happy being single.

When production got wind of the rumors and asked me about Benji, I told them that I wasn't comfortable asking him to be on the show. I even lied and said I wasn't seeing him when they wouldn't drop the subject. But they wouldn't accept it. One particular higher-up made me feel like shit, telling me, "If this guy cares about you at all, he should have no problem being on your television show." I knew in my head that that wasn't necessarily true, but in my heart I started to get paranoid. I was so self-conscious! Any guy who crossed my path couldn't win. If he was eager to be seen with me, then perhaps he was using me for publicity. If he wanted to keep things private, it must be because he was embarrassed by our relationship. Or at least that's what I thought.

Despite my adamant denials, the powers that be continued to do everything they could to put the subject on the show. They had my friends talk about him on-camera when they did scenes without me in hopes that it would force my hand. To be fair, Josh and Angel didn't even know how I felt about the situation. I hadn't confided in them how production wasn't letting the situation go. When Angel asked me on-camera if I was disappointed that Benji didn't come to a party we filmed, I responded that I wasn't because I wasn't expecting him to. I didn't think they would use that footage, simply because Benji had never been established on the show, so how would it even make any sense? I didn't know that they had already logged interviews with Josh and Angel talking about him. I refused to say Benji's name in interviews at all for the longest time, resulting in a major blowout. Eventually, one of my favorite producers even told me, through tears, that her boss threatened her with her job if she didn't get me to say his name on-camera. They simply refused to let it go.

It was a bunch of dirty dealing and, needless to say, was super frustrating. Here I was, thinking I finally had a reasonable amount of control over how I would be presented on television. After all, I was a co-executive producer and my name was in the title. It *was* my show, wasn't it?

This was a valuable lesson for me to learn. Perhaps I should have learned it by now, but on *The Girls Next Door*, there was such a narrow window of possibilities in which our one-dimensional characters could operate and Hef was so picky about what he would allow on the show that the parameters were different. However, after the Benji debacle, I was beyond careful about what I said in front of the camera, knowing it could be used out of context.

While filming the season, I was experiencing my first Vegas spring, and as any local can tell you, springtime in Vegas is rough on the allergies. The cottonwood, ash, mulberry, and olive trees are just a few examples of the nonnative plants brought to the Vegas Valley over the past hundred years, and all combined can wage a serious war on the sinuses. Between the pollen, dry air, heavy winds, and desert dust constantly kicked up by the never-ending ground-breaking and construction, the air was ripe for the allergy prone. Usually there is a "honeymoon period" of about a year after moving to town before the allergies take hold, and it appeared for me that the honeymoon was over. Singers even have a term for the effect of the allergies: "Vegas throat." Besides sounding like an STD, the "Vegas throat" can wreak havoc in the life of a performer.

I was regularly bogged down with the flu-like symptoms of recurring sinus infections. The infections would be so severe that it would hurt just to turn my head. My whole body ached. But as they say, the show must go on. I refused to miss a single performance or a day of filming, so I had my doctor on speed dial to keep me on a heavy rotation of house calls and antibiotics. When I wasn't needed in L.A. I'd spend my days off recovering in front of the TV with Laura, watching old episodes of *Vega$* over a giant dish of penne pasta smothered in cheese from room service.

After several weeks of being hotel bound, I was starting to get cabin fever. A road trip would be the perfect change of scenery! As a nostalgic tribute to *Girls Next Door*, production and I had decided to do an episode each of *Holly's World* with Bridget and Kendra. While Kendra flew out to coach me in baseball, Bridget and I opted to do a road trip from L.A. to Vegas, along with Josh and Bridget's boyfriend, Nick. Our plan was to stop at all the weird random roadside attractions I saw along the I-15 every time I did the drive, so I could write about them for a chapter in a coffee-table book on Las Vegas that I was working on.

Since Josh and I had only one day off to do everything on our itinerary, we flew out to Burbank (the more low-key of the Los Angeles area airports) Wednesday morning and picked Bridget and Nick up in a rented SUV. According to the show, our purpose for doing this road trip was to spend some time with Nick and figure out if he was "good enough" for Bridget. Of course, since she seemed happy, I already assumed he was good enough, but the plot line made enough sense. Why wouldn't I want to look out for one of my best friends?

We commenced the four-and-a-half-hour drive, stopping at a few places I had seen so many times on the drive back and forth but had never had reason to pull over at. We explored an abandoned water park, ate at Peggy Sue's 50's Diner, and took pictures next to the World's Largest Thermometer. The best part of the drive was having the time to catch up with my old friend and see places we wanted to visit. When we reached Baker, which was just an hour and a half away from Vegas, we were instructed to take a detour north up to Death Valley. For fun, production had arranged for us to stay at the haunted Amargosa Hotel.

The hotel is located in Death Valley Junction, a town surrounded by barren desert for thirty miles on all sides. Originally known as Amargosa (meaning "bitter water" in Paiute), the settlement began as a Borax mining community built in the 1920s. Today, Death Valley Junction has a population of less than twenty people. Smack in the middle of one of the most extreme environments on Earth, home to record-setting heat, Death Valley is not for the faint of heart. The town consists of one building, a U-shaped Spanish Colonial revival, without so much as a gas station to call a neighbor. The building was erected to serve as a dormitory for miners and company offices, but over the years has held a hospital and assembly hall, among other things. In 1927, Borax moved their headquarters and the community became a virtual ghost town. Today the building operates as the Amargosa Hotel.

After we drove the desolate road through Death Valley, our headlights landed on the austere, blindingly white building. The sudden vision was a bit jarring, since we were out in the middle of nowhere in the dead of night, having seen nothing but the road in front of us for the last hour and a half. A cracked hand-painted sign was propped up near the driveway. A few people sat at a folding table on the patio, sluggishly playing card games by eerie lantern light. There was an odd quality to the property, as if everything happened in slow motion.

We checked in and grabbed a seat in the lobby with some fast-food takeout the crew had grabbed for us in Baker, the nearest city with dining options. I happily dug into my chicken fingers with ranch and barbecue sauce. Josh and I peppered Bridget and Nick with every annoying question we could think of (marriage? kids? when?), but the questions felt silly. Sure, they were for the sake of the episode, but I was the last person who wanted people checking up on my marriage status, so who was I to grill someone else?

After dinner, we spoke a bit to the property's caretaker, who told us that because she was ailing, we would be unable to meet the hotel's fascinating proprietor, Miss Marta Becket. Marta became a bit of a legend in 1970 when *National Geographic* magazine made the journey to Death Valley and photographed her painting the newly acquired property. Born in New York, Marta studied piano, dance, and painting as a child. Her talent and love of the arts prompted her to become a Radio City Music Hall ballerina and Broadway dancer in her teens. In 1967, at the age of forty-three, Marta set out across the country on a road trip with her husband. While her husband tended to a flat tire, Marta found herself in Death Valley Junction, wandering around the colonnaded building, peering into a hole in the back door of the old assembly hall. Something spoke to Marta, and she knew, right then and there, that she was going to perform in that hall.

Marta and her husband decided to make Death Valley their home. They leased the building, eventually buying it outright. She then spent six years painting intricate murals on the walls and ceilings of the assembly hall, now renamed the Amargosa Opera House. She performed, dancing and acting in original plays, every Friday, Saturday, and Monday at 8:15 P.M. sharp, whether an audience appeared at the remote location or not. Marta's murals covered the walls with spectators, a Spanish Renaissance scene of nobility, clergy, and commoners alike assembled in box seating painted around the room, most of their faces trained toward the stage. For over forty years, Marta followed her passion and regularly performed each week.

Marta has since become a source of fascination for many who hear her story. She braved loneliness and the elements and did what she was inspired to do, even though everyone else might have thought she was crazy. She painted and she danced because she loved it.

I found Marta's story inspiring. In a way I could relate to her. I went to Las Vegas to pursue what I was passionate about, even though some of my L.A. acquaintances turned up their noses at the idea. There is a bit of snobbery toward Vegas from the L.A. crowd: sure, they love to visit, but they regard it as less than, a place they wouldn't want to stay in for more than three days.

But Marta's story also inspired me, the way I am sure it has awed so many who have heard it. For forty years, she has faithfully pursued her dreams and what makes her happy, for no other reason than that it was fulfilling. She wasn't pursuing fame, money, or anyone else's admiration. Could I ever get to that point? Sure, I followed my dreams out to Vegas, but I knew that there was still a part of me that felt as if I needed to prove something to the world. Even though I had already checked off the goals on the list I had made only one year ago, I still had an emptiness inside of me that I was trying to fill with more, more, more. I wondered what I would be inspired to do if I knew there was no chance of winning anyone's approval, no matter what I did. What path would I follow? Where would my heart take me?

After learning we wouldn't be meeting Marta, we got down to business and started exploring the haunted hotel. First, we walked down the hotel's hall, which was lined with black-and-white group photos, instantly reminding me of *The Shining*. A particularly creepy one showed the building's residents in Halloween costumes, taken sometime in the twenties. The guy dressed as a clown was enough to give me nightmares.

We spent the night hunting ghosts and scaring each other silly. One of the hotel's wings, which served as a hospital at one point, stood in crumbling disrepair. The caretaker informed us that they referred to that part of the building as Spooky Hollow, and it was no wonder why. The dark, decaying corridor was littered with personal items, as if there had been a sudden mass exodus, increasing the ghostly feel of the place. We explored it with flashlights, waiting for the unexplainable to happen. While we didn't experience anything particularly paranormal during the hunt, the spooky atmosphere was enough for us. We were already scared out of our minds, even more so when one of the crew claimed to have had a "sexual encounter" with a spirit in his room! Ooh la la!

The next morning, we packed up and got out before the midday desert heat could catch up to us. We drove back to Las Vegas, dropped Bridget and Nick off at the airport, since they had to get back to L.A. right away, and scurried back to our regular *Peepshow* schedule.

I WAS HAVING A blast shooting the show and reveling in my good fortune. But just as every cloud has a silver lining, everything good comes with a price. While I was living my dream, working on both of the projects I had wished for and living a life of luxury with the most fun group of friends I could imagine, I was neglecting my body. I worked hard and played even harder. When I was going through the chronic sinus infections, I refused to miss a show or a minute of filming. My diet left much to be desired. I wasn't exercising and had to make a real effort to get adequate sleep. My nerves were frayed. It was only a matter of time before something had to give.

I loved my life and all the opportunities I was getting. I never complained about anything. But not taking care of myself was taking its toll and was slowly sneaking up on me. The waters were rising higher and higher behind the dam, and that dam eventually broke.

I was in my bedroom getting ready to shoot a scene with Angel and my manager, Jason. We had only a few minutes to do it, as I would have to go straight downstairs to the theater afterward. I knew Angel and Jason were ready to shoot; I had seen them sitting at my dining table as I walked in, talking about Angel's upcoming World's Largest 21st Birthday Party at Tao. I knew the crew was there, too, and had touched base with them before going into my room. When I walked through the door, I expected everyone to be ready to go. Time was money and we were on the clock.

But they weren't. Laptop in hand, I walked out of my bedroom door and not one camera was up. The field producer that day was someone new. "Hey, what's going on?" I asked. "I thought we had to get this scene wrapped really quickly." The producer rolled his eyes and slowly stood up.

"Okay, we'll be ready for you in about five minutes," he grumbled, with the enthusiasm of a sloth.

Let me be clear: this was an anomaly. The entire crew of *Holly's World* had been more than a dream to work with, and I became close friends with many of them. They didn't devise the plot to get Benji on-camera; they were just following orders. They were always fun, creative, and professional. The rude reaction from this new member was the last thing I expected. All of a sudden, all of my stifled emotions flooded me at once. I went back into my room and promptly called a higher-up to let him know that we were on an incredibly tight schedule and the new person in charge that day hadn't been ready. The tears were flowing uncontrollably, and I think the man on the other end of the line was a little taken aback by what probably seemed to him like a massive overreaction.

He suggested we wrap for the day, as I was obviously not myself.

"No. I want to shoot a scene," I demanded through sobs. "I don't want to waste time." I was never a very outwardly emotional person, so I wanted to get this rare outburst on camera. "I just want to go out there and talk about how I'm feeling."

The crew was directed to start shooting again. I came out of the room and sat down at the table with Angel and Jason and let everything I was feeling pour out of me. Through the tears, I tried to explain to my friends why I was so upset, but I wasn't very articulate. All I could manage to say was how tired I was all the time and how I felt like I couldn't keep up with the demands of my work.

But articulate or not, it was by far the most emotional I had ever been on-camera. Even though that day may have felt like a lemon, we made lemonade out of it. Overall, I was proud of the season and couldn't wait for people to see it. I hoped it would do well, but I didn't count on anything. Maybe people would think I was too boring. Maybe I really couldn't stand on my own on TV without the backdrop of the mansion. Who knew? I was just grateful to have the opportunity to try.

Right before *Holly's World* premiered, the network scheduled a round of press to promote the show. It was more press than I had ever done before, not to mention of a better quality. I couldn't believe I was finally on magazine covers, solo! The team at E! was wonderful and everything went smoothly. E! even put up a *Holly's World* billboard near Planet Hollywood as a surprise. There I was, larger than life, perched on a giant disco ball. I couldn't believe my good fortune—I felt like I was being treated like a queen! The network's faith in me and the show helped to quell any nerves I might have had.

For me, the most challenging part of that round of press was the radio tour. For a radio tour, you wake up super early and call a coordinator, who patches you in to a different morning show every ten to fifteen minutes for two or three hours. Granted, most of the radio-show hosts I talked to were lovely, but you know the old saying: it takes only a few bad apples to spoil the bunch. Given that some morning shows tend to go for the shock factor, it's almost impossible for me to do that many radio interviews and not have someone ask an inappropriate question about my days at Playboy. I had my share of uncomfortable experiences doing these sorts of tours back when I was tapped to promote *The Girls Next Door*. I warned my PR reps about the situation and asked them to please let the stations know ahead of time that I didn't want to talk about Playboy, that I was just there to promote *Holly's World* and *Peepshow*. I figured I had plenty to talk about.

Most of the calls went well, but of course there was one host who insisted on going there.

"So, you lived at the Playboy Mansion for several years," one of the male DJs stated. "What was sex with Hefner like?"

Even though the question pissed me off, I answered in a calm, even tone. "You know, I've moved on to a new phase in my life, and he's moved on as well, so I don't think that's an appropriate thing for me to talk about."

I silently congratulated myself on the professional answer, but then the DJ spit out:

"But Kendra was just on the show yesterday, promoting her book, and she talked about it! She said Hef lasted, like, two seconds."

"Well, if she wants to talk about that, that's her business." I replied shortly, praying for this interview to come to a quick conclusion.

I was finding it more and more difficult to take the high road when it came to not kissing and telling. I was frustrated. I wanted to keep my private life private, but I couldn't because other people were out there telling their version of the story.

If only they knew the truth, I thought. One day I would tell my story, but I wanted to do it when I had a more complete story to tell. I wanted to accomplish things on my own, to truly be my own person first. Writing a tell-all the second after leaving the mansion just reeked of convenience. In Kendra's case, her tales were used to spawn countless tabloid bits to draw interest in her TV show, and the show in turn was used to push the book. Strangely enough, even though Kendra's description of Hef (or Bridget and me, for that matter) wasn't particularly flattering, he didn't seem to protest. Let's not forget, Playboy was a producing partner on her show, so I suppose the hype benefited everyone who had a hand in the pot.

"Are you ever going to write a book about the mansion?" one of the other DJs asked me.

"Maybe, but not for a while." And I meant it. I would do it when *I* was ready, not when it was convenient for someone else.

When season one of *Holly's World* premiered, it scored ratings so strong that all involved were pleasantly surprised! I was incredibly grateful that people wanted to watch this show—even though it wasn't a show about the mansion or Playboy or Hef.

It was a huge moment for me. Attempting to shed the Playboy stigma and asking people to reconsider how they viewed me was an uphill battle, and the success of season one was a major victory. It was a really good feeling. Oddly enough, I knew that despite the show's success, I couldn't do it forever. After what happened with Benji, it had become apparent that reality TV was not particularly conducive to a healthy personal life. I was stuck in a "damned if you do, damned if you don't" situation. The last time I had heard from Benji, he revealed to me that "my people" (not sure who, but I have my suspicions) had reached out to "his people," asking him to appear on my show. I was shocked, and honestly, pretty embarrassed. I knew they wanted him on the show, I just didn't think anyone would ever go behind my back to ask. I insisted I hadn't been behind the request and that it hadn't mattered to me if he appeared on the show or not.

The more I thought about it, the more embarrassed I became. The whole scenario made me look so desperate! Here I was, supposedly an adult in charge of my own life, and the powers that be were still trying to control it, as if they could pull the strings on my love life.

Sure, I had wanted fame and knew that a lack of privacy came as a result. I knew dating wouldn't be easy for me, but I never imagined it would be made more difficult simply because someone from behind the scenes was lurking behind me like a protective shotgun-toting dad.

The whole situation was lame, but it was a side effect of something I had very much wanted: my own reality show. It was something I was going to have to live with, and, for the time being, figure out how to work around. This scenario made one thing clear: if I ever wanted to have a *real* personal life, I couldn't do reality TV forever. Years earlier, I had taken on-camera hosting classes, and I decided to revisit my old ambition to be a TV host. It was time to add a new goal to my list.

As if by magic, I was offered a position as the Las Vegas correspondent for the TV newsmagazine *Extra*. Well, it wasn't magic, it was more like connections. *Extra* shot most of their segments at Planet Hollywood and had thought of me as a natural for the post, since I was the face of the property. Still, the opportunity couldn't have come at a better time! I took the position without hesitation. At least three mornings a week I could hone my on-camera hosting and interviewing skills. I also started taking singing lessons, hoping I could eventually do a song in *Peepshow*, if I worked hard enough. My schedule was now even more hectic than ever, but for me, it was worth it. After all, I still felt like I was making up for lost time.

Once again, complications in my personal life pushed me further into my work. In addition, in the case of the TV show, my work pushed my love life away. As much as I hated to admit it, maybe I couldn't have it all, at least not all at once.

Chapter 7

"Oh, I don't mind him a bit," said Dorothy. "But you are so beautiful," she continued, "that I'm sure I could love you dearly. Won't you let me take you back to Kansas, and stand you on Aunt Em's mantleshelf? I could carry you in my basket."

—L. Frank Baum, *The Wonderful Wizard of Oz*

"Can I play?" I asked, hopping over the back of a green velvet couch and landing next to the cute guy engrossed in a game on his phone.

"Hey, sure!" he blurted out with a big smile. He hadn't seen me enter the bar and I had taken the opportunity to sneak up on him. He leaned over to give me a big hug and proceeded to explain the game he was playing to me. I took this as a cue to lean up against him. *I think this is going to be a great vacation,* I thought.

Mark was a tall, gorgeous specimen I had met briefly at a concert, months ago. Even though I had gone to the concert with a date, I couldn't help but notice him. How could I not? He exuded the sort of casual confidence that I loved. Leaning up against the cement wall in a white T-shirt and ripped jeans, he draped one sculpted arm nonchalantly over a cooler and used the other one to simultaneously hold a beer and tuck his long, dirty blond hair behind his ear. First, I was drawn by his deep laugh as he surveyed the girls desperately trying to get the attention of the band, but once the most beautiful set of crystal-blue eyes I'd ever seen met mine, it was all over.

He caught me looking at him and smiled. I quickly averted my gaze. I figured the acknowledgment must have been because he recognized me from TV or something, since we were surrounded by a sea of beautiful young women and I was convinced I didn't stand out. A normal person would have smiled back at him and introduced herself, but I was nervous and there with another guy.

As the room filled up, our two groups somehow merged and I found myself standing close to him.

"What about you?" he directed my way as I tried to focus on a fake text I was pretending to type on my BlackBerry.

"Huh?" I replied. It was about as gracious as it sounded, a guttural interjection to the hot guy who was nice enough to include me in the conversation.

He repeated the question as my eyes darted between the floor and his striking jawline. His beard was about a week grown in, long enough to look hot, but short enough so that I could still make out the slight dimple in his chin.

"I don't really know," I replied, though I hadn't even heard what he was talking about. Scared that I had either come across as aloof or awkward, I excused myself before any further damage could be done.

I was telling Laura all about that night in L.A. when I was back in Vegas. As I typically did first thing in the morning, I scrolled through my Twitter mentions to see if anything interesting had happened overnight.

It had.

"Holy shit," I whispered.

"What?" Laura asked, raising an eyebrow in my direction.

"The guy from the concert said something to me on Twitter," I said, my face lighting up.

"The one you said was hot?" Laura asked, leaning in closer to read over my shoulder.

He had tagged me in a post about the concert a few nights ago, making a funny joke about the scene backstage. As I tend to when people pique my interest, I journeyed over to his profile page to see who had made the comment . . . and there was Mark and his spellbinding gaze.

Maybe he likes me, I thought. *He did go out of his way to try and get my attention.* Little did he know that he already had it.

Our friendly social media banter quickly escalated into direct messages, and within a matter of days we were texting incessantly. Just as with Jeffrey before, I was able to spend time getting to know this person from behind the safety of my cell screen—and without having to further reveal how socially awkward I was. For a phone junkie like myself, having a regular text buddy was pretty appealing—and again, just as had happened with Jeffrey, I quickly made what felt like a new best friend.

Mark was sweet, considerate, and crazy smart. I valued his insight and opinions, and I began turning to him as my constant sounding board, my confidant, and, maybe most important, someone to make me laugh. Mark had the most wicked, witty sense of humor—especially when it came to the topic of sex. I always found sex to be kind of funny, and historically had difficulty making it work with guys, who thought a woman should always be prudish and serious about the matter. We connected on so many levels, and I felt we complemented each other so well.

Mark was also a stage performer, an actor who landed a role in one of Broadway's latest hits. He confided in me that he had just moved to New York, and with the exception of his castmates, felt lonely. I could certainly relate. I loved my new Vegas friends, but they were just that: new. I was still rushing around to find more, more, more to bring into my orbit, things that could fill the hole inside that came from having lost touch with old friends and lacking a solid emotional foundation underneath me. My new life had been constructed so instantly that it didn't really feel stable and Mark was living a similar type of lifestyle.

Everything about Mark made me want to jump in headfirst, despite the chips that were stacked against us. (A long-distance relationship was the last thing either of us had room for in our busy lives.) But all I had experienced so far with guys caused me to keep a firm grasp on my reservations.

"This reminds me of you," he texted me one afternoon, along with a snapshot of a storefront he had passed, his reflection barely visible in the window. Through the smudged glass, I could see a display that included a beautiful photograph of Marilyn Monroe. She was uncharacteristically casual, wearing her iconic blond locks in two braided pigtails and staring at the camera with a wistful look on her face.

That kind of thing wasn't a rare gesture; that was just Mark. Throughout the day, he would send sweet random messages just to say hello and let me know he was thinking about me.

After a few months of back-and-forth, I started to wonder if we would ever see each other again. Both of us had schedules that were set in stone, but as luck (or fate) would have it, he had a few days off during my upcoming September vacation. As eager as I was to see him again, I wasn't going to change my plans or go out of my way to connect. I had given so much of my life to boyfriends in the past and had learned my lesson. Like a rubber band, I had been stretched too far and had now snapped back. These days, I wouldn't even think of compromising for a boy.

I refused to make any effort to meet anyone halfway (both figuratively *and* literally). Hannah and I had already booked our flights and hotel rooms in Florida for a week of relaxing and theme-park hopping. If he was interested in me, *he* was going to have to come see *me*. Even though I craved a boyfriend (or Mark in particular), I wasn't going to sacrifice a vacation with my friends.

When he mentioned his days off that happened to fall during my vacation, I decided to take the bait and just go for it.

"I'm going to Florida for the week. You should come," I basically commanded, as if it were the most normal thing in the world to fly across the country at the last minute. He had only a few days off, so if he was a drag in person, it's not like he would ruin the whole week, I reasoned to myself.

"That would be kind of the rock-star thing to do, wouldn't it?" he responded timidly. He wanted me to convince him. Clearly, he wasn't used to jet-setting for pussy.

"Yes, it would," I responded. After he found a flight that would arrive around the same time as ours, I sent him the hotel information, explaining that I had already taken care of the rooms. I booked three: one for me, one for Hannah, and one for him. Whether or not Mark and I would end up in the same room at the end of the day remained to be seen.

As our black town car slowly approached the sprawling luxury resort, a gorgeous white Victorian-inspired structure came into view. It looked like something from another time, or something out of a movie, as if this picturesque lakeside escape existed in soft focus. A VIP host clad in a coral seersucker uniform met us at valet and escorted us into the hotel. Music swirled around the pastel four-story atrium lobby as an orchestra played from the second-story balcony. The staff—clad in era-appropriate turn-of-the-century attire—bustled around the grounds, which included a white sand beach.

"This'll do," Hannah said with a smirk, before waving to a raven-haired beauty curled up on one of the lobby's antique couches. She unwound her long, tanned legs and in one fluid movement was up from the chair and heading toward us.

"This is Sarah," Hannah said matter-of-factly. Once it was decided that Mark would join us, Hannah had reached out to a friend who lived nearby. I liked her warm smile and could tell by her willingness to drop everything and join us that she had the same love for spontaneity that Hannah had.

Mark had already arrived earlier that morning and had texted to let me know that he had set up shop at the bar on the second floor. Our host had informed us that our rooms were still being prepared and would be ready in a few minutes, so we left our bags with the bellhop and jumped into the giant cage elevator and headed up to the second level to greet my latest lust interest.

Even though I had met Mark before (albeit only once), I started to get nervous as we approached. *What if things were awkward between us in person?* I wondered. With texting I could write, delete, and rewrite to make sure I was sending the perfect response. *What if he isn't mature in person and he gets on my nerves?* Did I mention Mark was twenty-three years old to my thirty-one? The age difference hadn't bothered me because we seemed like contemporaries . . . over the phone, anyway.

Of course, my most nerve-racking worry trumped that concern: *What if I wasn't all he expected?*

With a forced confidence but genuine excitement, I hopped onto the couch where he was seated and dropped next to him. "Can I play?"

"Hey, sure!" he smiled, lifting his arm to let me come in closer. "I'm playing Fruit Ninja."

Instantly my anxieties melted away as soon as I found myself lost in his striking blue eyes. My heart continued to race, but this time for different reasons.

I stared blankly for a moment and then got nervous again. *Had I stared too long?* I wondered. *Or was that normal?* I couldn't tell. Awkwardly I cut him off as he began explaining the game and introduced him to Hannah and Sarah. Mark stood up and shook each girl's hand. He politely introduced himself with a smile and immediately shifted his focus back to me. Hannah and Sarah attracted every set of eyes in the room—every set but the blue ones looking at me. Hannah curled herself up into the plush chair across from us. I could tell by the gleam in her eyes that she approved of my latest crush.

Sarah asked us what we wanted to drink, then proceeded to order beers for Hannah and herself, vodka on the rocks with lemon for me, and another martini for Mark. I leaned in closer to him, ostensibly to learn the intricacies of Fruit Ninja.

"Check this out," Hannah said, reaching into Sarah's purse and taking out her keychain. She threw it onto the coffee table between our seats and pointed to a long, skinny white object.

"That," she announced proudly, "is the bone from a raccoon's penis."

She let that hang in the air (and on the table), waiting for Mark and me to react.

"What?" Mark laughed, leaning forward to investigate.

"Don't tell me the South isn't interesting," Hannah said with a smirk and a raised eyebrow.

"So they literally get boners," Mark asked, looking quizzically at the object on the coffee table in front of us.

"No way," I said. "They have an actual bone in their penis?"

"They sell these in the gift shops down here." Sarah laughed. "Along with alligator skins and coconut monkeys."

Mark and I took to Google on our respective phones to find the answer. After determining that, yes, a raccoon does indeed have a bone in his penis, Mark and I got into another debate: iPhone versus BlackBerry.

"But how can you possibly answer all your emails without a keypad?" I asked, flipping his phone around to study it. "Trying to type on this screen would drive me crazy. Doesn't it take forever?"

"No way. I love Apple. These take *way* better pictures, too," he claimed, taking his phone back. "And besides, you can't play Fruit Ninja on a BlackBerry."

Before I could respond, our dapper VIP host approached us to let us know he had a surprise for us.

"Please follow me," he requested, smiling brightly before turning on his heels. We piled into the elevator and zoomed up to the top floor. We were buzzing with excitement. Mark's and my connection in person thus far had lived up to all my expectations. We were intrigued as to what our surprise was going to be. We followed the concierge down the long corridor to two giant wooden doors.

"We'd like to offer you our presidential suite," he announced as he pushed open the doors and gave us a small bow. Mark and I slowly walked through the massive, columned entry hall into the giant living room, with rich marble floors and antique chandeliers, but our eyes were immediately drawn to the floor-to-ceiling windows offering a panoramic view of the resort's lake. Hannah and Sarah followed behind.

"This'll work," Hannah said again, with a laugh. She turned and walked into the first bedroom; it had twin antique Victorian sleigh beds.

"Guess we're in the kids' room," she chided, tossing her monogrammed Goyard bag on one of the beds.

Mark and I wandered into the second room, which had a silk-covered king-size bed.

"So we're staying in here?" he asked shyly.

"I guess so," I said, trying to sound more nonchalant than I felt. It wasn't that I didn't want to sleep with him at this point; it was that I didn't want to *let on* that I did. I loved it that he wasn't as presumptuous as all the other guys I had been spending time with in the last . . . well, ever.

The concierge put our bags in the closet, and I excused myself to change for dinner. Our master bathroom was gorgeous: ornate gold hardware, beautiful pink marble floors and countertops, and a giant tub that just begged to be occupied by more than one person.

I caught my reflection in the antique mirror. *Guess I'll be wearing these all weekend,* I thought as I pulled a brush through my clip-in hair extensions. Ordinarily I would never sleep in these uncomfortable things, but suddenly it was super important to me that Mark *not* see me with my natural shoulder-length hair. I realized I had more of a thing for this guy than I had thought.

Which suddenly gave me pause. When I packed for the trip, I hadn't really planned on attempting to impress anyone with my appearance. Sure, I knew Mark was coming, but I hadn't counted on the mere sight of him throwing my feelings into overdrive.

Dressing up for dinner wasn't even an option. My suitcase was brimming with T-shirts, shorts, and Converse sneakers. *What was I thinking?* I asked myself. I had packed for a relaxing Florida vacation, but neglected to factor in the fact that a *hot guy* that I was *totally into* was going to be there.

I dumped out my makeup case on the marble countertop and shook my head. I hadn't even double-checked my stash of travel cosmetics to make sure all the pieces were there. *Fucking scatterbrain,* I swore to myself as I realized I was missing eye shadow and bronzer. Luckily I had brought one of the most versatile products I owned, the classic NARS Orgasm Blush. Using what I had and some inventive tricks of the trade, I touched myself up as best I could.

Just as I emerged from the bathroom, there was a knock on the door. Sarah's boyfriend had arrived with three grocery bags filled with booze.

"Awesome!" Mark shouted. I mean, we certainly could have cleaned out any bar in town if we wanted, but Hannah and I decided to adopt a full-blown spring-break mentality on this trip.

After a pre-dinner cocktail, we walked the scenic route across the resort to get to our dinner reservation. The restaurant came highly recommended, and we were not disappointed. Set next to the picturesque lake, with lighted barges parading by, the restaurant was the perfect romantic spot for my first dinner with Mark. Each dish that was brought out topped the last, not only in taste but in presentation as well. Everything looked like an exotic pastry, swirled and colored to perfection.

Sarah's boyfriend and Mark hit it off right away, making the evening even more enjoyable. When you bring together a new group of people, most of whom don't know each other, you expect a lot of awkward silences—but we had none! Mark was an engaging conversationalist, which was a huge plus. I always knew I needed a social animal to balance out my quiet, reserved personality, and Mark passed that test with flying colors.

After dinner, Hannah, Sarah, and her boyfriend were eager to get back to their booze stash, and we asked our tuxedo-clad waiter for plastic cups for our remaining cocktails. Without missing a beat (or making us feel like amateurs), he appeared with them and gave us a rundown of which bars were still open at the resort.

"Hey, I want to take you for a walk," Mark suggested as he gently elbowed me in the side. "That seems like the romantic thing to do, doesn't it?"

Was this guy for real? I wondered. The truth is, I didn't even care. This trip was off to such an amazing start that I was just going to let myself go with it. I mean, I was on vacation. I decided to put all my paranoia about men aside for the week. I was determined to relax and let down my hair (extensions and all). Mark was doing everything right, so why not have a good time for a little while? *This guy is way too young for me to ever be serious about, anyway,* I thought.

He grabbed my hand and we split off from the rest of our crew. He led me along a path that wound farther away from our hotel.

"I really like your friends," he said.

"Oh, good! I knew you and Hannah would get along," I said with a smile. "This is the first time I've met Sarah, but any friend of Hannah's is guaranteed to be a good time."

"I'm really glad I decided to make this trip," he murmured, putting his arm over my shoulders.

"Me, too," I confessed. "It's too bad you can't stay the whole week."

Damn it, I thought, *I sound so desperate. Pull it together!*

But I couldn't help myself from blurting out exactly what I was thinking. I was transfixed by this guy.

We came to a fork in the path and he guided me away from the hotel toward a quaint old-fashioned dock on the lake.

"Let's look at the stars," he suggested as he walked me back to the edge of the dock, laid down on the smooth wooden planks, and folded his perfectly toned arm under the back of his head. I paused for a second to take in his sculpted physique sprawled out on the dock before setting myself down as gracefully as I could.

I could feel myself being swept off my feet, but there was still a casual element to it. There were no *Rules* this time. I was just going to be myself. If he didn't like who I was, fuck it. I was no longer that young girl who would do what a lot of people do when it comes to new relationships: customize myself to be someone's dream girl for the first few months of seeing each other. I wasn't going to overplan this, I was just going to enjoy it. *Be in the moment,* I reminded myself.

"Oh my god, look!" I said, pointing up toward the stars.

"Bats!" he laughed. Swirling over our heads was a sea of nocturnal creatures. I'd never seen a bat outside a zoo before. The feeling of being in the *now* washed over me like a tidal wave. Finally I felt immersed and taken away from my usual anxieties and obsessions by this special, oddly romantic moment.

"This is unbelievable," I whispered as we listened to the sound of them circling in the sky above.

We lay there under the stars for what felt like hours, holding hands and talking. I found myself opening up to him about things that I hadn't shared with most people, simply because he was so easy to talk to. It was the most intimate I'd felt with a man in a very long time—and we hadn't even kissed yet. When we finally headed back to the hotel, we approached the suite and could hear Hannah and her friends laughing and listening to music in their room. Room-service trays covered in booze and gourmet grilled-cheese sandwich crusts littered the hallway outside our door. *How long had we been gone?* Without announcing our return, we let ourselves in, grabbed a bottle of wine and two glasses off the bar, and stole into our bedroom, closing the door behind us.

"Did you know we were going to hook up on this trip?" he asked as we awoke the next morning, looking at me with those intense, flawless blue eyes.

"Umm," I began, unexpectedly shy. "I figured there was a high probability," I admitted with a laugh. I felt a momentary flood of embarrassment, but then reminded myself that there was no need to play games. I just hoped he didn't think I was a slut for being so presumptuous, but . . . too late!

Besides, I had already made the decision to stop giving any power to the "slut" label. No one would think of a guy as a slut for hooking up on a first date. In fact, I was kind of blown away that *he* hadn't taken it for granted that we would hook up that night.

"Do you use one of those cervical caps?" he asked me.

This was totally out of left field.

"No!" I scoffed, with a huge laugh. It was such an odd question to ask. I'd never heard anyone talk about a cervical cap outside of a sex ed class before! No one I knew used them.

"Oh, okay, just checking," he replied.

Was he paranoid about birth control? I wondered. We had used a condom, but knowing his sense of humor, I realized his question could easily have been just a joke. I bounded out of bed, hoping to shower and make myself presentable in record time. We were on a mission to go to Universal Orlando for the Wizarding World of Harry Potter, which had just opened.

"So, how'd you get into Harry Potter?" Mark asked me on the drive to the park.

"When I was studying French a few years ago I was looking for children's books to read in that language because I thought it would be easy, and I latched on to the series," I explained.

"Oh, that's cool," he said before offering his own history with Harry. "I really got into it because every year a book would come out and Harry would be in the same grade as me, so I could relate to it."

That was the first thing that made me feel old.

His fascination with Harry Potter being a bit more age-appropriate for him than for me was the only thing that had felt out of place, though. Otherwise, I felt like we were on the same page. He was self-made and had been working full-time since he was sixteen, which gave him an intellect and a maturity that effectively closed the gap between our near-decade age difference. Most important, he treated me like a lady, which was more than I could say for most of the guys I had dated before (who had all been my age or older).

That night we had a romantic dinner at a rooftop restaurant that he found. I was impressed that he took the initiative to research a special place for our final evening together. He was heading back to New York the next morning and wanted our last dinner together to be memorable. From the terrace, diners could see a nightly fireworks display. In full-blown gentleman mode, he escorted me to the balcony and asked someone to take a picture of us together.

"I didn't know what to expect from this trip," he said softly, "but it was even better than I could have imagined. I'm so glad I came."

It was in that moment that I discovered what it felt like to actually be weak in the knees.

Before I could respond, he kissed me. I closed my eyes, and without realizing it, I was finally opening my heart.

"QUIT POUTING," HANNAH TEASED me.

"I'm not," I shouted, tossing a throw pillow at her. I was surprised at how much I missed him. Mark left early that morning to make it back in time for his show that evening, and the enormous suite felt empty without him. I had made a concerted effort not to mope, so I knew Hannah was just giving me grief. But on the inside, I was definitely pouting.

After Mark left, Hannah, Sarah, and I decided to take it easy. I booked a massage at the spa, which was in its own pavilion just a short five-minute walk from the hotel. When I emerged an hour later, I was blissfully relaxed, but when I opened the doors and stepped back outside, I was struck with an acute case of spa hangover. The bright sun came flooding into my eyes—and I immediately experienced that dazed and confused fog from reentering the real world too quickly. The afternoon was warm and humid, which made me feel drowsy. My body had been operating on hyperspeed for months, trying to keep up with all my work obligations, and now that I had actually gotten off the roller coaster, it was shutting down. After I had taken only a few steps outside, the strangest sensation hit me right between the legs. I could feel my heart begin to race and I started to panic. I had never felt anything like this in my life, and I couldn't quite pinpoint what it was. As I kept walking, the sensation got stronger. It wasn't exactly painful, but something serious was going on inside me. I got the distinct feeling that I was giving birth to an object the size of an apple.

A friend once told me about how her mom had to have surgery because of a prolapsed uterus. With a renewed terror, I froze and thought to myself: *Oh my god, my uterus is falling out of my vagina!*

Clenching as tightly as possible and holding my breath, I took small steps back toward the hotel.

Just get back to your bathroom. You can call for help as soon as you have a better idea of what is going on, I told myself. Thank god this hadn't happened while Mark was here. This would have made me feel even more geriatric than the Harry Potter episode. Not to mention, it would make me the poster child for loose vaginas. Organs were escaping out of it, after all!

Thankfully, Hannah and Sarah were out when I got back to the suite. I knew Hannah and her raunchy sense of humor would latch on to this tale, which was fine, but let me save my uterus before getting roasted, please.

And just as quickly as the sensation came on, it began to dissipate. I noticed the apple-in-my-vagina feeling had vanished. I pulled down my shorts to go to the bathroom, praying a wayward internal organ wouldn't fall in the toilet bowl And there it was: the red condom Mark had used two nights before. Mark might have gone home, but apparently the condom had decided to extend its stay inside my vagina.

After all those years of hearing from sex education classes and *Seventeen* magazine that the vagina is self-cleaning (no need to douche, girls!), I had finally seen proof. Why a condom felt like a giant mass moving through there, I don't know, but I was so relieved that it was nothing serious, I couldn't have cared less. I bounded out of the bathroom, jumped onto the bed, grabbed my phone, and dialed Mark. In my flood of relief, I was dying to tell someone about this, and this story was definitely one he and his twisted sense of humor would appreciate.

"So you won't believe what happened!" I exclaimed the moment he answered.

"What?" he asked with laughter in his voice, instantly matching my vibe.

"So I was walking back to the room after getting a massage and I felt like something MASSIVE was coming out of my vagina . . ."

"Uh, Hols—" Mark started, attempting to interrupt. *He had to hear this,* I thought gleefully.

". . . like I was giving birth to something," I continued, speaking a bit louder as he tried to muffle me out.

"Um, Holly . . . ?" he asked, starting to sound concerned.

I wouldn't let him finish.

"So I started to get worried and hurried back to the room," I laughed. "And the condom you used the other night fell out!"

"Oh my god, Holly!" Mark shouted. "I'm backstage with my friend, and you're on speaker!"

My jaw dropped as I sat there in total silence. I wasn't quite sure of what the appropriate icebreaker would be to his friend whom I didn't know, but who now knew more about me than he ever needed to.

"Oh, heeeeey!" I called out to his friend with a forced air of casualness as I heard him laughing in the background.

"Let me call you back in a minute," Mark managed through their eruption of laughter.

"Nice to meet you!" another friendly male voice shouted.

We hung up and I fell back onto the bed, smiling. I loved that I could laugh about stuff like this with him—and it wasn't a huge deal. I could actually say what I wanted to say without censoring myself at all. Frankly, I didn't even care that his friend had overheard it—and it was clear he and the friend didn't, either.

"That's why I asked you if you had a cervical cap," he explained when he called me back a few minutes later. "I thought I felt something weird!"

"Oh!" It was all making sense now.

"I didn't even notice that it wasn't on at the end. I guess you had me distracted," he said, laughing. "How did I not feel it last night?"

"How should I know?" I laughed. "I didn't even know it was there."

Ordinarily this would have made me feel insanely self-conscious, but not with Mark. You can say this about the guy: he certainly knew how to make a night memorable.

Well, I thought as I laid back on the bed, smiling to myself, *so much for just a vacation fling.* In fact, I couldn't remember ever having been so sure about wanting to jump in feetfirst with someone.

If we had been ravenous texters before this trip, our communication became practically constant after it. When he sent me our picture from our final evening together, I decided to get myself an iPhone to save it on—as the wallpaper, no less. I loved that we could share emojis and play the same games. I still kept my BlackBerry for all my real-world communication and saved my iPhone almost exclusively for Mark, as a kind of portal to the dream world that our new long-distance relationship occupied.

Despite the fireworks (figuratively and literally), I was done assuming I was anyone's girlfriend, no matter how they acted toward me. I had thought that Jeffrey and I were more than we had been and vowed never to jump to a conclusion like that in the future. I didn't want to feel that stupid again! So in this case, I used the term *relationship* loosely. I reminded myself that Mark was not my boyfriend, even though he felt more like a boyfriend than most of my previous relationships had.

So I was conflicted when Nancy asked me for what she called a "huge favor"—popping out of a cake for her boss's birthday. An antic like that was just the kind of corny thing I was into. However, if I had a boyfriend, I probably wouldn't pop out of a cake for another guy. Especially if that guy was the handsome Eric J. Parkington. *But you don't have a boyfriend,* I reminded myself ruefully.

"Please," Nancy pleaded. "It's for his birthday party. It'll be funny, nothing provocative. It's a total gag. Everyone knows he has a huge crush on you, so it will just be a surprise that you're there."

"Okay," I agreed, knowing that I'd be helping Nancy (who always dropped everything when I needed her). Eric and I had run into each other quite a few times since Nancy started working for him, including that night at the comedian's pool party, and had added each other to our BBM. *I guess he and I are friends,* I reasoned. "I'll do it!"

After *Peepshow*, I hurried to get ready for my "second performance." I quickly switched up my hair and makeup, changed into a white dress, and raced toward the Hard Rock with Angel in tow. I busied myself with preparations for my big reveal so I wouldn't have to deal with the growing guilt I was feeling. I really just wanted to be curled up on a couch somewhere with Mark as my boyfriend, instead of living out some weird, campy fantasy of being the girl who jumps out of a birthday cake.

I quietly waited outside one of the hotel's newest suites. They had just added a new tower of deluxe suites, including one with a bowling alley. Two hotel staffers wheeled up the giant prop cake and removed the top. Nancy and Angel helped me step inside. I hunched down to await my signal. Nancy handed me a cupcake before placing the top back on. They wheeled the cart into the room and I could hear the partygoers wondering who—or what—could be inside the giant wooden confection. A minute later, Eric was brought in, and everyone shouted "Surprise!"

"Now!" Nancy yelled to me from outside the cake. I exploded out the top of the cake, my arms in the air as the party went crazy with cheers.

Eric was standing directly in front of me, and I tossed the cupcake I had in my hand at his face and flashed him a bright smile. He dodged the cupcake and looked back at me with a face flushed and beaming with surprise.

"Happy birthday," I said when I made my way to the bar. He gave me a hug and thanked me, his face reddening as his friends crowded around him to pay their respects.

Angel and I grabbed drinks and hors d'oeuvres before retreating to a table to hang out and people-watch.

"Eric just broke up with his girlfriend," Nancy started when she joined us at our table with a cocktail in hand, clearly celebrating being able to pull all this off. "Everyone is *so* relieved. She really stressed him out. We haven't seen him this relaxed since before they got together."

It was clear that he was an alpha. His social circle revolved around him—the women all wanted to be with him, and the men all wanted to be him. As we observed the sea of adoring partygoers, we saw everyone *but* the birthday boy himself. He was constantly concealed by a crowd, each person in it offering him a drink, a shot, or a lingering hug. Angel and I remained on the fringes with our plates of food, taking it all in.

"Who's that?" I heard Eric's voice ask over my shoulder as he plucked my iPhone out of my hand.

"Umm, a friend," I said hesitantly, shocked to see him sidled up next to me out of nowhere. I was surprised at how embarrassed I felt that he had seen my revealing choice of home screen wallpaper. *What kind of a psycho puts a guy's picture as her wallpaper before they are even dating?* I berated myself, cringing. The screen was still lit up since I had texted Mark just a few seconds earlier to wish him a good night. I dropped my plate onto the table and snatched my phone back. I had seen Eric doing a ton of shots moments earlier, so I wrote his uncharacteristic lack of manners off as intoxication.

"Is that your boyfriend?" he asked. "What is he? Some actor?"

Obviously he'd already heard about Mark.

"No," I stammered, feeling my cheeks flush a bit. "He's just a guy I've hung out with."

I felt like Mark was more than a guy I had just hung out with, but I had to remind myself that technically, he wasn't. Until we had a discussion about where we stood, I could for all I knew be one of a number of girls he was hooking up with. In my heart, I suspected that Mark wasn't that kind of guy, but I had just been so burned before that I refused to let myself take any chances.

"I want to get out of here," Eric said to me. Despite the occasion, he was dressed more casually than I had ever seen him, in a flannel shirt, jeans, and a baseball cap. It was quite the change from his usual Armani uniform. "Surprises aren't really my thing," he continued. "It was nice of everybody and all, but I'd much rather go somewhere quiet."

"I've got to head home now, anyway," Angel said. "Do you guys want to walk me down to my car? It'll give you a good excuse to ghost," she said, looking pointedly at Eric.

We quietly left the suite without anyone noticing, walking Angel to her car. Eric shot off a quick text, and moments later his Mercedes town car appeared. A driver quickly emerged and opened the back door for us.

"Where should we go? Besides home," he asked, already anticipating my answer.

"Take me to the Double Down," I replied. The Double Down Saloon is the absolute best dive bar in Vegas and I wanted to see if Mr. Fancy Pants could hang. He looked amused by my suggestion, but without any hesitation, instructed his driver to take us there.

When we rolled up in his car, we were surprised to find the bar virtually empty. The tiny one-room establishment featured a bar, serving their signature Ass Juice shots, a few pool tables, and a small corner platform for live music. The walls were covered in graffiti, stickers, and signs that read "Shut Up and Drink."

I helped myself to a tattered barstool while he ordered us two fruity drinks. We attempted a bit of small talk, but Eric, like me, wasn't the most chatty person in the world, so luckily the bartender chimed in quite a bit and kept the conversation going.

After only a few drinks, I was practically spinning.

"Let's go," I decided abruptly while wobbling to my feet. "I need to get home."

"All right," he said, pulling a few bills out of his wallet and laying them on the bar. His was the only car sitting in the seemingly abandoned parking lot. I crawled into the backseat and shut my eyes. As we made our way to Planet Hollywood, I swayed back and forth at each turn. Finally, a particularly rough left turn forced me right into Eric, knocking my head on his shoulder. My tough-girl act was quickly fading because I was clearly being seen for what I was: a lightweight! I usually drank my vodka straight or with water because I could taste what I was getting, and it kept my pace slow and steady. Give me a booze-infused sugary concoction and I'll slurp it down without realizing how strong it is—and eventually end up paying the price. *I should have chosen my own drinks,* I thought regretfully.

As we pulled up to the Planet Hollywood VIP entrance, Eric insisted on walking me up to my room, which, considering my level of intoxication, really was the nice thing to do. To my embarrassment, though, all the hotel staff that I saw on a daily basis greeted him by name.

"Good evening, Mr. Parkington," I heard over and over again as we made our way up to my suite. When he tried to tip anyone (valet, doorman, etc.), they staunchly refused, as if they were in the presence of some sort of royalty. *This is so weird,* I thought. *How do they all know him? They all probably assume I'm taking him to bed. Ugh!* I predicted that my trip downstairs tomorrow would feel like a walk of shame.

We reached the top floor and continued down the black, velvet-flocked hallway. The intricately patterned black-and-azure-blue carpet swirled at the bottom of my line of sight, contributing to my feeling of dizziness. When we arrived at the door to my suite, I stopped, kicked off my heels, and kneeled, dropping my purse in my lap and digging through my tiny clutch in search of the key card.

"Aha!" I shouted as I produced the key card with my right hand. He offered me his hand and I pulled myself up, closing one eye with great concentration as I inserted the card into the slot. *These damn key cards never work,* I thought. On the third try, success! As I turned around to thank him for walking me upstairs . . . Smack! Just like that. Without my even realizing it happened, he planted a kiss square on my lips.

"Good night, Holly," he said, and pushed open the door so that I could walk in.

"Night," I mumbled.

I turned around and stumbled to my room.

Okay, it was nothing, I thought, *Just a peck.*

"Who was the boy at the door?" Laura called from her room in a mock-chastising voice.

"I'll tell you tomorrow," I yelled back, not feeling like getting into it.

It had been an interesting night, but truthfully? I would have rather stayed in, knowing Mark and I were an actual thing.

As it turned out, I was less than a week away from getting my wish.

"Are you seeing anyone else?" Mark asked me over the phone one evening. "Because I'm not and I don't want to."

"No, I'm not," I responded. He didn't ask me if anyone else had kissed me, so it technically wasn't a lie. Besides, it *was* just a peck. If Mark had only had this conversation with me a week earlier, I wouldn't have even gone to that party!

To be fair, I had no interest in grilling Mark about whether he'd been seeing other girls over the past few weeks, which was totally possible since he turned heads everywhere he went. Since we weren't officially exclusive, it was none of my business, and honestly, I didn't really want to know.

"So I can say you're my girlfriend now?" he teased me.

"Yes," I said, a giant grin spreading across my face. It seemed so strange to be having this conversation after spending only one weekend together, but we'd been in constant communication for the last three months, so it felt like I knew him better than the people I saw every day.

Isn't this how it's supposed to be? I reminded myself. I mean, I *had* already slept with the guy. Maybe I had finally met a gentleman for once.

And just like that, we were inseparable. Or as inseparable as two people with conflicting schedules in different cities could be. Any time he had a day off, he would come see me, and vice versa. He had recently joined a touring production, so his schedule varied, but my Wednesdays off were constant. I found myself looking forward to my days off more than ever . . . wishing they wouldn't end, in fact.

Our first Wednesday apart fell the day before Thanksgiving. He had promised his family he would be home for the holidays, so I decided to make the most of the day with my friends.

Since Josh and I performed Thanksgiving evening, it wasn't practical to have a huge turkey dinner before getting onstage. After doing that our first year, we decided never to make that mistake again! Instead, we created a new tradition: Thanksgiving would be the night before (which was our dark day).

I decided to make use of my new house by inviting a group of friends over for a day-before-Thanksgiving feast. Angel, Roman, and the rest of my little family of friends gathered around the table for our turkey dinner. We ate, laughed, and passed our phones around the table, going over the year's most outrageous pictures.

After dinner, we decided to go see a family movie and chose *Tangled*. Little Roman fell asleep as I became captivated by the cartoon. When I saw the animated baby Rapunzel, I was overwhelmed with a feeling of longing. Trying to wipe the tears away from the corners of my eyes, I wondered why I was getting so choked up over a cartoon?

Out of nowhere, baby fever was hitting me pretty hard—triggered by an animated movie of all things. *Damn,* I thought, *if that's what's getting me emotional, I'm in trouble!* At this point I was thirty-one years old, so it wasn't abnormal to be thinking about kids. While I might feel as if I were barely twenty-one, my biological clock was ticking.

I've got a few more years in me, I thought, and tried my best to forget that intense longing I was now feeling.

At first it was easy to brush the feelings away. I was too busy retreating into my fantasy world with Mark. It wasn't long before he decided to move in with a friend in L.A., so it was becoming easier for us to find time to be together.

"I probably should be out in L.A. full-time anyway after the show wraps," he said. "It's where I need to be if I want to get more roles, ya know?"

Deep down I suspected that L.A. living wasn't really the most practical thing for him financially, and that I was probably a big factor in his motivation to relocate to the West Coast.

Most Monday nights Mark would fly to Vegas, and on Tuesday nights we would drive to L.A. for my Wednesdays off together. On our first drive, we left at 11:30 P.M., after that night's *Peepshow.*

I knew that all of the Starbucks past the state line would be closed after midnight, so we stopped for gas and coffee at Primm, the town on the border of Nevada and California. Since it's the first place to gamble when coming from California via the I-15, two massive casinos welcome visitors on either side of the freeway. The I-15 largely replaced Highway 91, the original route to Vegas. When the highway was paved in 1937, the road was open for drivers, leading to thousands and later hundreds of thousands of visitors flooding Las Vegas from Los Angeles every year.

"I always wonder about the people who used to do this drive back in the fifties, before cars had air conditioning," I said. "How miserable."

"That sounds terrible," Mark agreed with a laugh. "It must have been pretty desolate. I wonder if they had many gas stations along the way."

"Well, supposedly there was one right here run by a guy named Whiskey Pete," I said, nodding toward the other side of the freeway, where a giant casino called Whiskey Pete's stood. There was a mascot sitting atop the Whiskey Pete's sign, a cartoon drawing of an old miner based on Pete MacIntyre, the man who owned the land the casino sat on in the early part of the last century. He ran a gas station on the property and supplemented his income by bootlegging (hence the name), cooking up his wares in the caves surrounding the area.

Before he passed away from miner's lung in 1933, Pete asked to be buried standing up so he could "watch over" his land. When the bridge connecting Buffalo Bill's and Whiskey Pete's casinos was built in the eighties, Pete's body was unintentionally exhumed. He still held a bottle of whiskey in his (now skeletal) hand.

"Supposedly he haunts the casino's hotel and customers will find their gas gauges mysteriously moved up to full after parking on the property."

"You love your ghosts and shit," Mark said with a smile.

"I know. Now it's your turn to tell me a ghost story," I said as we got back in the car. I loved being able to talk to Mark for the whole four-and-a-half-hour drive. The drive can be deathly boring, but we never ran out of things to discuss during those trips, which was one of my favorite aspects of our relationship. He could keep me totally entertained with whatever he was saying all the way from Las Vegas to L.A.

As December rolled around, I began the business of planning my birthday soiree. I couldn't help feeling anxious. Sure, there would be press photographers there, as there were at all of my bookings, but it wasn't just a typical club appearance. It was a really personal event—my birthday. While I wasn't into exploiting my love life for the press, I *did* want my significant other to be part of my big day. Things were so amazing with Mark, but how would he react to being linked publicly with me? It was about to be the moment of truth. Would the idea of being photographed with me send Mark running in the opposite direction? It seemed to have done the trick for every other guy I dated. After all, he did consider himself a serious actor. Let's face it, with reality TV and Las Vegas, my brand was about as cheesy as it gets. I was happy with who I was, but would he be?

Mark didn't seem like a fame whore, but I was petrified that he would end up being just like the rest of them: happy to slink in and out of my spotlight only as it was convenient for him.

When we arrived at the nightclub, I told him I was going to do the carpet with the cast of the show and that I would meet him at my table. After we were reunited inside, the ball would be in his court.

To my relief, he was completely supportive and normal, like a real boyfriend should be. He didn't jockey to get press attention or creep around like he was too cool to be photographed with me. His willingness to be present in my life and to accept me on my own terms, unlike the other guys I had dated, meant more to me than he could possibly know. He fit so perfectly and effortlessly into my world while still being his own amazing person.

This is easily the best birthday I've ever had, I thought.

The next day was unseasonably warm as Mark and I took a helicopter trip to the Grand Canyon for my birthday. As the aircraft rose above the city, we took in the beautiful sites, but the heat was so intense that I nodded off on his shoulder during the flight. We landed deep in the canyon with an amazing picnic lunch that we barely touched. The beauty of the canyon demanded our full attention. It was such a stunning backdrop, but I was more in awe of the realization that we didn't even need this amazing a sight. Anywhere we went, whether it was spectacular or mundane, seemed to come alive when we were with each other. I couldn't believe how at ease I felt with this person. I knew he would be back for the weekend of New Year's Eve, just a week away, but I couldn't help wishing that he wasn't leaving.

The previous New Year's Eve, I was single, hosting at the nightclub at Planet Hollywood. I hung out with Laura and Kent, who was back in town for the weekend, but something was missing: a boy to share a romantic first kiss of the New Year with. The night ended with me alone in my suite. There were no fireworks for me that night, literally or figuratively. I hadn't seen them on the Strip because I had been holed up in the club all night, and there certainly hadn't been any romantic fireworks, either.

This New Year's Eve fell on a Friday, which meant it would be a three-day extravaganza. Every year, visitors from all over the world flocked to Las Vegas to ring in the New Year. The city was a sort of mecca for the decadent champagne-swirling bashes that most people sought out to celebrate the festive holiday, with more options than there are hours in the day.

To welcome in 2011, the choice was a no-brainer: the grand opening of the Cosmopolitan hotel. With Jay-Z and Coldplay headlining a private, invitation-only concert, it was, without a doubt, the most exclusive ticket in town. Cost was very clearly not a concern for the owners (the hotel itself had a $3.9 billion price tag), as they planned to host an eclectic, intimate mix of celebrities and high rollers for the entire weekend, offering all of them their own accommodations.

Yet despite the lavish festivities happening around the hotel, Mark and I spent most of the weekend holed up in our luxurious suite, lounging on our balcony (an unusual Vegas amenity), which offered a picture-perfect view of the Bellagio's fountains. While we were invited, along with the rest of the hotel's VIP guests, to the grand ballroom for the formal New Year's Eve dinner, we opted to host our own little party for two on our velvet pin-tucked marine-blue couch and ordered in pizza from the unnamed joint in the hotel that locals had taken to calling "Secret Pizza" (aka the worst-kept secret in town) and one of the hotel's signature offerings: a giant steamer trunk full of booze. Even though we decided to be hermits—despite having arguably the most desirable New Year's ticket that year—we could still feel the energy rushing upward from the concert directly below (Beyoncé, Kanye West, and John Mayer all made appearances on stage with Jay-Z and Chris Martin). What's more? My standard fear of missing out wasn't a factor—even though on this occasion most people would have agreed that we were crazy for forfeiting our access to the world's best New Year's party. But for once I didn't care.

Apparently Jay-Z called the weekend a once-in-a-lifetime experience, and I couldn't have agreed more, but for different reasons. Mark and I shared our first kiss of the New Year, and the night was absolutely perfect. Part of me could have stayed in the moment forever, but we were moving forward into 2011 and I was certain that it was going to be the best year of my life so far!

Chapter 8

"As a matter of fact, we are none of us above criticism;
so let us bear with each other's faults."
—L. Frank Baum, *The Marvelous Land of Oz*

My self-proclaimed "best year ever" was already off to an eventful start. After the holiday break, cameras were up and rolling for season two of *Holly's World* . . . and just in time to capture me getting a few bits of New Year's news.

The first was that my most infamous ex, Hugh Hefner, was now engaged to the leader of his live-in Lollipop Guild, Crystal Harris. While that part of my life was ancient history, not to mention the fact that the news didn't surprise me that much, everyone assumed I must be devastated about it and was watching me, waiting for a reaction. It was clear that people took it for granted that I would be mad or upset, expecting me to be caught crying in public or ranting on Twitter. My reaction was silence, while inside I was glad I dodged that bullet. That wasn't the reaction anyone expected or wanted, though.

Suddenly, my social media was exploding and my publicist was being inundated with requests for interviews and comments. I was irritated, but the engagement wasn't what bothered me. This assumption about how I felt was. I felt like I had come so far to reinvent myself and to build my own world that for me it was a huge setback to once again be labeled as Hef's lovelorn ex-girlfriend when I really didn't give much thought to what was going on up on Charing Cross Road anymore.

The second piece of news that greeted me was from *Peepshow*: I was instructed to lose weight. There was no "or else" tied to this, just the request itself. Despite my own discontent with the photos I had shot less than a year earlier, this news totally blindsided me.

While word of Hef getting engaged rolled off my back, being told that I was fat (at least that's how I interpreted it) launched me into a full-on spiral of grief. It's no exaggeration—I began going through the textbook five stages.

Stage one: Denial.

"I do not need to lose weight," I huffed to Nancy, who shook her head vigorously in solidarity. "I happen to think I look good!"

"You look better than good," she said enthusiastically. "You look fucking great!"

"I've never been a stick figure, anyway!" I whined. "That's not me. This is ridiculous!"

Upon hearing the news, I immediately decided that I would *not* be losing any weight. It was *my* body and I was incredibly happy with it.

Stage two: Anger.

Who are they to tell me I need to lose weight? I fumed. *Tickets are selling better than ever!*

I'd seen my fair share of nasty tweets or comments, but I hadn't noticed one online hater ever criticizing me for being "fat." I thought I had broken free from a world where how I looked was dictated down to the pound, so my rebellious streak rose up when anyone dared to make a suggestion in that direction.

Stage three: Bargaining.

Because the news came to me through my manager, I thought if

I vented to him, perhaps he would take my concerns right back to the producers.

"I have a really full schedule and it all ties into promoting the show," I complained, "I barely have time to sleep, let alone work out! When do they expect me to find the time?"

The truth of the matter was that when I wasn't onstage, I was filming, doing press, or doing promotional events—all things I thought contributed greatly to the success of the show. Just when I thought I was doing everything I could for the production, it was pointed out that I didn't even look the part anymore. Being told that something that I was doing (or in this case *wasn't* doing) might be adversely affecting the show was a major blow. I know that's not what they were implying, but it's how I felt. I lived and breathed my career, and the suggestion made me feel like a failure.

"Isn't this show supposed to have some diversity in it?" I finally added, pulling out every stop I could think of. I knew damn well that my arguments were going to fall on deaf ears, but the embarrassment of being called out for being "overweight" made me scramble to defend myself.

Stage four: Depression.

I'm not talking about major depression, mind you, I'd been through that before. What I was experiencing was more a cocktail of shame, embarrassment, and sadness.

Have I really been prancing around onstage looking completely out of shape? I wondered. *Have I been making a fool of myself all this time?*

I began wondering if I was surrounded by yes people who just said what they thought I wanted to hear. Maybe the *Peepshow* executives were finally telling me what everyone else had been thinking all along?

Where were you two when I started to pudge out? I thought, staring at a picture of me with Hannah and Lindsay.

I felt like I had let myself down. After finally regaining control of my own life and achieving all my goals, how was it that I couldn't even control my own body?

How can I continue to hold my life together if I can't even control five to ten extra pounds? I thought. I was feeling particularly defeated. When Mark came to town for a visit, I was too embarrassed to share with him what I had been told. I was afraid that if I told him that I had been designated "Fatty of the Month," the curtain would fall and he would think less of me.

Stage five: Acceptance.

After expressing myself in every way that I needed to, I finally decided that I should at least try to lose the weight (*How much do I even need to lose?* I asked myself. *Five pounds? Ten pounds?*), but only because I knew I wasn't at *my* ideal weight, anyway. After all, hadn't I been unhappy with the last set of performance photos? Hadn't I been sucking in my stomach like crazy, feeling self-conscious at photo shoots? In the end, the show did expect their star to be in top physical form. They were certainly paying me enough money for it.

Just because I had accepted that getting in shape wouldn't be a bad idea didn't mean the feelings from the earlier stages were completely wiped out. What made me most anxious about this request was that I knew healthy weight loss took time. And time was something I had less and less of these days. I now had a complex bundle of emotions tied to my weight, but I tried my best to forget about them for now and instead to devise a plan to make lemonade out of this newest batch of lemons that had been dumped in my lap. I decided that my weight journey should be documented on my TV show, which had been renewed for a second season a few months earlier.

Production agreed, but they also wanted my reaction to Hef's engagement covered on the show. Initially I balked at the idea. Even on my own show I couldn't get away from people wanting to hear about my relationship with Hef, and the last thing I wanted to do was give that part of my past any weight in my present.

But after talking this over with production and giving it more thought, I figured, *Why not?* This would be a good chance to show people just how much I *didn't* care about the engagement. In fact, I was happy everyone was moving on! I could use it as a platform to show viewers and the press that I was thrilled in my own life and not pining away, as people erroneously assumed I was. After taping *Extra* one morning, I flew into L.A. to film the "congratulations" scene.

Walking into the mansion for the first time since I had moved out was a bit surreal, to say the least. I couldn't get over how quiet the place seemed. *Had it always been this quiet?* I asked myself. Sure, there had never been parties going on 24/7, but I didn't remember the quiet times being *this* quiet. The great hall was like a morgue. A giant dollhouse I had commissioned as a gift for Hef two years earlier (a replica of the home he had grown up in in Chicago) was placed on a table in the middle of the hall, taking center stage.

If there was anywhere on the mansion property that could make me feel comfortable, it was Mary's office, the location of the first scene we shot. I welcomed the chance to catch up with my old friend, but as we were on a shooting schedule, we had to concentrate on a few specific topics in a short period of time, so the producers could get the content they wanted.

We were on our best behavior. Mary said nice things about Crystal and I said nice things about Hef. It was funny, because Mary made a comment about my leaving being hard on them and said, "You know, there wasn't really a fight or anything . . ." as if to imply that Hef was confused as to why I left.

There were plenty of fights, I thought. But now wasn't the time, in front of the cameras, to remind Mary of my laundry list of grievances. If Hef truly was confused as to why I left and forgot there was any fighting, he either had the world's most selective memory or thought talking down to his girlfriends and making them cry on a regular basis was normal.

After my scene with Mary, I strolled around the zoo and said hello to the monkeys and birds I used to spend so much time with. It was wonderful to see these little creatures, but I couldn't help but see the parallels between the animals in the cages and what my life there had been like. It reminded me of the young woman I used to be, who wanted so much but spent her days tiptoeing around the grounds, talking to the animals.

"Are you ready?" the producer asked. I smiled and nodded, a pit growing in my stomach. Filming with Hef was beyond awkward. For so many of the years that I had lived with him, I had forced myself to look at him through rose-colored glasses. Now that I saw the real person, though, it was like interacting with a stranger. Thank God we had the dollhouse to talk about; otherwise I have no idea what I would have said.

Did Hef seem more frail than he had two and a half years ago? Or was I just seeing him through different eyes? He seemed a different man, dramatically changed from the person I knew just a few years ago. It made me wonder if there were stresses behind the scenes that I wasn't aware of causing him to seem less robust than usual. The economy had crashed since I left, and even before that, the company had been walking a financial tightrope.

Crystal finally came down to say hello. She too seemed different from the few times I had met her. Reed-thin and wearing little makeup, she was dressed in basic jeans and a long-sleeved shirt. She seemed tired and mellow, gracious and not snotty as she had come across to me in the past. I congratulated them both on the engagement, and the scene wrapped. Overall, I was happy that we had decided to do the segment. I felt like it was a dignified way to leave that part of my past behind.

Naturally, all of that was counteracted when, in the finished version, producers added a gag-worthy montage of Hef and me to the end of the scene (similar to one they had used at the end of *GND* season five, which they knew I had hated). But, montage aside, I was happy with the scene and thought it was a nice opportunity to show the public how I really felt about the situation.

I jumped back on a flight to Vegas from Burbank and landed with just enough time to get backstage and get ready for the show. After disembarking, I walked through the airport with my head down, continuing the text conversations I'd been having with Nancy all day. I made my way to the escalator that I knew would deposit me on the baggage-claim level right in front of Starbucks, since I needed fuel for this evening.

I had no more than stepped on the escalator when I got a text from Eric.

Look up, it read.

I scrunched up my face. *What the hell does he mean by that?* I thought.

When I actually did look up from my phone, I saw him standing at the base of the escalator, looking as suave as always, his hands in the pockets of his suit pants.

Damn, he looks handsome, was my first thought. *Maybe I should try and set him up with one of my friends,* was the second, reminding myself that I was taken.

"Hey!" I exclaimed as I hopped off the escalator. "Where are you headed?"

"I'm not headed anywhere," he stated. "I'm here to pick you up."

"Really?" I asked, incredulously. "Why? What's going on?"

"Because I felt like it. You are too big to be taking flights on Southwest and taxis to film things."

I nervously laughed off what he said. I didn't know how to respond to him. Was he making fun of me? I certainly didn't think of myself as "too big" for anything. It's not like I was a movie star. *Nancy must have put him up to this,* I thought.

He led me to valet, where his Bentley was waiting for us. As he drove me to Planet Hollywood, I tried as best I could to make conversation, though there were a lot of awkward silences. It was the first time I had been alone with him since the night at the Double Down.

Is he as socially inept and quiet as I am or is he just trying to be mysterious? I wondered. *There's no way someone as popular as he is, is this nonverbal.*

"We should go on a trip together sometime," he offered woodenly as we pulled up to the VIP entrance. "Have you been to London? It's one of my favorite cities."

"I can't," I laughed, trying to hide the fact that I was blushing. "I have a boyfriend." I stepped out of his car and thanked him for the ride. My "thanks for the ride" came out as if there were a question mark attached to the end. It was so odd that he had shown up at the airport to greet me. Had he been bored, looking to impress me, or what? Was it even appropriate that I accepted the ride? It would have been rude to turn it down, considering Eric and I were friends. I thought holding Eric firmly in the "friend zone" while I had a boyfriend meant I was in control of the situation, even though his flirting was inappropriate.

A few days later, I was back in L.A. on my day off. Mark and I curled up in our designated booth at the Polo Lounge for dinner. As if purely to torture me, a wire basket sat in the center of the table, overflowing with pieces of lavash and blue cheese bread.

"A McCarthy Salad, please, no meat," I ordered when the white-coated server appeared at our booth. That was all I planned on eating.

I hadn't mentioned my new diet to Mark, hoping he wouldn't notice my drastically different dining habits. He didn't need to get caught up in my tailspin, plus I couldn't think of anything that would be more boring to this confident guy who just so happened to have a perfectly fit physique.

"So," Mark began, "a friend of mine was talking about Crystal Harris, that girl that got engaged to Hef." He broached the topic gently, without even a drop of judgment in his voice. "How are you feeling about that?"

"You know, I really don't care about it as much as people think I do," I responded quickly. "I'm not surprised by it either. He seemed to be slowing down even back when I was still there, so it was only a matter of time."

I looked directly into those breathtaking blue eyes, gave him a smile, and shrugged, hoping my response sounded as unattached as I was to the matter.

"So, tell me about this audition," I asked excitedly, eager to change the topic. Mark recognized my shift and launched into an animated story. No one is really comfortable talking about their ex-boyfriends with their new ones—and I was no different. Unfortunately, mine wasn't your standard awkward situation; it was made increasingly more uncomfortable by the amount of press this news received. Underneath my discomfort, I was really amazed at how cool Mark was being. *You know,* I caught myself thinking, *no one I know personally ever asked me how I felt about the engagement . . . not even my closest friends.* Everyone just assumed they knew how I felt or avoided the topic altogether. We had staged a scene about it for the TV show, but no one had bothered to discuss it with me in real life.

Mark's ability to see past his own ego in order to make sure I was doing okay just proved what a well-adjusted and caring person he was. In some ways, he was almost too good to be true.

All I ever wanted was a partner who respected me enough to value my opinions and thoughts, instead of rushing to judgment. Part of me wanted to explain to him how annoying I thought all the public assumptions were, but for some reason, I just couldn't manage to get the words out. Automatically I shut him out. I wasn't ready to open up that can of worms. Being told for years that I wasn't quite good enough was only one issue out of a whole host of dysfunctions I had bottled up inside.

I wasn't yet comfortable enough in my own skin and feared Mark would find those elements of me unattractive.

My earlier resolve to just be myself in that relationship had exited stage left. Mark had become my escape. When I was with him, I was in a space where my concerns about body issues and public scrutiny weren't allowed to enter. I didn't want our relationship to become this heavy thing where we suddenly threw our baggage on the bed and started unpacking. I didn't want to risk losing what we had, which was light and fun. I wanted to be that adventurous girl he fell for months earlier.

After changing the subject to one I was more comfortable with (work),

I had plenty to talk about. For the second season of *Holly's World*, producers wanted to bring in two new cast members. First was Claire Sinclair, who arrived in Vegas in January. Mary O'Connor had told me about Claire, who was coming to Vegas to guest-star at Crazy Horse Paris, just as I had planned to do a few years earlier.

"Maybe you could be like a big sister to her," Mary suggested. "She's a wonderful girl. She's just a breath of fresh air around here," she had said, referring to the mansion. Claire was a quirky nineteen-year-old who had recently been published as a Playmate. She was intelligent, outgoing, and had an offbeat sense of humor.

With her porcelain skin, naturally buxom figure, button nose, and brunette bangs, she looked like a modern-day Bettie Page. Claire had recently been cast as the protagonist in a pilot (produced by the same company that did *Holly's World*) called *The Bunny House*, which wasn't picked up by E! There was only so much room for these Playboy-related, advertiser-unfriendly shows, and *Holly's World* and *Kendra* were currently taking up that space. A producer had told me that they hoped that putting some cast members from *The Bunny House* on my show would make them popular enough for E! to reconsider. I could have felt threatened or used by this move, but I didn't. I knew E! wouldn't order another Playboy show, and frankly, I liked Claire. I thought she could be a relevant cast member, not because she was a Playmate, but because she was a budding Vegas showgirl. Plus, I loved *Crazy Horse Paris* and was excited about featuring it on an episode.

Claire needed a place to crash for filming, so I was happy to offer her my room at Planet Hollywood, much to Laura's dismay, who had been enjoying having the whole suite to herself since I spent most days at my house. After a year of back and forth, I was finally ready to make my house in Southern Highlands my sole residence.

The second cycle of the show was set to air in just a few weeks, and E! spared no expense sending a team to Las Vegas for an elaborate promotional shoot. Planet Hollywood's largest ballroom was transformed into a dreamland. One setup was a pink, sparkly candy land; the other one was a giant yellow-brick road to Oz, complete with a field of poppies.

The producers wanted to include Jayde Nicole, a Playmate of the Year who was also joining the show for our second season, in the promo shots. But since she was hired to assume the role of resident Vegas villain, I put my foot down because it seemed so unnatural.

"If she's supposed to be our enemy, why would we be posing for photos with her? That doesn't make any sense," I asked, which seemed to put to rest any argument they considered heaving my way.

Production wanted Jayde on my show for the same reason they had wanted Claire. Jayde had been cast as the antagonist on *The Bunny House*, and some of the executives at E! thought she was great at being "the girl you love to hate." At first I was fine with the decision to include Jayde. I know reality shows thrive on drama, and if she was willing to come in and play the role of the shit-stirrer, great! After all, I'd much rather have fake drama in my life than real conflict.

However, when it was announced she was going to be joining the show, the drama became a bit more real, as the addition itself created tremendous tension among the existing cast members. No one felt like their place was secure anymore. If we had such a good thing going, my costars were unclear on why we needed new people. As filming went on, I started to feel less and less in on the joke when it came to Jayde's role. Between local gossips, manufactured drama, and lack of communication, any friendship I had with Jayde before we started filming quickly evaporated. Just as I had with the Benji situation the season before, I felt out of control of what was supposed to be "my own show."

In fact, everyone in the cast was feeling strained and uneasy about the situation, but there wasn't much I could do about it now. I figured that when the season was wrapped, everything would hopefully go back to normal.

* * *

MY NEXT VACATION COINCIDED with the Super Bowl, allowing me to book a hosting job in Dallas that weekend, which left a few days for Mark and me to make a pit stop in Mexico before heading to Dallas. What could have been more perfect?

I chose the same resort that we had filmed at a year prior. Without my wild and crazy crew present, the whole property was incredibly quiet and relaxing, as if the energy had been dialed down several notches.

Our first stop? The spa. Because we were both performers, we were constantly exhausted. Naturally, we opted for the ninety-minute couples massage. But after an hour and a half of detoxing, we decided it was time to retox!

I had successfully shed about ten pounds in the last four weeks, due mainly to the crash diet I'd subjected myself to, so I happily climbed into my bikini for some beach barhopping. We walked along the white sand beaches, and Mark filled the air with talk of our plans for the rest of the year.

When we wandered around the resort, our heads fuzzy with margaritas and our skin warm from the sun, we happened across an arts and crafts workshop on the beach. A beautiful older Mexican woman with deep cocoa brown skin and wiry hair the color of ash gestured for us to come closer.

"Sit," she playfully commanded, flapping her hands to encourage us to kneel in the sand. Without preamble, we both dropped to the beach. She pushed a set of paints in front of us.

"Married?" she asked, pointing from Mark back to me.

"No," I replied with a polite smile. I knew she wasn't being presumptuous and could immediately feel the kindness in her eyes. "You?" I asked, attempting to replicate the warmheartedness in which she asked us.

"No," she responded, a small but sincere smile framing her face.

"Here, you should do this seahorse and I'll paint the lizard," Mark offered as he grabbed the statues and reached for the purple and black bottles of paint.

We sat side by side, painting our silly sculptures, laughing, and teasing each other against the beautiful backdrop of the clear blue Caribbean. When we finished our self-proclaimed masterpieces, we handed them to the tiny woman to bake in the kiln.

With long fingers covered in leathery skin, she reached out for my seahorse, then the lizard. Deep lines creased the skin surrounding her eyes, which beamed a radiant, almost shimmering black as she nodded her head ever so slightly as a thank-you, and in that moment, I was struck by her beauty. She wasn't trying to fit any conventional or trendy beauty standards, but she was radiant standing there on that beach—and I felt ashamed. I had spent the better part of a month obsessed over my weight, and here this woman was perfectly content, beautiful, and unique just as she was.

After we thanked her, we walked to the pool bar and ordered two frosty margaritas while our sculptures baked.

"Hey, are you okay?" Mark inquired, a concerned look on his face. "I've noticed that you've lost a lot of weight. I've been meaning to ask you about it."

"Yeah, well . . ." I started with a smile and roll of the eyes, proceeding to pour out a condensed version of the story. I confessed that the ordeal was going to be a story line on the series and even how I had crash-dieted in order to quickly lose the weight I needed to in order to reveal the kind of "transformation" I wanted for television. Attempting to play it cool and brush it off as no big deal, I proceeded to gloss over the situation. Mark did not seem convinced.

When I finished sharing the whole saga, Mark sat quietly for a moment, clearly contemplating what to say next. To be fair, this was a difficult tightrope for any guy to walk, because there really was no right answer.

"Well, I think you've always looked amazing," he said earnestly. "You never needed to lose any weight. I mean, you can do what you want, but I always thought you looked perfect just as you are."

I smiled, and leaned down to take a sip of the jumbo-sized margarita, less concerned about calories now that I had reached my desired weight.

"You can talk to me about this kind of stuff, you know," he added, hoping that this would spark further dialogue. I knew that he was trying. His blue eyes, the same ones that had first bewitched me months earlier, gazed with genuine compassion into my own, begging me to let him in.

"I'm good, really," I insisted, playfully patting the top of his hand as if to acknowledge how cute his concern was. "It's just really not that big of a deal." I felt like I had opened up enough for that day, I wasn't ready for an emotional deep dive. I didn't want to ruin our vacation.

"Hey, we should go check on our pottery. I bet it's done now," I suggested, standing up and walking away from the bar before he even agreed.

After that first day, we spent the majority of our time tucked into the large king-size bed inside our luxury villa, sleeping most of the day away. We were both so exhausted from our respective schedules that we desperately needed the rest. A hectic workload was one of the major things we had in common, but it was still disappointing to wait all this time to see each other, only to spend the lion's share of it passed out.

Maybe we are too *similar,* I wondered. I had tremendous respect for his work ethic and realized, for the first time, what an enormous effort he was making just to be able to spend time with me. It gave me pause to think about what my intentions were toward him beyond just having a good time. It seemed like he was pretty serious about me . . . but was I that committed to him? I certainly liked him well enough, but would we still be a good match in a few years? And, in the meantime, was I even *ready* to settle down and be serious with someone? Instead of continuing to live in the moment, as I had done with this relationship so far, I reverted to overthinking things, marking every aspect of my life down on one of my mental to-do lists.

"When's your next vacation?" Mark asked. He was wrapped in a fluffy white robe. The sun was setting and we were holed up on our patio to bask in the last few minutes of warm sunlight.

"The second week in March," I replied. My voice was soft and groggy, having just woken up from our late afternoon nap. "That's usually a slow week, right before spring-break season starts."

He scrolled through the calendar on his phone and landed on that week.

"I'll be in Oklahoma and Nebraska then. Will you come visit me?" he asked, burrowing his scruffy face into my neck.

"Of course," I answered, immediately feeling a twinge of regret.

The truth was, I had already been thinking about going to Paris on my next vacation; in fact, I desperately wanted to go. Ever since my first trip years earlier, I had fallen head over heels for the City of Light. I had been there twice, but always for filming and always on someone else's schedule. Now that I was finally independent, personally and financially, I wanted to do *my* dream trip to Paris, *my* way.

I started to wonder, even though I really liked this guy, if I was ready to be tied down *at all*. I knew that any serious relationship would require compromise, but was I even ready to compromise? I decided to brush those thoughts away for the time being, resolving to deal with them another time. I closed my eyes and laid my head on Mark's chest, listening to the waves against the shore.

I've heard more than one person say that if your significant other carries more than one cell phone, chances are he or she is cheating. I can't say that's true all the time, but in my case, things definitely started to get out of hand.

When I decided to get an iPhone, I did it out of enthusiasm for Mark. I was so swept away by him after our first weekend together that having matching technology seemed like just the thing to make me feel a little closer to this new long-distance crush. It was the perfect accessory to a budding romance. I always intended to keep my BlackBerry for most other communication, including emails.

I certainly didn't get a second phone with the intention of deceiving anyone, but simply having two phones lent itself to that. They became like two different extensions of me. Without realizing it, I started to compartmentalize my life according to what I used each phone for. Since Mark hit me up only on my iPhone, the ever-so-persistent Eric quickly became the man of the hour on my BlackBerry.

In the beginning, I found Eric's attentions flattering, particularly because he was the type of guy who could have any woman he wanted. He asked me out routinely, and I would constantly remind him that I was taken. I wasn't completely rude. After all, we were friendly acquaintances.

For years, I had been craving a career and someone special—and when it rains, it pours. Between *Peepshow*, *Holly's World*, and *Extra*, I had three jobs, not to mention a beautiful, sweet, amazing man who seemed to care a lot about me. I felt so lucky to have Mark, but I was also starting to have my doubts about the relationship. Now another charming, handsome man was knocking on my door and really beginning to become more aggressive in an attempt to capture my attention. I started comparing Eric and Mark in my head. One was local; the other wasn't. One was five years older than me, one eight years younger. Instead of listening to my heart, I started to wonder who the more "practical" choice was.

Mark's tour schedule meant that he wouldn't be attending my season two wrap party, but he made sure to send me a beautiful bouquet of orange roses (my absolute favorite). When Angel carried a second gigantic, breathtaking arrangement into the kitchen I was utterly blown away. Two bouquets! If Mark wasn't the most thoughtful . . .

"They're from Eric," Angel said knowingly, rolling her eyes.

Oh, shit, I thought. Mark's sweet bouquet looked like a grocery store bundle next to this enormous, artistically crafted display. *Poor Mark.*

As I sat there staring at these two offerings, I started to get annoyed. *How dare he?* I thought. It was completely inappropriate for Eric to send me these! I felt defensive of Mark, who, unbeknownst to him, had been belittled in my own home by what looked like a floral monstrosity, now that I knew who it was from. I shook my head and went upstairs to choose a dress for the night's after-show festivities.

The cast and I were ready to get a little crazy. We'd been working on overdrive and were excited to celebrate our last day of filming at LAX, the nightclub inside the Luxor.

We were led into the cavernous space, under the black glass chandeliers and past the wrought-iron balustrades that decorated the club. We arrived at our booth on a second-story balcony, looking down at the pulsating crowd below. My friends and I danced, laughed, and snapped photos like crazy people, reveling in our moment together. Cakes, flowers, and complimentary bottles of Cristal were brought to the table all night as we tossed party favors to the crowd below us. After the cameras wrapped, none other than Eric appeared at our booth, looking impeccable and crisp.

Had he been refreshing my Twitter feed just to find out where I'd be? I wondered, at once thinking that his behavior was a little much, but also feeling kind of flattered.

"Did you like the flowers?" he shouted into my ear over the blaring music, snatching the opportunity to fill the seat that had just become vacant next to me.

"You shouldn't have sent them. I have a boyfriend, remember?" I replied, still refusing to thank him for the flowers. *Perhaps I haven't been sending a strong enough message,* I thought.

"Then where is he?" he asked, a devilish grin on his chiseled jaw.

I shot him an evil look.

"If you were mine, you wouldn't be able to keep me away," he continued. I was determined to keep Eric at arm's length, but his persistence made him hard to ignore. He partied with my friends and me through the night, intermittently disappearing for brief periods to socialize with other people he knew in the surrounding booths. We had a limo waiting to take a bunch of us home, and Eric spontaneously jumped in as we were leaving. My best friends, who like everyone else in town had fallen hard under this guy's spell, were happy for him to join us in the raucous ride home as we popped a few bottles of champagne so that we could each have a nightcap on the way.

The first stop was Hannah's mansion on the Eastside. Next, Josh and Lindsay were dropped off at their lofts farther south. Finally just Angel, Eric, and I were left in the limo. I knew Angel and I would be dropped off first, as we were heading south and Eric's luxurious condo was located in Turnberry Place, on the north side of the Strip.

As we pulled up to my house, Eric walked us to the front door. Angel darted in first, leaving me with an extra moment to say good-bye to Mr. Persistent.

I quickly ducked inside my house and reached for my M-embossed doorknob. The interior of my home illuminated behind me as Angel flipped on the lights and went upstairs.

Eric leaned towards me and then pulled back . . . and I just watched him as he looked behind me, a devilish grin appearing on his face as his eyes locked on to something.

"Good night, Holly," he murmured.

"Night," I said. I was confused, but as I turned around, I quickly understood.

Sitting on the coffee table were the two arrangements.

"WHY DON'T YOU EVER send pictures anymore?" Mark asked.

"I will, I've just been so busy," I explained.

"We should talk on the phone more," he added.

Truthfully, these were perfectly reasonable requests, but I somehow couldn't find the motivation to up my game. I was having trouble juggling everything in my life, but I couldn't admit it and Mark was feeling the slack. Picking up the phone to call Mark should have been easy, but something was keeping me at bay. Deep down, I felt guilty and unworthy of all the effort Mark put into making the relationship work, since I was having my doubts about us. I respected him too much to not let this imbalance bother me, but I was still at a loss for how to actually handle it.

I grew vague when the subject of my coming to visit him during my next vacation came up. I desperately wanted to go to Paris, and Mark wasn't free to come with me. The urgency was mounting for me, as if this were the last vacation I would ever go on in my life.

Something about my behavior was eerily familiar . . . I was reminding myself of Jeffrey, pulling away from Mark in the same way that Jeffrey had pulled away from me. It wasn't fair. *Mark doesn't deserve someone who treats him like this,* I told myself. I wasn't as invested in the relationship as I should be. I knew now that I had to figure out a way to let this one down easy.

I can't continue to lead him on, I thought after texting Claire and asking her if she had the second week of March free. *It's not like we had a future together, anyway. I'll get to the point where I want to start a family way before he will.*

For me, having a talk about the future and kids with Mark was totally out of the question. I didn't want to be seen as that "crazy" girl who's trying to convince their man to settle down. During my time on *The Girls Next Door,* I had become known as the marriage-obsessed girlfriend, with babies constantly on the brain. It soon became a running joke on the show, which I was happy to play into. I thought the gag worked and there was a root of truth to it. I *did* want marriage and a family one day. But unfortunately it worked *too* well and the joke was soon inextricably attached to my public image. I couldn't bear the thought of Mark thinking of me that way, too.

Besides, his career was just starting to take off, and he had everything ahead of him. I felt he *shouldn't* want a family any time soon.

Yes, I would be doing him a favor if I set him free, I thought.

Maybe I was scared of getting hurt again. Maybe, in my own way, I wanted to preserve our relationship and freeze it as a perfect moment in time, breaking it off before he could ever have a chance to tire of me and leave me heartbroken.

He had the following weekend off and had already planned to come to Vegas. I knew I should have canceled it, but I didn't. For some reason, I couldn't pull the plug. I tried to tell myself that it was because he didn't deserve a long-distance breakup, but I really shouldn't have let him spend the time and money to come out and visit, either. The truth was, I was nervous and didn't know how to say what needed to be said. I hoped that seeing him in person would force me to face reality and help me find the right words.

"Let's grab sushi," Mark suggested as soon as he jumped into my car when I picked him up from the airport. We went to one of his favorite spots, which had a gorgeous, sweeping view of the Las Vegas strip.

After we ordered, we gravitated toward the corner of the booth and I leaned up against him as I usually did, but it felt awkward and forced, as if there were a large space between us. Our conversation was unusually stilted. I was walking on eggshells trying to avoid having the talk right before I had to go onstage, and while I couldn't tell you what he was thinking, it was clear something was on his mind. He just wasn't as talkative as usual and I'm sure he could feel the distance between us as I lay in his arms . . . how could he not?

"I have this friend whose wife was cheating on him . . ." he started awkwardly as he stared out the window.

I knew exactly what he was doing . . . and I can't say I blamed him. My throat began to close up. I knew that wherever this conversation was going, it would end with us saying good-bye. I was selfish, terrified to have it right before going onstage; I was scared that I wouldn't be able to dry my eyes and jump into character on time.

"Angel is hosting over at Chateau," I interrupted with forced cheer, attempting awkwardly to change the subject. "You should really go see her while I do my show. It'd be fun." Angel, in addition to acquiring my understudy role in *Peepshow*, had also landed a role in a neighboring production, *Absinthe*, and was now booking nightclub appearances of her own. Somehow my ploy worked and our conversation veered in another direction for the time being.

Hours later, after the show, I grabbed Mark from Chateau and drove down the I-15 toward home. He kept talking about how Hannah and her new boyfriend had been there and how happy they seemed. He also told me how Angel had confided in him that her relationship with the guy she was seeing was better than ever.

He's going to ask me if I'm happy in our relationship, I thought, panicking.

I changed the subject as quickly as possible. It wasn't just the idea of discussing our relationship with him that triggered my anxiety; it was the thought of anyone's questioning my happiness, period. Just that thought terrified me for some reason.

The next morning, my alarm began chiming at eight A.M. on the dot, and immediately I popped out of bed.

"Where are you going?" Mark mumbled sleepily.

"I gotta go do *Extra*," I reminded him as I began to get ready for the day. Our conversation very quickly turned into a heated discussion about how I hadn't made any time for him on this visit (true) and his asking me if I was seeing someone else (not technically true), both of which I vehemently denied.

He wouldn't let it go. Suddenly he asked me bluntly what he had been trying to ask over the past fourteen hours.

"Are you cheating on me?" he asked

.

"No!" I cried, my eyes suddenly welling up.

"Have you ever cheated on me?"

"No!" Tears were streaming down my face now.

I could have easily taken control of the conversation and communicated like an adult, but all I did was shake my head while the waterfall of tears poured from my eyes. I couldn't believe how incapable of any mature communication I was in this moment. And wasn't *his* age my issue? If it hadn't been so heartbreaking, this preposterous situation would have been laughable. It was as if I was having an out-of-body experience, watching myself do everything wrong.

"We need to break up," he finally conceded, unable to get through to me despite his best efforts. "I came all the way out here to see you and you can't even make time for me. I'm busy, too, you know."

"I know," I croaked, my voice barely audible as I wiped the tears from my face. "I'm sorry."

As he got up off the bed to get dressed, I felt heartbroken, yet oddly detached at the same time, as if I was watching someone else's life happen. Was I really just letting this relationship with this amazing guy end without giving him the explanation he was owed? Was I really letting this perfect creature walk out the door and out of my life after every asshole guy I'd already survived? Why was I so heinously self-sabotaging?

Looking back on this, I'm not sure I had the self-esteem to let myself be loved the right way. And simply by failing to communicate, after years of dating douche bags, I became the douche bag.

Chapter 9

"It's no use screaming at a time like this. Nobody will hear you."
—The Wizard of Oz (1939)

I ran my fingers through my hair and rearranged the off-the-shoulder neckline of my oversize cashmere sweater as I approached the giant slatted-wood double doors. It felt more intimidating than inviting—an odd choice for a restaurant.

As usual, Eric had popped up on my BlackBerry that week to rib me about the latest episode of *Holly's World* before asking me for a dinner date. He knew that Mark and I had called it quits, or at least I assumed he did. Gossip travels at light speed in Vegas. It had been a few weeks since Mark had caught a plane home and I was finally ready and free to accept Eric's offer.

Guy Savoy was one of the most exclusive restaurants on the Strip. In recent years, Las Vegas had become a hotbed for foodies and now had offerings from some of the world's most esteemed chefs. I was counting the days until my Paris trip with Claire, but in the meantime, this French cuisine was a tantalizing appetizer.

A statuesque maître d' guided me to "table number three." We strolled through an impeccably chic dining room, with high ceilings and a wall of windows with a glittering view of the Strip's lights. It was modern but somehow warm, with rich wood panels and bright artwork on the walls. Eric stood up to greet me, radiating charm and chivalry and offering me a slight kiss on the cheek.

He waited for me to sit as the maître d' pushed in a sleek dark brown chair behind me. As if out of thin air, a server in a gray suit appeared with a small stool on which to place my tiny black clutch.

"Champagne?" Eric asked with a sly smile as he reached for the bottle of Cristal that had been chilling next to us.

"Sure," I murmured before adding, "but just one." My *Peepshow* choreography was ingrained in my muscle memory at this point, but I never wanted to give anything less than my full attention to the performance.

As he filled our glasses, politely and discreetly waving off the server, who was attempting to take over, my gaze drifted from the golden bubbles to the top two buttons of his white shirt, which were open and allowed the collar to frame his jaw. His thick dark hair was perfectly in place and he had not an hour's worth of stubble on his smooth skin.

"Cheers," he said, bringing his glass to mine. "To the first of many evenings to come."

I clinked his glass, our eyes locking as we took sips of the champagne.

"I already ordered us the Prestige," he stated. "You will love it." I nodded, suddenly feeling a bit like a fish out of water. Prestige was the restaurant's ten-course tasting menu. Normally I wouldn't have selected such a lavish dinner before heading onstage, but I figured, *What the hell.* I wasn't going to decline when being offered the royal treatment.

I felt like Katniss Everdeen arriving by speed train to the Capitol, quietly taking in the absurd decadence around me. Each course appeared before us looking more extravagant and otherworldly than the last. From the silky artichoke and black truffle soup with mushroom toasted brioche and French burger canapé, to a marinated lobster salad, green apple sorbet palate cleanser, and an artfully crafted strawberry rhubarb gelato with basil granité, the meal was simply exquisite—and superseded only by the company with which I shared it. Truth be told, we didn't say much over dinner, as we were too busy raving about each dish. Even the bread cart was a masterpiece, sprouting up like a wild garden of golden baked treats.

Throughout dinner, Eric's BlackBerry stayed dutifully in his pocket. At least that's where I assume it was, because I never saw it once. In turn, my phones stayed inside my clutch the entire meal (something they hadn't done in quite some time).

Why had I been so hesitant to go out with him? I wondered. He defied my expectations. With his devastating good looks, impeccable style, and success, he was the type of man most women would want to be with. After my string of less-than-typical boyfriends, there was something exciting about being with Eric, someone it seemed everyone else wanted, the proverbial "catch," if you will.

I was having such a good time that I almost didn't want to leave to do my show.

"I hate to be rude, but I really have to head over to start getting ready," I told Eric.

"Absolutely," he said, placing his linen napkin on the table and standing up. "Let me walk you to your car."

We walked out of the tower toward the south entrance of Caesars. Someone must have alerted valet, because my car was already waiting for me. Eric walked me to the driver's-side door.

"Thank you for dinner," I said as he opened my door for me.

Without saying a word, he leaned in and kissed me.

"I'll see you soon," he said with one of his seductive smiles. He held open the door, and I slid, without saying a word, into the driver's seat . . . and cruised the one long Strip block south toward Planet Hollywood. On my way up to the theater, I checked the phone that had been cooped up for hours in my purse and found a new text from Eric.

"When can we go on another date?" it read. I had to admit, I was flattered by the persistence. I decided to wait until after the show to answer him, and while I was waiting, Nancy texted me telling me she would be bringing a certain Eric J. Parkington to see my performance tomorrow. *Okay, then*, I thought with a smile on my face.

The next day, I decided to take a few extra minutes getting ready at home before I left for work. I leisurely sat down at my vanity and began applying my makeup. It was a big night for me. Not because Eric was coming to see the show, but because it was the first night I would be performing my latest number. I had taken over the role of Goldilocks in addition to the part I already occupied. What was challenging about this role was it required singing. I am not a gifted singer by any means; in fact, I have to work hard and rehearse for months just to be able to put one song over. I could have been nervous to have Eric there on my first night, but oddly enough, I wasn't. I was confident in his feelings toward me. And you know what? I actually identified with my job so much, it eclipsed what a guy might happen to think about my performance.

As I dusted powder over my foundation to keep it in place, Napoleon started barking like crazy. *What's that all about?* I wondered while I reached over to grab a lip liner. Suddenly, I heard an urgent pounding at my front door.

That's weird, I thought. I paused, torn between running downstairs to answer the door and acting like I wasn't home. On one hand, the urgency called, but on the other, the forcefulness of the knock alarmed me. I glanced at my phone quickly to see if anyone had texted me saying they were at the door. No one had. Before I even set my phone down, there were more knocks at the door, harder this time. It was as if someone very large, very strong, or very angry (perhaps all three!) were determined to knock down the door.

"Madison!" a male voice yelled. "We know you're in there! Your car's out front!"

I didn't recognize the voice. I grabbed my phone, in case I needed to call the police. I didn't dial right away because there was a part of me that still wondered if it could be someone I knew, or a neighbor who needed help. Slowly, I tiptoed downstairs to assess the situation. I crept through my entryway, approaching the peephole I had recently installed for just these sorts of occasions. Knocks on my door weren't uncommon. Somehow, my home address seemed to have become public knowledge. Not only did I receive regular fan mail and packages at my home address, but visitors would drop by consistently, usually friendly neighborhood kids wanting an autograph.

Those deliberate visits were some of the only times I ever saw anyone from the neighborhood. Due to the extreme nature of the Vegas weather, I rarely spotted anyone outside. I had met very few of the other residents. Usually, the community resembled the set of a Western town in an old movie, just before a shoot-out. The streets were almost always empty, waiting for the cliché tumbleweed to roll on through, emphasizing the loneliness of the setting.

"Answer the door!" another adult male voice yelled.

I cautiously peered out my peephole and saw two ordinary-looking men, both wearing baseball caps. I had never seen them before in my life.

"We know you're in there!" one of them yelled gruffly, knocking again. The knocks were so forceful, the pictures in my entry hall rattled against the wall.

Irrationally afraid that they could somehow see me through the door, I tiptoed around the corner into my family room and crouched on the floor, waiting for them to leave.

If they knock one more time, I'm going to call the police, I told myself. Suddenly, I regretted my decision to buy a house. Living in the hotel felt so much safer. As my heart raced, a million thoughts ran through my head. *Why did these men sound so hostile? Were they here to hurt me? What could this be about? Why did I have to be alone in the house right now?*

Suddenly, Napoleon grew quiet.

After what seemed like five long, slow minutes of sitting in silence, I heard a car start and drive off. I slowly approached the door again, looked out, and didn't see anyone.

Thank God they left, I thought. I decided to leave while the coast was clear. I quickly ran upstairs to grab my bag, raced back to the door, opened it, and looked around to make sure the uninvited visitors were nowhere to be found. I sprinted the few steps to my car and locked the doors the second I was inside. I drove off to work, eager to get back into a more populated area where I felt safe.

Since I arrived backstage early, with my makeup already done, I had some time to kill. I decided to check my Twitter mentions while I waited for the rest of the cast and crew to trickle in. Among the mentions were a few from an (judging by his profile picture) average-looking young man in a baseball cap.

Read in sequence, his tweets mentioning me chronicled his afternoon adventure, first with him declaring he was going to my house to see if I would buy a newspaper from him. *He looks too old to be selling newspapers, but okay.*

The next tweet was a victorious exclamation of how he and his buddy had so easily followed a resident into my gated community.

The few after that were more of the hater variety, calling me disparaging names for not answering my door.

Why did he think it was okay to do that? I wondered. I took a screenshot of the tweets and sent them to my neighborhood's security staff. I was assured they would keep an eye out for him and not let him in if he approached the front, manned guard gate, but, unfortunately, if he were to tailgate in behind a resident through the unmanned side gate, there wasn't much they could do about it.

Lot of good that does me, I thought grumpily, though I was grateful that this guy had thought his escapades worth tweeting about. How else would I have ever found out who he was?

After venting to a few people about it, I decided to put it out of my head and start warming up my voice. In fact, I was so nervous I never stopped warming up except when I was onstage. I was in my own little bubble, singing the same song over and over again in between scenes. When it was finally time to do the new bit, it went by in a blur.

As I wrapped up the number, crossed my glittering gold Louboutins, and waved at the audience, I spotted Eric and Nancy in their seats. His gleaming white smile seemed to light up the theater as he applauded enthusiastically. He seemed to have really enjoyed it! A feeling of accomplishment swelled up in my chest. Just when I thought I didn't care about Eric's opinion, I practically started glowing.

When the cast and I came out in white feathers and rhinestones for the finale, Eric was one of the first to rise up and lead the standing ovation. I couldn't believe how supportive he was! I suppose, because he was the alpha type who always liked to appear in control, I had expected him to be more macho, more dismissive of what I had going on in my life. Happily, that didn't seem to be the case.

After the crowd had let out, I was walked to my meet-and-greet and ran into Eric and Nancy in the corridor. Eric surprised me with a bouquet of red roses. He went on and on about how much he liked the show and how he couldn't wait until we saw each other again. Needless to say, I was on the same page.

Seeing Eric after my meet-and-greet would have to wait, though.

"Holly, there are two policemen here who have a matter they need to discuss with you," one of the security guards told me after I signed my last autograph and snapped my last photo of the night.

"What is it about?" I asked, my mind racing, trying to figure out what I had possibly done wrong.

"Don't worry, you're not in trouble," he reassured me with a smile. "The theater has been getting some strange calls and they want to talk to you about it."

"Okay," I agreed, relieved that this didn't seem serious.

I followed security back to my dressing room, where two police detectives were waiting. After introductions were made, they told me what had brought them there.

"The box office at this theater has been getting some unusual phone calls," the first detective told me.

"The caller has mentioned your name several times," his partner chimed in, "so what we're here for today is to try to find out if you have noticed anything suspicious. Anyone loitering around the theater, sending you messages over the Internet, any letters?" He trailed off.

"Ummm . . ." I started, "I haven't received any messages. What have they said over the phone?" I asked, dying to hear more of the story. I had the feeling that they were downplaying the situation so I wouldn't be scared.

"Well, we don't want to alarm you, but they were threatening messages," the dark-haired officer said. "They mention you and Tiger Woods . . . do you know what that connection might be about?"

"No," I replied. "That sounds completely random. I've never met the guy." Tiger Woods had been all over the news for the past few years due to his cheating scandals. The Vegas press took exceptional interest in the story, as many of the women involved were locals.

"The caller was threatening to take a gun and kill you and Tiger Woods," the second, lighter-haired officer said calmly, as if not to alarm me. "They have also mentioned bomb threats."

A chill ran down my spine. Clearly the person on the other end of the line wasn't all there, but something told me this wasn't just a harmless prank, either. I remembered how scared I had felt in my house earlier.

"We came down here to check this out. Also, a suspicious package was discovered by your stage manager earlier," the detective continued. "It was an unmarked shabby-looking box left in the theater, centered in front of the backstage door. He was worried, because of the phone calls, that it might be an explosive device. The package turned out to be harmless, but we're keeping an eye on the situation, so any information you can provide would be helpful."

"I haven't received any threats personally," I offered, shaking my head. I was still taking it all in. I couldn't believe this was the first I was hearing about all this! I related the incidents of people knocking at my door, but admitted there had been no actual threats issued.

"Do you ever see anyone loitering around the theater or notice anything strange?" the dark-haired detective asked me.

"Um, just Peter?" I said, ending the statement with a question mark as if I wasn't sure he counted. I looked at security for confirmation, knowing they knew Peter on a first-name basis as well.

Peter was an unusual but seemingly harmless man who regularly frequented *Peepshow.* He came to my meet-and-greets roughly once a month, always with a small trinket gift. That part was sweet, but when he started showing up at some of my *Extra* tapings in the morning . . . well, that struck me as a little excessive.

When I took my vacations and Angel stepped into my role, he would show up to see Angel as well, bringing her similar gifts. Alarm bells went off when he followed me out of an *Extra* taping, asking if he could "stop by my house" because he "had a present for Angel."

"She doesn't live with me anymore!" I had lied, quickening my pace and losing him in the crowd that covered the casino floor.

"But Peter has a really distinctive voice," I added. "And he's such a regular, I'm sure anyone who works at the box office would recognize it." Plus, just because Peter had been the first person to pop into my head didn't mean there weren't others. There were other regulars who brought me roses frequently. Who's to say they were any less suspicious?

"Can you describe Peter for us?" the sandy-haired detective asked. I went on to describe Peter as best I could. He was tall, lanky, blond, and always wore a tan suit. The detectives thanked me for my time and gave me their cards, urging me to please contact them if I thought there was anything else they should know.

"Would you like me to escort you down to your car, Miss Madison?" one of the security guards asked me.

"No, thank you," I replied with a smile. "I'll be fine. It's kind of you to ask, though."

I appreciated the offer, but I was sure I would be all right while I was still in a public place. When it came to my empty house in the suburbs, though, that was a different story. Ever since Angel had started in *Absinthe*, she and Roman had been staying at her mom's, which was closer to the Strip, leaving me by myself. I texted Eric and asked him if he would stay over that night. I told him I had reasons for not wanting to be alone, but that it was a long story and that I'd fill him in once he got there.

So much for waiting until the third date, I thought.

Chapter 10

"Oh, yes; I am anxious," returned the Scarecrow. "It is such an uncomfortable feeling to know one is a fool."
—L. Frank Baum, *The Wonderful Wizard of Oz*

"My goal is to make enough money so that I can spend half the year on a yacht," Eric declared to his friend who sat opposite us.

I cringed on the inside, trying to hide the fact that I thought his dream sounded like the most boring thing on the planet.

"Yeah? My goal is to hire all the *Sports Illustrated* swimsuit models to appear at my nightclub," his friend shared, as if they were having a *Lifestyles of the Rich and Famous* fantasy pissing contest.

Jesus, I ditched Mark for this? I thought. He had been so much more interesting! These guys seemed like they were more obsessed with trying to impress each other than anything else.

Less than a month into dating Eric, I was bored. Sure, he was handsome, but we had nothing to talk about. I needed some kind of substance! He had been mysterious and charming from a distance, but up close, we had no chemistry.

Since I didn't feel safe alone at my house, I had taken to staying at

Eric's place more often than not. I still felt unsafe alone in my home, even though the threatening calls to the theater had been traced back to a mental care facility (clearing Peter of any suspicion). I still had strangers knocking on my door regularly and received unusual fan mail and notes at my home address.

At first, staying at Eric's was fun. He lived at Turnberry Place, a luxurious high-rise on the north end of the Strip. Getting to know Eric better wasn't so much fun, though. It seemed the charming, debonair gentlemen I had fallen for was a bit of a facade. At home he was a cranky, sleep-deprived mess who spent most of his time saying he was "working," but really he was just googling girls on the Internet. Our physical intimacy quickly dwindled. I started to suspect he was addicted to the chase.

It was quite humbling to realize, so quickly, what a major mistake I had made, trading Mark in for Eric. Eventually, I started sleeping at home again and hired a security guard to keep watch outside my house at night. Eric and I hadn't officially broken up, but we were seeing each other less and less and I was fine with that. We still texted daily, but I no longer thought of him as an ideal boyfriend.

"I have something amazing to tell you," Eric texted me one evening as I was applying my makeup backstage.

"What is it?" I shot back.

He replied instantly. "I can't tell you over text. I have to tell you in person."

Shit, I thought, *this is intriguing.* When I didn't reply right away, he texted: "Come to Marquee tonight. Please? I really want to see you."

I told him I would stop by the club after my performance. I hadn't brought a change of clothes with me to the theater, and I wasn't exactly looking resplendent in the black leggings and Space Mountain T-shirt I had left the house in. But in the end, my own curiosity got the better of me. I was dying to know what the big secret was! So after that night's *Peepshow,* I headed straight to the club. I was anxious to find out what he was so eager to tell me, but when I finally slid into his booth, Eric was nowhere to be found. He had to know I was there; Nancy had greeted me at the door and led me to his table, after all. My eyes darted around the room, half expecting to see something spectacular go down. I mean, whatever it was, Eric certainly made it sound like a big deal.

Just then, he plopped down next to me, his eyes locked on his BlackBerry, and let out a halfhearted, "Hey."

"Hey! What was it you wanted to tell me?" I asked, eagerly waiting for him to cough up this big news that he couldn't wait to share.

Without looking up from his phone, he launched lazily into the story. "So, remember that awesome thing I wanted to tell you?" He asked the question as if it was a conversation we had weeks ago, instead of just hours earlier.

"Yeah . . ." I said, resisting the urge to remind him that it was the only reason I showed up to the club at all.

"Well, remember that bitch I told you about?" he asked.

"Uh-huh," I muttered. *Where was this going?* I wondered. The last time I had stayed over at his house, he had been angry about an ex-girlfriend.

"Well, I may or may not have had drugs planted on her in Mexico," he said matter-off-factly, still not bothering to look up from whatever message he was ferociously typing.

"What?" I shouted. He had to be kidding. Right? And even if he had wanted to do that, how was he capable? What kind of weird connections did this guy have? "Are you serious?"

"Yeah," he said, still not looking me in the eye.

"What happened?" I asked incredulously. "Is she in jail?"

"No," he said, finally looking up, his voice dripping with annoyance. "She somehow managed to get away with it."

Cue a long, awkward pause as he waited for me to respond.

"Wow," I finally offered. "That's pretty insane."

I had so many questions: Was she at the airport? At a resort? Did he phone in the tip to the Mexican police? Who planted the drugs? What kind of drugs? I thought it *had* to be a tall tale he was telling in hopes that I'd somehow be impressed with the reach of his power. Or maybe this was his way of scaring me off. If it was, it was working! If this actually turned out to be true, I thought it was in my best interest to know as little as possible, as I was becoming increasingly unfamiliar with the man sitting next to me.

I knew then and there that I needed to formally—and carefully—call things off with Mr. Parkington. He'd now gone from surprisingly boring to straight-up sinister. My initial reaction was to run out the door, but as the experts say, when you meet an animal in the wild, back away SLOWLY. I finished my drink, dropped a few hints about how exhausted I was, and then after about fifteen minutes told him that I needed to catch some sleep.

As soon as I walked out the door, I pulled Twitter up on my phone. I needed to know if there was any truth to this crazy story. I searched the name of the woman in question and her account came up right away.

Sure enough, she had recently landed back in the United States and began tweeting a slew of messages about her run-in with the Federales, how outraged she was that a bag of marijuana had been planted in her purse and how #blessed she was to be back in the U.S. In one post she tagged the name of the friend she was traveling with. When I checked out that woman's account, I saw the most recent tweet: "Thank God! Back home safe! No jail for my bestie!"

Holy shit! I thought. *It seems to have really happened.*

For the next few days, I eased up on Eric's and my communication and came up with excuses that would keep me as far away from him as possible. When he texted me to tell me that he would be going to L.A. for a few days, I used it as my opportunity to break things off. Knowing that he would be out of town would make things less awkward.

Okay, so I know that it's super cheesy to break up with someone via text message . . . but how often has that ever stopped me? In this case, I didn't feel I had a better option. Eric and I never spoke on the phone, and I knew it would be at least a few days until I could see him in person, so I decided to message him that since we're both so busy with work, it's probably not the best time to be seeing each other and we should just stick to being friends.

I hit send and braced myself for his response. I hoped he wouldn't be upset. I wondered if he would ask me to reconsider. Hopefully he would agree and say it had been nice getting to know me. I waited . . .

and waited . . .

and waited.

For someone so addicted to his damn BlackBerry, I knew he saw my message. He didn't respond, though. Not a single word. I knew our relationship had lost steam, but that didn't mean I expected him to ignore my breakup text. I had wanted this guy to exit stage left from my life, but when he totally blew me off, it drove me nuts! In fact, I couldn't stop obsessing over it. Just a few months earlier he had been bugging me for a date and I was putting him off like a snobby cheerleader—and now he couldn't even be bothered to acknowledge my text? Had my stock fallen that far? Just as I had with Jeffrey, I found myself hurting more over the lack of a reaction than over the actual loss of the guy.

The ball was in his court, and I was stuck wondering why he was so completely unfazed by my calling it quits. Or was he playing games with me? Even though I had plenty of reasons to be glad this guy was out of my life, my head was swimming and my ego reeling. Was I so worthless I didn't even deserve a response?

The following Saturday, Lindsay asked me to meet her for drinks. We sat around pouring our hearts out to each other. She had quit the downscale topless show she had been performing in and was feeling unfulfilled in her new job as a go-go dancer. Just when I was about to remind her that she had flaked the last time *Peepshow* held auditions, I spotted Nancy making her way toward me.

"Hey, girl!" she said, with a big smile plastered across her face. "Are you coming to Marquee tonight? Eric's going out."

"No," I said soberly. She must have known that Eric and I broke up, right? Nancy gave me a puzzled look, so I told her that going to Marquee, Eric's favorite club of the moment, probably wasn't a good idea since Eric and I were no longer seeing each other.

Her jaw dropped to the floor. She told me she was sorry to hear that and asked what happened. *He didn't even mention it to her?* I wondered incredulously. If this guy was trying to make me feel like I had never existed, he was doing a damn good job. Eager to get it off of my chest again, I confessed to her what I had already started to tell Lindsay: how shitty I was feeling over this latest breakup.

"I guess I'm so hurt because he just disappeared. He could have at least texted back something like 'I'm sorry it didn't work out,' or 'I agree, I'm glad we can still be friends, hope to see you around.' Ignoring me completely is beyond rude."

Nancy listened sympathetically, nodded, and gave me the unsolicited assurance that she was sure Eric wasn't seeing anyone else—even though up until that moment the idea hadn't crossed my mind.

A few hours later, after I had arrived back at my house, I heard my phone vibrate. I was already in bed, but I reached over to my mirrored bedside table to see who felt like talking. I was surprised to see that it was Eric. Quickly I read the message.

"Hey, I'm sorry it didn't work out. I agree with you and am glad we can still be friends. I hope to see you around soon."

It was pretty much word for word what I had said to Nancy. She must have run back to him and told him everything! I was too embarrassed and angry to confront her about it. I clunked my phone back down on my nightstand and threw the covers over my head. I was frustrated with Nancy and decided I needed to sleep on it before opening my mouth. It was all so ridiculous. Why was Eric even bothering to try and smooth things over at all at this point?

I tried to tell myself that I shouldn't care so much. Eric hadn't been right for me anyway. When I decided to go out with him, I thought it was a no-brainer. After all, he was good-looking, successful, local, only a few years older than me, and he'd been pursuing me for a long time, which had to mean he really liked me and would appreciate me once he had me, right?

Wrong. In fact, I started to wonder if the real reason I had been attracted to Eric was that he fit a dangerous pattern I had been drawn to before: a successful alpha male with women throwing themselves at him everywhere he went. It was as if, deep down, I felt like a nice guy like Mark was too good to be true and that I didn't deserve him, so I shoved myself back into my comfort zone . . . even though my comfort zone wasn't good for me.

I was having a hard time truly accepting it, but I needed to admit that while Eric looked good on paper, I had taken a big chance on him before I even got to know him.

But perhaps most important, I learned to always check what's in my purse before heading through airport security.

Chapter 11

Dorothy looked him over. Yes, he was shaggy, all right; but there was a twinkle in his eye that seemed pleasant.

—L. Frank Baum, *The Road to Oz*

"Cougar?" I scrunched up my nose at the very idea.

"Yes," Hannah confirmed, using her glossy onyx nails to flip through the pages of one of the gossip magazines littering my coffee table.

"But I'm only thirty-two," I protested. "How can I be a cougar at thirty-two?"

"You're going on a date with a guy who is eight years younger than you," Hannah answered matter-of-factly.

"Mark was eight years younger!" I exclaimed.

Hannah looked up from her magazine for the first time to give me a quizzical look.

"You knew that," I said, cutting her off before she even had time to respond. "I told you that!"

"I guess I forgot," she replied, turning her attention back to the tabloid in her hands. "He always seemed so mature. I thought he was, like, twenty-nine."

She took a deep breath as if to say *c'est la vie* and continued: "Anyway, yes, you are a cougar . . . at least in this scenario."

"I thought you had to be at least forty before being considered a cougar," I complained, dropping myself into one of my antique side chairs covered in a soft plum velvet. "The word *cougar* just feels so old. Can't I be something else? Like a tiger?"

Even Hannah had to smile at this. "Or a kitten," she offered with a laugh.

Being called a cougar felt to me like being labeled as some sort of predator—a woman on the hunt for a younger piece of meat. Sure, a cougar is simply a liberated woman, one comfortable with her sexuality and age, who prefers the company of younger men. But it still made me feel old. I suppose when you spend your twenties as a Playboy bunny, a warped sense of what constitutes *old* for a woman becomes ingrained in you.

"Then don't go out with him," Hannah volunteered, tossing the magazine back on my white marble table. "If you don't want to be a cougar, then don't be one. It doesn't even sound like you're that into him."

She was right. I wasn't crushing particularly hard on Ray, but something about him seemed intriguing, nonetheless.

"I don't know. I think it will be nice to have someone to talk to who is outside of the regular Vegas social circle."

"Sick of us so soon?" Hannah asked, her eyes wide and playfully alarmed.

"You know what I mean." I tossed a throw pillow at her. Eric Parkington dominated the Vegas social scene and seemed to be buddies with every eligible guy in town, so I was eager to step away from that particular clique.

The guy I was about to go on a date with, Ray, just sort of appeared out of nowhere. Dressed all in black with a shaggy nest of reddish-blond hair on top of his head, he was lurking at the lobby bar at one of my favorite casinos.

Nancy and I noticed the cute but unusual-looking young man staring at me from the bar. He sat quietly for most of the night, looking out of place among the upscale crowd in his ratty clothes with his clunky giant turtle shell of a backpack defining his silhouette.

Who is that character? I wondered.

Before Nancy and I parted ways, he asked for my number out of the blue and without saying more than ten words to me. He had an endearing stutter and a charming smile. There was something likable about this cute oddball at the bar.

I had to give him credit for having the balls. Most men didn't approach me directly. Sure, people would come up and ask me for a picture or an autograph, but I hadn't been asked for my number in person by a stranger in about ten years.

What the hell? I decided. Ray shared that he was currently living in Orange County, but visited Vegas regularly. He was an up-and-coming painter making a name for himself in the art world. He was in his early twenties, with a quiet voice and mannerly deportment.

The next day, as I was making my way toward the *Peepshow* theater, he called. Not texted, not tweeted . . . actually called.

Nope, I thought, hitting the decline button. *Who actually calls people anymore?*

Look, I can't be the only phone-a-phobe out there. Personally, I rarely see the need to actually speak to people on the phone.

I quickened my pace, and when I finally got backstage, I texted Nancy. "Ray's calling me!"

"Did you answer?" she texted back.

"No!" I replied instantly.

"That's kinda fucked up. You should have answered. He seems like a nice guy."

I'd heard that before.

"Yeah, you're right," I responded. "I'll let you know how it goes."

"I'm coming out to Vegas next weekend!" Ray exclaimed when I finally returned his call.

"Oh, really? What's the occasion?" I asked.

"To see you!" he shot back.

"Okay!" I acquiesced with forced enthusiasm. I had thought it might be fun to go out with Ray next time he happened to be in town, but if he was truly coming out just to see me . . . that felt like a little too much pressure. I wasn't really feeling up to entertaining someone I barely knew for three days. What if we didn't hit it off? I decided I would return to my suite at Planet Hollywood while he was in town. It was going to be a busy holiday weekend for me, with shows and nightclub hosting obligations, so it would be convenient for me to be on the Strip the whole time and not have to battle Memorial Day weekend traffic.

I ALMOST IMMEDIATELY STARTED regretting committing to seeing Ray. Over the next few days, I was bombarded with requests from him: *Can you pick me up at the airport? Can you take me to the best mall? I can stay at your place, right?* This weekend was going from busy to overbooked. On one hand, I felt sorry for him. *Maybe he just didn't know how to communicate and was asking every question he could for the sake of conversation,* I thought. I could certainly relate to that. *Or maybe he really is too young for me,* I wondered. Was he incapable of renting a car, booking a room, googling his favorite stores? All this dependence was starting to make me feel like more of a mother figure than a date.

Nancy kindly offered to accompany Ray to my show and take him to dinner during my second performance, before heading over to XS, where I would meet them when I finished my meet-and-greet.

When I arrived at the club later that night, the VIP host, an impeccably dressed, olive-skinned young man with spiky black hair led me through the entrance to the Encore Tower Suites to take advantage of the low-key, private entrance. He discreetly escorted me into the club, past the golden sculptures of the female form lining the entrance. We made our way to my usual spot, among a group of tables on an elevated platform next to the DJ booth.

Looking much more animated than the first time I met him, Ray was holding court at a roped-off VIP table of local nightlife veterans, all of whom I knew well enough, with Nancy at his side.

"How's it going?" I shouted over the music before leaning down to pour myself a vodka soda. A server immediately appeared and politely took the glass to continue fixing me a drink, even throwing in my usual lemon wedge. She knew what I wanted without even asking.

Did she see what I was reaching for? I wondered. *Or am I just that much of a regular?*

Clubbing was starting to get old. I went out regularly after work and usually had a fantastic time. However, I was beginning to recognize, as my partying schedule started to outpace even my hardest-partying friends, that I was going out simply to avoid returning home to an empty house. Furthermore, I had become such a fixture on the nightclub scene that tabloid rumors were starting to pop up that I was dating a few of my buddies, nightclub hosts or managers. It was irritating to think that I couldn't have a social life, or heterosexual male friends for that matter, without becoming romantically linked to them. *No one would assume that a man frequented his favorite nightspot because he was dating one of the female managers,* I thought grumpily. As a woman, it seemed, a man had to be the motivation behind everything I did.

Ray crept through the crowd, a huge grin peeking out from under his hat.

"You were amazing!" he exclaimed in my ear as he wrapped his arms tightly around my torso and twirled me around.

"Thanks," I said, surprised at how gregarious he was. What happened to the shy little hipster I met at the lobby bar? Sure, I was happy that he enjoyed the show, and of course I appreciated that he took the time to see it, but suddenly, I felt awkward. It hit me that I had just committed to spending an entire weekend with a virtual stranger.

He smacked a big kiss on my lips before setting me down and turning back to the person he had been talking to. Now that the crowd had parted, I could see who it was—none other than Mr. Eric J. Parkington.

What the fuck? I wondered. I had been so grateful to Nancy for offering to entertain Ray, but I hadn't realized she was taking him to hang out with Eric.

Suddenly a gorgeous blue-eyed brunette stepped in front of me.

"Hi, I'm Kate," she said, offering me a hug. "I'm from L.A., too. I saw that you follow a few of my friends on Instagram." She went on to talk about a DJ she used to date and listed a few of the people we knew in common, most of them friends of Eric's.

"Cool!" I smiled. "It's nice to meet you!"

"So, are you still seeing Eric?" she asked, a confused look on her face.

"No," I responded, my guard immediately raised. She had to have seen Ray embrace me just a moment earlier, so it felt like a loaded question. "We stopped seeing each other a while ago."

"Oh!" she said, seemingly surprised. "That's too bad. My boyfriend and I stayed at his house last time we were here. He couldn't stop talking about how much he liked you."

Somehow, hearing that Eric had said that about me stopped me in my tracks. Despite how things had unfolded, my ego desperately wanted to believe that Eric once felt something for me. In retrospect, I'm pretty confident that gushing about his girlfriend was just a slightly more tactful way of letting Kate and her boyfriend know who he was banging, but there was still that part of me that wanted to believe it.

Before I could spiral too far into my own psyche, Ray plopped down next to me and threw his arm over my shoulder. He was busy talking to Nancy, who was sitting on his other side, when I felt someone tap my shoulder. I looked up and saw a group of girls dancing up next to the rope that divided our areas.

"How old are you, anyway?" she slurred, obviously drunk enough not to realize she had screwed up her face into an exaggerated, quizzical stare that made her resemble a Treasure Troll.

"Thirty-two," I replied coldly, turning away from the ropes. Not that it mattered, but this lady didn't look like a spring chicken herself! Why was she asking about my age so rudely? Was she implying I was too old for Ray?

Thankfully, just when I was starting to feel like this crowd was too much for me, Nancy suggested we migrate to a dive bar downtown. When we arrived, I walked in ahead of Ray and took a seat at one of the beat-up red pleather booths.

"Hols!" Ray shouted at me as he stumbled over people on his way toward me, resembling a bowling ball slowly meandering down an alley.

My insides suddenly froze. That was Mark's nickname for me. *How could I have felt so at home with Mark,* I wondered, *but so awkwardly old with this guy?* They were the same age, but the difference in maturity was staggering.

"My buddy here," he said, sloppily patting the shoulder of a nightclub promoter I vaguely knew and he most certainly had just met, "invited us out back for a smoke."

"I'm okay," I shouted, waving my hands to signal I wasn't interested.

"Come on, babe," he pleaded.

"I'll go with you, but I'm not going to smoke," I conceded.

Ray's face lit up like a Christmas tree. He stood upright, pulled his shoulders back, and said to the promoter: "Lead the way, good sir."

The promoter was flanked on either side by two women he had obviously recruited to help "entertain" this up-and-coming artist who had graced the bar with his presence. I smiled at the ladies and started to introduce myself, but one of them rolled her eyes and shot a smirk at the other before I even opened my mouth.

I followed them through the door and leaned against the concrete wall of the cold, empty hallway, as the two girls plopped down onto two metal folding chairs, chattering away.

After fidgeting around—crossing and uncrossing her fishnet-stockinged legs a few times, the one nearest me squealed as she theatrically lurched away from me, rolling her eyes and shooting over-the-top exasperated looks to everyone in the circle, as if I had just done something wrong.

"Ew," she snarled in an ear-splitting baby voice. "That's cold!"

She was referring to the oversize metal-studded bag on my shoulder, which she had brushed up against while I had been standing still.

What am I doing here? I asked myself. I'd been in snotty, immature "Mean Girl" situations like this before and no longer had any tolerance for them. I was getting too old for this.

"Are you okay?" the promoter asked the girl, leaning in to her ear to whisper something. His lips remained at her ear as her eyes widened.

"No way!" the girl gasped before quickly turning to the other girl and whispering in her ear.

"Oh my god!" her friend squealed.

"Holly, oh my god, it's *so* nice to meet you," the girl with the fishnets purred, suddenly slapping the widest, most fake smile she could muster on her face. "We're so sorry, we didn't know it was *you*."

"That's okay," I replied, thinking, *You shouldn't have to know who someone "is" to be nice*. "It's nice to meet you."

"Oh my God!" her friend exclaimed. "You have to tell us ALL about the Playboy mansion!"

I took a deep breath, smiled, and said, "I don't live there anymore."

If Ray can't see how snobby these people are, he's got a serious problem, I decided. And it appeared that he chose not to.

"Wow, those two were a little much, right?" I proclaimed after finally convincing him to go back to the booth.

"They were okay," he noted before launching into a short diatribe.

"You seem like a loner. I have a philosophy: I let *everyone* hang out. Then everyone has a good time. Everybody wins."

Maybe I wasn't the social animal people assumed I was. Maybe I *was* easily put off, but I wasn't a snob. It was my way of protecting myself. For the past decade, I'd foolishly opened myself up to a lot of people who didn't have my best interests at heart. Neither Ray nor I was wrong to be the way we were; we were just different.

Too different to be a couple, I thought.

"So what's next for you?" he asked me the next morning. His flight was in a few hours, so we had some time to kill. I busied myself by pouring two iced coffees from the room-service tray, then stirring mine frantically with a straw, even though I took my coffee black.

"Like . . . today?" I asked, trying with all my might to avoid the question.

"No," he said, a boyish grin on his face. "Like, in life. Like, next year? What's after *Peepshow*?"

"I don't really know yet," I confessed as I handed him one of the iced coffees. It was true. *Holly's World* had yet to be reordered for its third season, and while I loved *Peepshow* and *Extra*, I knew I would eventually want to move on to something new and wasn't really sure what that would be. It felt like just yesterday I had struck out on my own and landed those jobs. But more important than simply figuring out what was next was figuring out what I really *wanted* to do. And after spending the last few years proving myself to the world, it was now time to figure out what *I* wanted.

"More TV?" he asked, his eyes searching me for an answer.

"Maybe. We'll see what happens."

"You know why I like you so much?" he asked, setting his glass on the table with a flourish. "You are *killing* it. For real. Like, with the TV show and the stage stuff. It's like . . . awesome. I just couldn't be with someone that doesn't know what they want to do in life, you know?"

"Yeah," I agreed hesitantly. "Thanks."

But I really don't know what I want to do with my life, I thought. Obviously it's possible and quite common to be attracted to someone's ambition, creativity, or work ethic, but I suspected that Ray was just blinded by the glitter of it all. I couldn't shake the feeling that he was interested in me because I was on TV, not because of who I was. Hey, I couldn't blame him. After all, I'd been the same way when I was his age!

His comments raised some questions. I was already in my third year at *Peepshow*, and I had given myself four years in Vegas. Would I want to stay longer? Somehow that wasn't sounding as appealing to me as it may have a few months earlier. As attached as I was to so many of the things that came with my life (the friends, the money, the excitement, the notoriety), I started to wonder if I wasn't ready to grow up a little bit. Perhaps going on a date with a younger man had made me realize that I might be ready for the next step, whatever that may be.

And ready or not, fate was about to force my hand.

Chapter 12

"She must be a witch," exclaimed the girl.

"I do not think so," declared the Wheeler. "But there is some mystery connected with her, nevertheless . . ."

—L. Frank Baum, *Ozma of Oz*

"You know," the bartender teased, "this place is haunted. There are secret apartments behind the restaurant where Lee used to stay overnight, even though his house was only a few minutes away."

The "Lee" in question was Liberace, who was now peering at me from behind the bar, in the form of a cardboard cutout.

"We should totally have a slumber party here. We could do some ghost-hunting and film it for the show," I mused as I walked around the giant piano-shaped bar, taking the room in. I looked up at the black ceiling, dotted with fiber-optic stars, and around at the mirrored walls. "It would be hard to film, though, with all these mirrors. It would be impossible to not see the camera people."

"Or . . . we could just have a sleepover and not film it," Laura said wryly, taking a sip of her cocktail. Out of the entire cast, Laura was by far the least attached to the TV show.

I sat down at the bar next to Hannah, face-to-face with the cardboard cutout. We had just finished an amazing lunch at Carluccio's and had migrated to the adjacent "Piano Bar" to toast Laura, who had recently bought herself a condo. I was finally turning my room keys back in to Planet Hollywood after a very memorable two-year stay.

"I saw your 'at home' piece in a magazine at the salon," Hannah began. "Are you happy with how it turned out?"

I let out a sigh and laughed simultaneously. "Yeah, I like the pictures, those turned out great, but the headline is another story."

"I figured," Hannah said with a smirk.

"It's just so frustrating that everything has to be about 'finding a man,'" I complained. The piece, which was supposed to be about my newly decorated home in Las Vegas, had been titled "Waiting for Prince Charming," and the slant of the story had been how I had everything but a man. It turned a piece I would have ordinarily been proud of into one I was kind of embarrassed about. I had been excited to show off my new house, one I had purchased on my own, as a single woman, but instead of highlighting my busy work life, the article made it sound like I was pining away in my perfect home, waiting to be saved.

"Yeah, that sucks," Hannah commiserated, stirring her cocktail.

"Where's Lindsay?" Nancy asked.

"She's MIA," I answered with a shrug, as if her absence didn't bother me . . . but it did.

I had invited my sandy blond friend to dinner, but she hadn't returned my text. She had seemed cranky and stressed the past few times I had seen her.

I had been trying to reach her for the last week, in fact, and had been receiving only minimal responses. I was bummed because I could have used the extra shoulder to cry on. Months after our breakup, I still couldn't stop complaining about Eric. I had major regrets about ever going out with him. I had let Mark go, and for what? Not only was I shitty to Mark, but the guy I had basically left him for, Eric, turned out to be a total ass. *Talk about instant karma,* I thought.

Earlier, at dinner, over a plate of stuffed shells, I bitched to Nancy about Eric's lack of post-breakup sensitivity, partly because I was hoping she'd have some reassuring words for me. I didn't even care if she went back to him and repeated what I said. He deserved to realize how insensitively he behaved. Deep down, I was hoping that Nancy would tell me that Eric really *did* miss me and that he was just trying to act tough or give me my space. Even though I knew he was a dick, my ego still couldn't get past that need for approval.

"Just wait until your TV show's back on," Nancy replied flippantly. "He's thirsty. He'll be pursuing you again for sure."

That was just what I didn't want to hear. Sure, it was further proof that Eric was not someone I should be wasting my time on, but it still hurt my feelings. It made me feel like I was nothing without my show.

"Are you coming to Blush tonight?" I asked her. "You know, I asked Lindsay if she was coming and she said no and that she was still upset about last weekend. I asked her what she meant and she refused to answer. Do you know what she's upset about? Not telling me is kind of a bitch move."

"Yeah, I'm coming, and I don't know about Lindsay," she said, suddenly a woman of few words.

Okay, something's up, I thought. The Nancy I knew would have agreed with my "bitch move" comment and carried the shit-talking to a whole other level. I had a sinking feeling she was going to repeat what I had said to Lindsay, but threw that thought out of my mind. *Nancy has my back,* I reassured myself.

After a moment of silence, talkative Nancy returned. "Can I tell you about the DJ I hung out with who pulled down his pants in front of me?"

Nancy blurted out, downing the last of her Jack and Coke. "You know who he is, he just got a billboard next to the I-15. Anyway, he bent over next to his bed, spread his ass cheeks, and said, 'I'm better than you!' "

The pure absurdity of the story made me laugh so hard I almost snorted my own beverage out of my nose. The rest of the table was less amused. I was beginning to notice that my other friends weren't always as entertained by Nancy's wild-card personality as I was.

I had forgotten all about DJ Ass Cheeks by the time dinner was over and we were all gathered at the bar. Hannah was looking at her phone and describing all the dick pics her boyfriend was sending her when she remembered something.

"Hey, Nancy, I found a picture of this actress from the sixties," Hannah said, scrolling through her photos. "I think she looks like you." Hannah pulled up a gorgeous picture of Natalie Wood and held her phone up for Nancy to see.

Nancy leaned forward to inspect the photo, squinting as if she were already too drunk to see straight. Just when I expected her face to light up (who wouldn't want to be compared to Natalie Wood?), her visage contorted in disgust and she glared at Hannah.

"Fuck you," Nancy snarled. "I'm way hotter than that."

"You should be saying thank-you," Hannah snapped back. "I'm never giving you a compliment again."

The bar went silent, as we were the only ones in it at seven P.M. Nancy's bizarre reaction was completely uncalled for and made no sense. It was as if she had been waiting for a reason to go off on Hannah, whom I had long suspected she was more than a little jealous of. Perhaps this was a sign that Nancy's drinking was getting out of hand. I'd noticed her getting more and more wild, but had been so busy filming that I hadn't given it much thought. I decided I would take Nancy aside at dinner that night and have a talk with her. Angel would be there, and I could use her help. She was good at the heartfelt stuff.

"Well, I'll take Natalie Wood!" I said to Hannah with a smile, trying to smooth things over. "Nancy, if you are meeting me for dinner, you might want to leave. We need to get ready."

"Yeah, I'm coming," she answered. "But I'm gonna go home and take a nap first."

"That's probably a good idea," said Hannah, barely hiding her irritation as she stood up and grabbed her purse. "I'm not sure if I'll be seeing you guys out tonight."

I stayed quiet, not wanting to fan the flames. I asked the bartender to please call a cab for Nancy, then said good-bye to everyone cheerfully as if nothing had happened and headed home to get ready for the night. I chose a neutral-colored fringed bohemian-style dress to wear with color-coordinated Dior heels. I held my flowing hair back with tiny braids on either side of my head and wove a few small daisies through them. I was happy that Angel was coming with me to the appearance. I was looking forward to catching up, since it seemed like I saw her less and less these days. In fact, the whole group was rarely ever together anymore, and I missed it.

"Where is everybody?" Angel asked as we took our seats at a table with a lake view.

"Lindsay's pissed at me or something, Josh has a gig, Laura hates going out on the Strip all of a sudden, and Hannah's pissed at Nancy, who was supposed to be here, so I'm not sure if she'll show up tonight," I said, shrugging. We had all been so inseparable just a few months earlier and now we were drifting apart. Hannah's new boy toy was taking up more and more of her time and I missed my partner in crime. Laura was no longer my roommate and had taken a new job endorsing a pole fitness class. When she went out these days, she preferred dive bars and a new clique of friends she had met on her own. "I don't know what happened to Nancy. She's not answering my texts." I shrugged. "Maybe she passed out. She was pretty drunk at lunch today and snapped at Hannah. I was thinking we might need to have a talk with her."

It wasn't until we had finished dinner and been seated at our table at Blush that Nancy finally appeared. No sooner had Angel and I been given our first glasses of champagne than a familiar screech hit our ears.

"Hey, strangers!" Nancy yelled as she hopped over the back of the banquette.

"Oh, hey!" Angel shouted back over the music. She excused herself to go say hi to Hannah, who had just walked in, making room for Nancy, who reached for the magnum of champagne at our table and clumsily poured herself a glass. She was wearing a leather minidress and her hair was disheveled. It was clear she was completely wasted.

"You won't believe what Lindsay said about you," Nancy shouted as she plopped down next to me.

"What's that?" I asked, my spine stiffening. I could tell Nancy was already too far gone this evening. She clearly hadn't taken a nap.

"She said you lied to her about the *Peepshow* auditions and that you must be jealous of her to want to keep her out of the show," she stated, unable to conceal the slow, sly smile spreading across her face. "She also said that you are so self-centered that all you can talk about is Eric and that you don't even give a shit about what your friends are going through."

"That's ridiculous. I practically beg Lindsay to come to those auditions!" I said, trying not to look like I was too interested in what she had to say. It was obvious to me that she was trying to start a bad-mouthing fest, and I wanted no part of it. Nancy was quickly becoming less and less trustworthy in my eyes, though parts of what Lindsay supposedly said rang uncomfortably true.

"And she said you were rolling your eyes and laughing because her show closed," Nancy continued, her eyes barely able to keep focus, let alone eye contact.

"That's definitely not true!" I exclaimed, growing more and more frustrated as I grabbed my phone out of my clutch. "I'm just going to text her and ask her what the hell her problem is."

"Don't say I told you!" Nancy screeched like a hellcat as she lunged at me and tried to wrestle my phone out of my hands.

I threw Nancy off me and stood up. Nancy's forward momentum nearly landed her on the floor.

"Then quit talking so much shit!" I yelled as I quickly wove my way through the crowd toward the manager's booth. I was furious—how dare she try to snatch my phone out of my hands! I rarely raised my voice, but something in me snapped. I didn't have patience for the bullshit anymore. Lindsay had dropped hints that she thought Nancy had become jealous of our friendship not long after introducing us and that Nancy was scared I would "steal" Lindsay from her. I had brushed that off as too immature for Nancy, but now I was seeing that perhaps Lindsay had been on to something. I spent the rest of the evening at the managers' table, simply to avoid Nancy.

"What happened?" Angel asked when she finally found me at the other table.

"Nancy said she told you off for talking shit about Lindsay and that you stormed off in tears!" Hannah exclaimed, a concerned look on her face.

I burst out laughing. "Not exactly," I said. I filled them in on our exchange. "I'm not getting great service right now, but I'm texting Lindsay as soon as I get out of here."

"What are you ladies doing?" I heard a familiar voice say behind me. It was Doug, the one who sprayed champagne on me at the MGM Mansion, looking uncharacteristically crisp in a white dress shirt, the sleeves rolled up to his forearms adding a casual touch to his otherwise dressy ensemble and showing off a deep tan.

"Nice tan," Hannah teased.

"Thanks," he smiled, flashing his blindingly white veneers. "I just got back from Saint-Tropez."

Oh, here we go, I thought.

"Anyway, how are you ladies?" he schmoozed, throwing a beefy arm over my shoulder. "How's Eric?" he asked, looking pointedly at me. "Or are you not seeing him anymore? I thought I heard you were dating a DJ or something?"

"No." I sighed, annoyed at him for quickly drawing attention to the mess that was my love life.

"I gotta get home soon," Angel interrupted with a yawn. "I have to be up early with Roman tomorrow."

"I'm down to leave, too," Hannah added.

"I have to be here for an hour still," I said, looking at my slim gold watch.

"I can give you a ride back to your house if you want to have your driver take Angel and Hannah home," Doug offered, looking toward me for an answer. It was customary that nightclubs sent a driver to bring their hired hosts to and from the club. Ordinarily I wouldn't have wanted to commit to sharing the drive home with Doug, but I knew Angel needed to leave, and not only was I obligated to stay, I wanted to. I was still fired up about Nancy's behavior toward me and felt more like venting about it to anyone who would listen than going to bed.

"Ladies, I'll walk you to the car," Doug said, suddenly a gentleman. "I'll be back!" he said to me with a gleam in his eye.

I conversed with the nightclub staff over champagne until Doug returned. He was actually surprisingly well behaved that night. He listened to me complain about Nancy and offered good advice. He wasn't coming on as strong as he usually did and mentioned a girl he had started seeing. He talked about the stand-up shows he had signed on to do in Vegas and the great house he rented in the same golf course community in Summerlin where Hannah's new boyfriend lived. Suddenly, I felt better about being in his company. *Perhaps we could be comfortable in the friend zone,* I thought.

When my gig was over, Doug walked me out to valet, where he had a limo waiting, complete with a cheesy, neon-lined interior. We laughed a little about it as we got in and he quickly started telling me stories about his latest European jaunt. I had had a few drinks that night and was quite distracted by my anger toward Nancy, so the car ride flew by in a blur. *This drive is taking a while,* I thought. I cracked the tinted window to get a better view.

"Where are we going?" I shot at Doug, interrupting his sales pitch on Ibiza in August.

"We're gonna go by my place real quick," he responded. "I gotta pick something up."

I could see where this was going from a mile away as he scooted closer to me. I pretended to be fascinated with his stories as I whipped out my phone and BEGGED Hannah to drive over to Doug's house to pick me up. I had known Doug was renting in the area before he even mentioned it to me. I remembered Hannah mentioning to me that she was soon to be "neighbors with the douche bag" back when she started spending more time at her man's house. The douche bag in question was too busy telling me how much money he had spent furnishing this new pad to notice that I seemed more than casually interested in my phone.

Hannah's Mercedes was idling in the driveway when we pulled up.

"Who's here?" Doug asked, squinting his eyes at the beat-up car.

"Hannah. She's staying around here," I explained. "She's picking me up."

"But . . . hey," he stumbled, grasping at straws. "She can hang out, too!"

"Thanks for the ride!" I shouted, throwing my hand up into the air for a distant wave as I trotted over to Hannah's car.

"Goin' back to Doug's, are we?" she playfully admonished, backing out of the driveway.

Doug was left staring at us, his arms out in an exaggerated shrug.

"No!" I cried. "You heard him offer to take me home. I didn't know he meant *his* home."

"Gross, what a tool," Hannah said, rolling her eyes. "I've heard he has a big dick, though."

I swatted Hannah on the shoulder and we laughed all the way back to my house.

When I awoke later the next day, I pointed the remote toward my windows to lift the blackout shades. *The same blackout shades Eric convinced me to buy,* I thought ruefully. I didn't even need them. I could sleep through anything. The bright sun poured in, bouncing off the crystal chandeliers and illuminating my baby-blue damask-covered walls and mirrored furniture. Napoleon took the cue to wake up and started barking and jumping around wildly. I reached over to the nightstand to grab my phone and the first text I saw was the kind you just don't want to start your day with. Hannah had sent me a screen shot of an Instagram photo Nancy had posted the night before. It was a picture of Nancy and three women I had never seen before crowded into a diner booth with one dainty piece of cheesecake in the center of the table. Under the photo, the caption read: "I love these ladies! Friends worth having! #MyTableIsFull #NoBasicsAllowed."

I rolled my eyes. I wondered if this was a passive-aggressive dig aimed at me. Even though it wasn't a very masterful burn, it still hurt. Not to mention, once I checked Twitter, I realized that that post was the least of it. Nancy and Lindsay seemed to be subtweeting about me like crazy. They weren't mentioning my name, but I believed they were talking about me, and slamming me pretty hard, at that. Well, Nancy appeared to be slamming me. Lindsay seemed to be agreeing. My heart was in the pit of my stomach. I didn't know how I was going to concentrate on the show tonight. Here were two of my closest friends appearing to hate on me, suddenly and viciously. My emotions plunged. I couldn't wait to get backstage to tell Josh about what was going on.

So now I'm basic, I thought. I suppose she thought she was just the epitome of wild, crazy, fun—the opposite of basic. If I had been speaking to her then, I would have had news for her: having a drinking problem doesn't mean you aren't basic. In fact, it had made her horribly predictable and boring.

What had gone wrong between Nancy and me?

Was I bad at communicating? Sure, but I couldn't remember ever not being straightforward with Nancy. Her open-book mentality was what I admired about her, so I naturally tended to mirror that when I was with her. If anything, I should have staged an intervention by now.

And I'd always been there for Nancy when she needed something. I was confused and couldn't understand where her resentment was coming from.

And why am I basic? I wondered. Since when did *basic* become the go-to insult? And is anyone on the same page about what it means? Is a basic just someone who likes what's popular? Are you basic if you like pumpkin spice lattes, Ugg boots, and infinity scarves?

How was I to interpret this insult? I wondered as I threw back my baby-blue satin comforter and rolled out of bed. Instead of brushing off the post, like I should have, I proceeded to turn it over and over in my mind, analyzing it to death.

Napoleon trailed at my heels as I descended the staircase en route to the kitchen to get his food. *I was never basic,* I thought to myself. I was always the kid getting suspended from the cheerleading squad for dying my hair purple or ruining the vintage prom dresses I wore to school by "hemming" them with a lighter. I wasn't popular. I always had my nose in a book or my head in the clouds and would find joy in random small details other people wouldn't notice. I was a Phoebe in a world of Rachels and Monicas. Oh, whoops, I made a *Friends* reference! How basic of me.

As I showered, I contemplated why I always had a natural aversion to doing what was popular or what was expected of me. It wasn't that I thought I was cooler than anyone else, it was more instinctual than that: I simply wasn't interested in dipping my toe into a flooded market.

Strangely enough, I think the search for the offbeat is what led me to Playboy in the first place. I saw it as vintage glamour with an illicit twist. Nothing basic about that! Of course, as I went deeper and deeper down that rabbit hole, I started losing myself in the quest to become the "perfect Playmate." Sure, the platinum-maned, spray-tanned, blow-up doll look might not be the norm in most social strata, but it was definitely, at the Playboy mansion, basic. I was a Playboy basic bitch. But I also knew that those days were well behind me.

I couldn't stop thinking about this as I got dressed. After I laced up my shoes, I picked up my phone and looked at the mean post one last time. As I stared at it, I told myself, *You know you're not basic. Don't let this insecure woman get to you. Why is this bothering me so much?* I wondered.

Maybe it hurt because I felt like she was trying to say I was not special. And deep down, perhaps I didn't feel like anyone thought I was special. Maybe the "basic bitch" insult hit an unexpected nerve. Clearly it went deeper than how I was feeling about Nancy to how I was feeling about my life in general. All of us want that person who makes us feel like one of a kind, and I had thrown Mark away, the only guy who ever had. *Good luck finding another one,* I thought to myself as I grabbed my giant tote and walked out the front door.

After work, I met Lindsay at the Chandelier bar at the Cosmo so we could speak in person and get to the bottom of whatever our overblown misunderstanding was. I ran through what I wanted to say to Lindsay in my mind as the escalators pushed me up amid the million Swarovski crystals of the giant chandelier that encased the bar like a massive spider web.

I spotted Lindsay on one of the royal-blue damask sofas with a lemon drop martini in her hand.

"Nancy told me you called me a bitch for not telling you why I was mad," Lindsay blurted out self-righteously as I sat down next to her.

"I'm sorry," I apologized, "but I was frustrated. How am I supposed to know why you are mad or what I did wrong if you just go silent?" I said, pausing to order a vodka soda from the bartender.

"You're one to talk!" Lindsay exclaimed, practically spitting out her drink. "That's what *you* do to people! Don't even get me started! You are the queen of going silent!"

"Well, that's not what I'm doing now," I shot back, though I realized that what she was saying was totally spot-on. "I'm trying to fix this. What's the problem? And what's Nancy's problem?"

Lindsay opened her mouth to say something, but I wasn't finished.

"I know you've been friends with Nancy longer than me," I continued, "so you can believe what you want, but she was telling me that you were saying all these nasty things about me. It's like she doesn't want us to be friends."

"You are totally right about that," Lindsay agreed after a few moments. "She has been complaining for a while that she thinks you are trying to steal me from her."

"Who steals friends?" I said, throwing my hands in the air with exasperation. "This isn't high school!"

"I know," Lindsay said quietly. "It's ridiculous. To tell you the truth, Nancy and I have been growing apart for some time now. She just gets so wasted whenever we go out together that I end up having to babysit her. Remember when I told you she kicked my car a few months back and left the dent in it? That was kind of the last straw. But I think she blames you for us growing apart when really that's not it at all."

"So she's going back and forth between us . . ." I started.

"And playing us both," Lindsay finished. "I kind of suspected that in the back of my head, but I didn't want to believe it. It pisses me off."

"It makes me really mad, too," I agreed. "The one thing I liked best about Nancy was that she was always so honest. No matter how much of a hot mess she was sometimes, or no matter how unconventional, she just didn't give a shit. She was straight up about it. I loved that about her."

"I know," Lindsay said. "But let's face it, that's been changing for a long time."

"You're right," I said, "I didn't want to see it. I'm slow to let go sometimes, but it got to the point where she's so mean to people . . ."

". . . that it's embarrassing," Lindsay finished. "It was only a matter of time before she turned on us."

"Yeah, I guess I just stupidly thought I was, like, special and immune to her wrath or something," I reflected, crumpling up my cocktail napkin.

"Well," Lindsay said, lifting her martini glass, "here's to letting go."

WHO'S CALLING ME? I wondered. I could hear my phone buzzing before I was ready to wake on this hot summer's day. *This must be important for someone to be calling over and over again,* I thought. *It's the Fourth of July weekend, after all.*

I finally reached over and grabbed my phone, peering out from under my comforter to see who the persistent caller was. It was a producer from *Holly's World*.

"Hello?" I answered.

"Holly, we've got some unfortunate news," he began before going on to tell me that with a new network president at the helm of E! and the Playboy-related advertiser problems that had lingered since the *Girls Next Door* days, the decision had been made to not renew the show.

I expressed my disappointment as I let the news slowly sink in.

"You seem to be taking this well," my bearer of bad news said. "I think I'm more upset about it than you are."

"It's not that I'm not upset about it. I knew it would come to an end sometime, I just wasn't expecting it to be so soon," I replied, trying to sound strong.

In truth, I wasn't taking it that well. I've never been a very outwardly emotional person and I didn't see the point in throwing a pity party over the phone, but that didn't mean I wouldn't be bummed about this for some time to come. I tried to reassure myself that it wasn't that bad. Sure, it would have been fun and productive to do another season, but I never planned on doing reality TV forever. Hadn't I got everything I wanted from it anyway? The TV program had helped make *Peepshow* a hit, I had established myself on television as a single woman, I'd attracted several endorsement deals, and the show had bought me time to figure out my next step. The only problem was . . . I hadn't figured out my next step yet! This made me feel terrified and not ready for the change. I felt uninspired and out of control of the situation, two feelings I was terribly uncomfortable with.

After we hung up, I wallowed in sadness by taking my vintage Corvette out in the blistering heat (no air conditioning in a 1960!) and ventured to the nearest McDonald's drive-through. I proceeded to load up on junk food and stuff my face like the proverbial girl who's just been dumped. Only instead of a pint of Ben & Jerry's, I had my favorite McDonald's Extra Value Meal and a handful of barbecue sauce packets. I drove back home feeling sorry for myself. It was the Fourth of July and I desperately needed to get out of the house and forget my troubles. I knew Hannah's boyfriend was having a barbecue and a few other people we knew were throwing parties in his neighborhood. When Hannah invited me, I hadn't committed to anything. But after being on the receiving end of a rough blow, I was eager to get out of my house.

"Hannah!" I texted, noticing that it was already noon, "I'm on my way!"

As I drove across town to the party, I let the news sink in. Then it hit me. So many of my friends depended on the show. *Friends,* the word echoed in my mind. Were they my friends? What if they wouldn't be now that the show was over? I felt a sinking feeling worse than the one I had when I got the news. After all, hadn't most of my former Playmate "friends" exited stage left once I was no longer first lady of the mansion?

"So, I got some bad news today," I told Hannah after I found her at the flagstone bar in the backyard. The view of the Strip and the mountains beyond the pool and golf course was breathtaking, even in the daytime. "My TV show got canceled."

"What the fuck? Why?" she asked, wrinkling her forehead as I filled her in on why and how bummed I was.

"I'm so sorry. That fucking sucks. Woman, you need a drink," she said shoving a vodka shot at me.

"Thanks," I said. "I'll see if I can't change their minds or revive it some other way, then I'll tell everyone else as soon as I know there's no hope."

"Don't stress," Hannah said, throwing her arm over my shoulders. "You'll find something else to fill that space in no time."

Even Hannah knew how desperately I needed a full schedule.

"Thanks," I said, not feeling an ounce of the confidence that Hannah had for me. I envied her lack of insecurity.

Lindsay showed up and grabbed the lounge chair next to us. Hannah and I had already gotten comfortable, she in a black string bikini and me in a white tank top and denim skirt.

"Oh my god, you guys, check this out!" Hannah gasped as she scrolled away on her phone's screen.

She flipped the phone around so we could see the bright pink blog page set against black, the unmistakable look of her favorite local gossip site. What was unusual about this particular entry was that the photo featured was one of Nancy accompanied by her latest instant bestie.

I couldn't believe the headline I read, as it was particularly salacious and scandalous.

"What?" I exclaimed, grabbing the phone from Hannah as Lindsay leaned in to see what it said.

I was silent as I scrolled down and saw the flood of comments that had exploded on the blog since it was posted only a few hours ago. Cruel posts flooded the page, and I winced at reading particularly hurtful ones. It appeared that Nancy had pissed off a lot of people, far more than just Lindsay and me. As I read the comments, it was clear that these people seemed to know her, at least casually. Some described what her apartment looked like inside; others mentioned her pets by name. I felt awful for Nancy. I knew too well what it was like to be torn apart in a public forum where any of your haters or frenemies could pore over it and laugh. I wanted to reach out to her, but was hesitant. Would she think I was secretly gloating if I tried to express empathy? Nancy had never been one to talk about her feelings.

"Jeez, this is heavy," I said, passing the phone back to Hannah. "I wonder if any of it's true."

"I dunno." Hannah shrugged. "But she's obviously aware of it. I just went to find her on Twitter, and all of her social media is gone. She deleted everything."

"No way!" I gasped. Lindsay and I both searched Instagram, Twitter, and Facebook for any sign of Nancy. We couldn't find a single one. It was as if she disappeared off the face of the planet.

"Someone should text her, make sure she's okay," Lindsay suggested.

"I agree. Do you still have her number?" I asked, looking at Hannah. I still made a habit of deleting the contact info of people I no longer wanted as part of my life. There was no need to be tempted back into conversation, whether for friendship or feud.

"Not her new one," Hannah replied. "She tweeted that she was changing her number about a week after you guys had your falling-out."

"Sometimes I miss her." Lindsay sighed.

"Me, too," I agreed. I couldn't help but be angry at her for breaking up this amazing little family we had created. "We had a lot of good times. It's like she ruined all of those memories by turning into a giant shithead."

"She was *always* a shithead," Hannah grumbled. "I suspected it the very first night, after the show! She got major attitude when you invited me along. Nancy was mean to everyone. You avoided her wrath the longest because she always hoped you would put her on your show or something. And when she realized she couldn't get anything else out of you, she turned on you, too." Hannah shot me a look that said *You know I'm right* before turning her attention to her maroon metallic nails. "Anyway, where are the boys?" she asked, looking around at the suddenly female-dominated pool.

God, I thought. *Was Hannah right?* I had focused so much of my energy trying to ward off any guys who might have an agenda that I didn't even think to look at my own friends. I guess I just didn't want to be that cynical. The thought made me feel so stupid.

I was jolted out of my thoughts by the thunderous clap of a bright red firework blooming in the sky. In the distance, we could see the brilliant display exploding over the Strip. I was starting to feel antsy, like there was somewhere better I could be or something more productive I could be doing . . . but what? Aren't you supposed to spend holidays with your closest friends? And here I was, with Hannah and Lindsay . . . so what else was missing?

Plenty, whispered the creepy little troll in the back of my head who was never, ever satisfied.

Instead of having an angel on one shoulder and a devil on the other, I constantly heard a critical, overly ambitious, always unhappy voice that was fueled by all the online haters, by the toxic manipulators in my life, and most of all, by me.

Lindsay yawned dramatically, announcing she was ready to head home, and Hannah had wrapped herself around her boyfriend, so I took that as my cue to leave, too. The night still felt young and I wasn't very excited about going home to my empty house, but I figured it was probably for the best.

I called a cab, said good night, and waited on the brick stoop in front of the Tuscan home. The night was dark, but still as hot as if it were midday. The bricks burned my legs as I sat, but I didn't care. In moments of stagnant frustration, I didn't mind anything that made me feel alive or snapped me out of a funk. The cab pulled up and I directed the driver to Southern Highlands.

I don't want to go home, I lamented to myself in my head.

As I gave the friendly, talkative taxi driver directions through the twists and turns of my suburban community, I wondered if I could be happy growing old in this house alone.

What if I never found anyone? What if all my friends moved on and settled down, building families and new lives of their own, and I was still a lonely workaholic until the day I died? Could I be happy? Could work, pets, and a few friends make my life feel complete, even if I never got married and had kids? I know plenty of people choose to live their lives that way and love it, but deep down, that didn't feel like what I needed. I wanted a balance between the personal and the professional. I realized, though, that at the end of the day I might not have a choice.

Had spending my twenties at the Playboy mansion spoiled my chances? Had I missed my chance to meet "the one"? I wondered if setting Mark aside the way I did spoiled my karma as well. Perhaps I was in for a world of hurt because I had so carelessly hurt *him.* I made the decision then and there that if I was lucky enough to ever meet someone like that again—someone I had amazing chemistry with who was smart and fun and treated me the way I wanted to be treated—I would NOT take him for granted.

When we pulled up to the seemingly lifeless house, the driver cheerfully announced our arrival.

"Here we are!" he exclaimed as I handed him the cash I had carefully folded in my hands and thanked him for the ride.

"Hey, thanks, miss!" he said. As I trudged up the cobblestone walkway, I dug around the bottom of my bag for keys. *Why do I always have to burden myself with a bottomless purse?* I wondered resentfully. *I need to get my shit together.* I'd spent a few minutes on the ride over carefully selecting the right amount of cash for the driver. Why couldn't I have thought to pull my keys out of this mess too?

Shit, I thought. It was too dark to see what had hooked onto the fabric inside my bag, so I tugged and tugged until I felt it finally spring loose, in the process turning my entire bag inside out all over my porch. *Perfect. Just the perfect end to the perfect day.*

I looked up and noticed the taxi had already turned around in the cul-de-sac and was speeding off before I could even begin to open the door. *Even the driver, who had seemed so friendly a moment earlier, doesn't care if I get inside safely,* I thought, half-jokingly.

As I searched the overcrowded chain for the front door key, it didn't immediately register that tears had begun to fill my eyes and drip down my face. With the right key in my hand, I went to unlock the door, but my arm dropped limply to my side.

I felt so alone—so *very* alone.

Suddenly I felt heavy and allowed my body to crumple to the ground. I curled myself into a ball, pulled my knees to my forehead, and had a good cry.

Had I spent so many years desperately trying to prove my value for myself or for others? For the people who told me I wouldn't amount to anything? Why did I care so much about what they thought? As if anything I could do would change their minds.

When would I be satisfied? I asked myself. When would I feel like what I had was enough? I knew what I had achieved . . . so what else was there?

I was so confused. I couldn't even explain what it was I wanted or needed in order to fill the massive pit that was inside me.

I thought I should have been happy, with this nice house I bought for myself, but it felt like an empty shell. *What was I thinking, buying a house with so many bedrooms?* I scolded myself. *I had no need for a house this big.* Part of me just assumed, I suppose, that the rooms would somehow get filled up. *Why did I buy a house so far away from the Strip?* I continued. I felt disconnected, lonely, and abandoned in the quiet suburbs, surrounded by people I never saw.

My dreams had been realized. Hadn't they? Wasn't this everything I wanted? The world I had worked so hard to create around me was growing and changing, as things always do, but I wasn't ready for change. At least I didn't think I was. I was panicking because I didn't have a precise idea of what my next step would be. Without knowing exactly what I wanted, how could I ever move forward?

One thing was certain: I wouldn't find it sitting here crying like a baby on my front porch. *I'll think about it tomorrow,* I told myself.

Exhausted from the long day in the heat, I pulled myself together and made my way inside. I flipped on the crystal chandelier in my entryway and heard manic barks and the clicking of doggy toenails across the travertine floors. At least someone was happy to see me!

Chapter 13

"Hush, my dear," he said; "don't speak so loud, or you will be overheard—and I should be ruined. I'm supposed to be a Great Wizard."

"And aren't you?" she asked.

"Not a bit of it, my dear; I'm just a common man."
—L. Frank Baum, *The Wonderful Wizard of Oz*

"Ouch!" I yelped as Lindsay shoved a bobby pin behind my right ear.

"Sorry!" she shrieked.

I laughed as I wove my fingers through the blond knee-length braided wig, carefully helping Lindsay position it on my head.

"There," I announced, pointing to a spot near the crown of my head. "Can you stick one in right there?"

"That's what she said," Hannah deadpanned.

With surgical focus, Lindsay, in a black tutu, navigated the large pin through the wig. Summer had transitioned into fall, taking with it the oppressive desert heat. It was Halloween and I was set to host the annual

"HollyWeen" costume party at Studio 54 in the MGM Grand . . . a venue (and resort) that held a lot of memories for me.

As I began tucking a handful of colorful blooms down the braid, Hannah, a "sexy zombie" clad in a ripped dress and fake dried blood, popped a bottle of champagne. Lindsay, as a picture-perfect Black Swan ballerina, began idly flipping through one of the books on my end table.

The book she was holding was a Vegas guidebook I had written after spending my first year in the city. It included a bit on my first trip to Vegas, which happened to be with Hef and his girlfriends. The volume lauded the luxury of the trip (private planes! exclusive hotels! bottle service!) but omitted the behind-the-scenes drama that had made the trip almost unbearable.

"Can you believe I've still never been inside the MGM Mansion?" Lindsay pouted, thumbing through the chapter on luxury suites. "I've been everywhere else."

"The Mansion is okay." Hannah shrugged. "But I'm really feeling the Imperial Palace for my next tawdry one-night stand," she joked.

Lindsay looked at me and rolled her eyes.

"I saw that," Hannah cautioned, with a small smile.

"What was it like?" Lindsay asked, ignoring Hannah. "It must have been so nice."

"Not really," I grumbled. "It actually wasn't a fun trip for me."

Hannah and Lindsay both looked at me quizzically, since the book had only detailed how glamorous it all was.

"Sure, everything was top of the line," I conceded. "The rooms were out of this world, we flew private . . . We had the best of everything, but when you are with the wrong people, all that stuff is meaningless."

"Do tell," Hannah purred, hungry for a bit of scandal.

"But in the book it sounds like you had a great time . . ." Lindsay began, her voice dripping with an innocent naïveté I couldn't very well fault her for.

"Well, it's a travel book. It wasn't an appropriate place to air all my dirty laundry," I explained. "Besides, I'd end up having to deal with Hef and all those girls if I were to actually say anything honest. The last thing I want is to invite them back in my life in any way."

"What's the worst he can do?" Hannah pressed. "Write you a letter?" she teased, rolling her eyes.

"All of those people who watched *The Girls Next Door* just wouldn't get it. They thought I was happy with Hef. They wouldn't understand if I had anything bad to say. It would seem so out of left field, so sudden. Plus, when it looks like you are living a life of luxury, no one wants to hear you bitch about it. People don't care about what went on on a deeper level. They think if you are holding a glass of champagne everything must be okay."

"People aren't that dumb," Hannah interjected. "It's not so black and white."

"It's not that they're dumb, it's just not what they want to believe." I tried my best to explain. "They are used to seeing everything between the girls and Hef painted like it was some sort of fairy tale. Actually, even though the show was very good for me in many ways, I kind of get disgusted at how much people buy into it. They never saw any of the dark side: how we were treated, how we treated each other, or what people thought of us. They think living at the mansion must have been heaven on earth and expect me to be out here pining away for that lifestyle or something."

Lindsay and Hannah were quiet, riveted by what I was saying. They had never really heard me go off on this topic before. Sure, I alluded to not being happy there—hence my departure—but I never divulged any specifics. I had put my past so firmly behind me that I rarely spoke of it . . . and tried to think about it as little as possible.

"But, anyway," Hannah began, "what happened during that trip?"

I started laughing, which caused Hannah and Lindsay to breathe an audible sigh of relief. I hadn't realized how tense the room had become.

"Right, sorry," I started. "Let me tell you about my first trip to Vegas . . ."

I had just moved in with Hef a few weeks earlier, and contrary to popular belief, I didn't *really* know what I was getting into. All I had seen, before I became a girlfriend, was the other women making it sound like they loved it there, which I believed, because Hef had the perfect-gentleman act down pat. No one briefs you on the rules or expectations before you make the decision to move in, so I was still learning my way around.

It was the birthday of one of Hef's favorite girlfriends, Lisa, and she had asked for a trip to Las Vegas to celebrate. I didn't realize it then, but it was almost unheard of for him to agree to such a grand gesture for any of the girls. Just a few weeks earlier, another one of the girlfriends had celebrated her birthday, and her gift from Hef was a handful of gold-plated Playboy-brand costume jewelry.

"He got a cake for his birthday in every country we went to in Europe last spring!" she had erupted after opening her gifts, throwing things around her room, yelling that he refused to do anything special for her birthday. "Spoiled little man! He *knows* I hate gold jewelry!"

"So he gave her gold jewelry as a fuck-you?" Hannah grilled, fascinated by the inner workings of the bizarre world that I so rarely reminisced about.

"No," I answered. "I don't think he had any idea about her taste in jewelry, or any of our specific likes and dislikes for that matter. We were flattering ourselves if we thought otherwise. He knew roughly four things about each girl. Her name, her age, where (approximately) she was from, and how well she behaved and followed the rules.

"Anyway, there was some pretty clear favoritism going on—not everyone got a lavish trip for their birthday. One of the girlfriends, Vicky, eventually pointed out to me that he liked to play favorites to keep everyone on their toes."

"That's messed up," Lindsay interjected.

"I know," I agreed. "But that's exactly what he was doing. How else could he stay in control of seven women? It prevented us from banding together and staging a coup. He needed to somehow maintain the upper hand."

"Oh, yeah," Hannah reasoned. "That actually makes sense."

"So, anyway, we were off to Las Vegas for Lisa's birthday," I said, attempting to get off of my tangent. *I could go on for days,* I thought. "Since it was my first time, I had no idea what to expect. I was excited to be doing my first trip to Vegas in such style. I didn't really know what the city had to offer. I had visions of the Rat Pack and Marilyn Monroe dancing in my head."

Hef chartered a small but luxurious private jet to make the trip. He absolutely refused to fly commercial for any reason. Being from modest means myself, I was overwhelmed by how grand it all seemed. Flying private was an entirely new experience for me. When we pulled up in front of the plane, we were prompted to pose for photos in front of the aircraft. As soon as Hef's photographer announced that she had the shot, we turned to board the tiny plane. I happened to be one of the first to climb aboard after Hef, so it was up to me to choose my seat. Even though I was still a newbie, I was already aware that sitting in the wrong place was a major misstep.

Knowing how low I ranked on the totem pole as the newest girlfriend, I chose what I figured to be the least desirable seat available: the seat furthest from Hef. The two girlfriends with the most clout (Tina, his "main" girlfriend, and Lisa, the "baby") sat next to Hef at all times, which actually worked for me since I was still extremely intimidated by him.

I buckled my seat belt and got comfortable in the spacious, soft leather chair, anxious to see the infamous Vegas skyline.

We barely had time to drink our champagne and enjoy the platters of gourmet hors d'oeuvres that were passed around before the captain informed us that we would be landing in just a few minutes. I looked out the window and was surprised to see a tiny, toylike city. Most cities I had flown into had such a large urban sprawl you couldn't see where they started or ended, but Las Vegas was very compact, an oasis in the desert. The Strip was even more so. Each one of the city's iconic casinos was laid out one right next to the other. I spotted a pyramid, a castle, and the "emerald city" that was the MGM Grand. It was like a tiny jewel box spilled open in the middle of the Mojave Desert, leaving a pile of colorful gems littering the ground one on top of the other. I never expected the Strip to be so dense! It looked like a world of excitement that I couldn't wait to tear into.

"This is so cool!" I said under my breath to Carolyn, the girlfriend who was sitting across from me.

"Yeah, I guess," she said, rolling her eyes and glancing out the window before taking a final swig from her champagne glass.

A long, sparkling limousine met our jet and we were immediately whisked away to the MGM Grand.

"I can't believe that was your *first trip*," Lindsay bemoaned. "My first time to Vegas I stayed at the Tropicana."

Hannah burst into laughter.

"I'm well aware that this wasn't normal," I acknowledged. "And trust me, my jaw hit the floor when we pulled in to the MGM Mansion."

The secretive, exclusive hotel, accessible only to invited guests, had a private, unmarked entry—virtually impossible to discern for an unknowing eye. Our limo was met by a small army of staffers, all on hand to greet us, including the personal butler who was assigned to our room. He escorted us to a private elevator that arrived at the door of a four-bedroom villa. Hef and Tina stayed together in the decadent master suite, while the other girlfriends quickly crowded into two of the other rooms. Clearly, they had already decided amongst themselves who was rooming with whom, neglecting to include me and Bobbi, one of the other new recruits who were rounding out Hef's girl squad that week.

Bobbi was one of two women being considered for the spot a former girlfriend named Adrianna had vacated a few months prior. I found Bobbi to be kind, noncompetitive, and not catty. She and I were sharing the "smallest" room, which offered two queen beds swathed in silk duvets and encompassed by large four-poster bed frames, complete with a sitting area. Attached to our room was an oversize white marble bathroom, with two sinks, a rain shower that could have easily accommodated half a dozen people, and a giant Jacuzzi bathtub.

After we unpacked, I wandered around the villa to see what other marvels were yet to be discovered. I decided that before I did, I should probably get the itinerary and figure out where I was expected to be and when.

Hef and Mary had set up shop in the suite's executive boardroom to go over the evening with a few of Hef's security detail. As soon as I poked my head in, Mary spotted me.

"What are you looking for, honey?" Mary asked.

"Oh, I just didn't know what the plan was today. Are we doing anything?" I inquired, my voice meek and low.

Mary's smile disappeared momentarily.

"The other girls took a limo and went shopping. Why don't you book some spa services or something?" Mary suggested. Her gentle and careful tone made it obvious that she felt bad that I had been so clearly excluded from the other ladies' plans.

"Oh, we can do that?" I asked about the spa services.

Mary nodded cheerfully. "And order in some room service, too."

"Great. Thank you!" I exclaimed, directing my appreciation toward Hef, though he didn't acknowledge my presence.

When Bobbi and I scheduled massage appointments, we were surprised to find out the practitioners could come to us! I had never had the means to visit a nice spa before, let alone order a massage to my hotel room. While I was in awe of how luxurious this all was, I couldn't help feeling terribly insecure.

Why had they excluded us? I wondered. *Did they not like me? Had I accidentally offended someone?*

In the beginning, I always tried my best to be friendly to everyone in the house. I believed that my life with Playboy would be the sorority experience that I had never had.

Maybe they had just been really anxious to get going, I consoled myself. *Maybe it was just an oversight.*

After our massages, Bobbi and I began getting ready for our first night out in Las Vegas. With the clothing allowance we were given, I was able to stock up on a few items suitable for our club nights. I kept it practical with reasonably priced mall fare and versatile pieces that carried just enough flash to align with Hef's less-than-classic taste. That evening, I wore a black lace Bebe dress, which I liked because it reminded me vaguely of a Dolce & Gabbana number Britney Spears had recently sported at an awards show. When it was time to leave, we took our obligatory group photo in the villa's entryway and piled in the limo to get to our destination. We were headed to Bootlegger Bistro, an Italian restaurant at the south end of the Strip, to celebrate Lisa's birthday.

When we entered the restaurant, the host led us to a long table next to the dance floor. I waited for each bottle blonde, including Bobbi, to take her spot at the table. After everyone was seated, I claimed the last empty chair, next to April. Since no one bothered to include me in the conversation, I kept myself occupied by reading about the family restaurant's history on the paper place mat in front of me. Suddenly, the piano player serenading the room started playing an upbeat jazz tune.

"This is called 'Playboy's Theme,' " Hef informed us. "It was the theme song to a show I did in the sixties called *Playboy After Dark*."

"It must be bizarre," Lindsay pondered, "to barely ever leave your house, and when you do, everyone treats you like you are visiting royalty."

"Yeah, that could turn just about anyone into an asshole," Hannah added. "Then what happened?"

Hef asked Lisa to dance, and April, who was sitting next to me, suddenly got teary-eyed "I wanna dance, too," she said sadly, a single tear rolling out of one of her heavily made-up eyes. At the time, I thought she was being drunk and dramatic, but it was really a foreshadowing. Being one of seven girlfriends can make even the most confident person feel extremely unspecial. Feeling a loss of identity was pretty much a standard symptom among all of us. It didn't matter if you *thought* you knew what sort of a situation you were getting into or how much money and glamour would be thrown your way. At the end of the day, everyone wants to feel valued, respected, and loved.

After the birthday dinner, we headed back to the villa to change. Well, five out of the eight girls changed. I was one of the ones who didn't. I had only thought to bring two outfits per day, a casual one for daytime and a dressier one for the evening activities.

"Don't forget your IDs," Mary warned us, "the casinos are strict. You can't get into a club without an ID here." This was new to us. No one ever carded any of Hef's girls when we went out in L.A., allowing him to routinely bring women who were under twenty-one out to the clubs. April quickly scrambled back to her room in a panic, certain she'd left her ID in L.A. After about ten minutes, she finally emerged victorious, driver's license in hand.

When we arrived at Studio 54 at ten-thirty, it was empty. By Vegas standards, we were used to going out super early, so there was literally no one there. We were placed in a balcony table overlooking a giant moon that was meant to be a replica of the "moon and the spoon" that hung in the original New York club (minus the infamous spoon, though).

"I guess I'll bring mine tonight," Hannah joked.

"Sh," Lindsay hushed. "I wanna hear!"

Once again, I grabbed an empty spot next to April and we dove into our first round of vodka cranberries. I decided to try and strike up a conversation, telling her the story behind the moon, which I had heard on a documentary I had seen a few years earlier.

"You know, the moon that hung in the original Studio 54 had a giant cocaine spoon leading up to its nose," I shared, thinking she'd get a kick out of the trivia.

April looked at me witheringly, with glassy, drunk eyes. After staring at me for a beat, she said, "I know *everything* about sex and drugs." She stood up, grabbed her drink briskly as half of it sloshed to the ground, and walked away from me, squeezing into a seat on the other side of the table.

This was an alternate universe. I was feeling so insecure and out of sorts, I did the only thing I could think of to help me get through the night.

"You drank," Hannah chimed in.

"I drank," I repeated.

When the evening was over, we arrived back at the villa and Bobbi and I changed into our pajamas before deciding to check out the gourmet dessert spread that had been set out for us on the dining room table. The villa was oddly quiet. Bobbi peeked through the open door of Vicky's room and noticed it was empty.

"I don't think they're here," Bobbi shrugged. Once again, the girlfriends had decided to take the limo out but failed to invite Bobbi or me. I wasn't quite sure why we were on the receiving end of five sets of cold shoulders, but I decided that I was much happier settled in the villa, getting a good night's rest in the most comfortable bed I'd ever slept in.

The next day was quiet. Bobbi and I slept in and ordered room service. At one point, Mary popped in to let us know what time we were expected to be ready for dinner that evening. I put on the other outfit I had packed for a night out: a pair of knee-high black boots, a black miniskirt, and a crop top with a dark faux-fur vest.

On the ride over, I tried making small talk with Vicky, attempting to perhaps mend any fences that may have been disrupted. She shot me an annoyed glance, rolled her eyes, and made a noise like she didn't want to be bothered having to talk to me. Suddenly, she turned toward Carolyn and April to chatter loudly about how amazing their night had been.

Are they just trying to make me feel worse? I wondered as I listened to their stories of debauchery. Apparently they had visited a strip club one of the girlfriends had worked at previously and got crazy wasted. Lisa and Tina were making small talk with Hef as he bobbed his head, clearly not hearing what the others were reminiscing about.

"That sucks!" Lindsay said with a frown. "To talk about it right in front of you like that."

"I think that was the point," I said. "I felt like I didn't belong, and the other girlfriends were trying hard to make it clear I was an outsider. I couldn't figure out what I had done to piss them off."

We started the evening in a private dining room atop the Rio. The restaurant, which sat on the fiftieth floor, offered a dazzling panoramic view of the city. Bobbi and I smiled when the server arrived with our whimsical Witch's Brew cocktails that were gigantic and overflowing with steam from the dry ice.

After dinner, we were whisked away to the Luxor to catch the Blue Man Group. As we filed into the theater, I dutifully followed the bleached-blond pack in front of me to our seats. One by one, each girlfriend took her place, and I ended up next to April, who occupied the aisle seat. Throughout the show, she kept leaving and coming back with daiquiri after daiquiri—which wasn't out of the ordinary for any of us. We all routinely turned to drinking out of boredom or to escape our personal demons. By the time the show was over, April had gotten pretty wasted, stumbling over her stilettos on the way backstage to meet the cast.

The Blue Men were posed on a giant metal staircase behind the stage. As the girls gathered around the stairs to surround Hef and the performers, I was crowded out of the shot. It didn't really matter to me, but Hef's photographer, Elayne, was a kind woman who always went out of her way to make sure everyone was included.

"Holly, go up one more step so we can see your face!" she instructed.

I obliged, climbing a stair and peeking my head over the towering platinum bird's nest of an updo in front of me. *Were they crowding me out on purpose?* I wondered. *No,* I thought, *they probably just want prime place in the photo.* Hef's personal photos sometimes ended up in "World of

Playboy," the social page in the front of the magazine every month, so if a girlfriend hadn't yet scored a centerfold, she could thrill to the fact that her name and photo were at least *somewhere* in *Playboy*.

After dinner, we were expected to hit one of the largest, most popular clubs in town, Ra.

"What's Ra?" Lindsay asked, wrinkling her nose.

"Ra was a nightclub at the Luxor," I explained. "There weren't nearly as many nightclubs in Vegas back in those days. In fact I think Ra and Studio 54 were the only two major ones."

Ra was an absolute blur. We all got pretty wasted, and when Hef made the decision to call it an early night, not even the "mean team" attempted to stay out any later.

We filed into the limo, one after the other, in a drunken stumble. Like I said, it was understood that Tina, the main girlfriend, always sat on one side of Hef, and Lisa, his second favorite, on the other. When it came to the other girls sitting down the length of the limo, I was usually relegated near the far end, but I hadn't noticed a specific hierarchy past Tina and Lisa's positions. I sat down somewhere near the middle of the seat and paused for a moment to unzip one of my brand-new stilleto boots, which had been killing my feet all night.

"Move over," one of the girlfriends barked at me.

"Hang on, I really need to get this boot off," I answered, fumbling with the zipper.

"Too big for your britches!" she spat angrily as she flopped past me.

She immediately starting hissing to the rest of the girls about me, and they all laughed loudly and made nasty comments as if I wasn't even there. Bobbi just looked down at her hands and kept quiet. I didn't expect her to stick up for me. She was new and wanted to keep a low profile.

As the limo pulled back through the unmarked gate and into the exquisite MGM Mansion driveway, I couldn't feel any less glamorous. I knew we were expected to go back to the bedroom with Hef, but there was just *no way* I was going to participate in that farce with this vicious horde of girls. I was the last girlfriend to trail into the villa, suddenly acutely aware of my place in the group, and broke off into my bedroom to get ready for bed. I really wanted to be under the covers before Bobbi came back from the master bedroom. I didn't want to talk to anyone.

"Yoo-hoo," squeaked a voice as the door to my suite slowly lurched open. It had been twenty minutes or so since we had gotten home, and Tina apparently had been sent to come look for me. She said that Hef was really concerned that I didn't come to bed.

Tina so far hadn't been catty toward me, so I felt reasonably comfortable explaining to her everything that had happened since we arrived, capped off by the childish display during the drive home.

"I'm not comfortable," I told Tina. "I don't want to be in there with them." As the "main girlfriend," Tina was expected to play the role of "mother hen" and wrangle all the girls according to Hef's whims.

Tina attempted to appease me, insisting that Hef just felt terrible that I was hurting.

"So why didn't he say so himself?" Lindsay inquired.

"Tina had just walked through my door a few minutes earlier to see what the problem was," I reminded her. "Hef didn't even know what the issue was yet. How could he be upset I was hurt? She was probably just saying what she thought she had to say to smooth things over."

Tina reported back to Hef about what had transpired, and he in turn scolded the girl in question for being rude and hurtful. The reprimand spurred her into survival mode. Trying quickly to save face, she accused my close friend Britney of trying to steal her spot as a girlfriend. She hinted that she thought it would be appropriate for Britney to be banned from the mansion.

Her accusation packed a punch. Not only was she taking the focus off her behavior, she was also striking a blow that would hurt me. If Britney got banned, which in essence meant I would lose the last friend I had, I wasn't sure I could last at the mansion. Maybe that's what she was aiming for all along.

The truth was, Britney had no interest in becoming a girlfriend. The other girlfriends seemed to simply resent the fact that one of my friends had access to the mansion without paying any of the dues that they had to. None of them ever regularly brought friends to the mansion. I'm not sure why, but maybe it had something to do with not wanting to show people what their lives were really like there . . . or perhaps they didn't want any more competition.

"And Hef fell for this," Lindsay gaped.

"Apparently." I shrugged. "Although I'm fairly certain he just liked the idea of Britney vying for girlfriend status. Either way, I started thinking that maybe my days at the mansion were short-lived, but even if I was to leave, it wasn't fair for Britney to get the blame."

I knew that broaching the conversation with Hef meant that I risked getting kicked out. But I couldn't let my friend be thrown under the bus.

I took a deep breath and marched my way down to Hef's office (after clearing it with Mary, of course—I wasn't *that* ballsy).

"Hi," I said, squeezing through the opening in the doorway.

"So . . . you wanted to talk to me about Britney?" he said, taking off his reading glasses and looking up from his papers.

"Yes," I announced in a shaky voice, as nervous as if I were back in high school, about to give a speech in front of the entire student body.

"Britney isn't trying to steal anyone's spot," I blurted out. "And she's never had an unkind word to say about any of them. I don't know why the girls are saying that, but it's not true. Please don't ban her over this. She's my friend."

Hef scrunched up his face, took a moment to think it over, and finally said, "Well, if you feel that strongly about it, I won't ban Britney."

I was so relieved I barely heard the rest of what he said, but it was something like a few disclaimer sentences on how important it was for him to have "harmony" among the girls and how he would have to keep an eye on this situation.

"It's kind of sad, really, because it would be years before I felt confident enough to stick up for myself again." It wouldn't be much longer until the mansion politics and the manipulative way Hef treated us would completely break me down.

It was all such crap. I had to wonder if Britney and I were on her shit list for an incident that happened weeks earlier. Britney had been hanging around waiting for me one afternoon and overheard a heated exchange between her and Hef. Apparently she had broken the curfew the night before and Hef said something to her like "Why can't you just try to be a good girl, like Holly?" The second he turned his back, she made a gagging face and said, "Fuck that!" Hef had poor hearing, and the girls knew it, so they would often say things just out of earshot that they would never say to his face. When she strutted out of the room, she spotted Britney and realized Britney had heard everything.

That trip was kind of the end of any hope I had that I would ever get along with these girls. The fact that they would try and get my best friend banned just to take attention off themselves seemed unnecessarily cruel.

"You should have written *that* story," Hannah decided. "Bitches of the Playboy Mansion."

"Maybe someday." I shrugged. "I'm just afraid of how everyone will react to the truth."

"Okay," Hannah began, "so because of all those years of being fucked with, now you feel like you have to be quiet and lie, saying everything was so great there. Why? Because of what 'everyone' will think of you? Who gives a fuck? When are you going to start telling the truth? It's like you're letting your past control you."

She was right. And she was saying something I needed to hear. No one had ever forced me to look at my demons head-on. I had the same uneasy feeling I had as when Mark tried to broach the subject, although here, eight months later, I felt closer to being able to admit the truth.

"I don't know," I confessed. Hannah looked at me, sincerity in her eyes. She was here for me. She was my friend and this was a safe place,

I tried to remind myself. I'd been skipping over the truth for years to avoid facing these dark, painful memories that I wasn't quite ready to deal with.

I made checklists and set constant goals to feed this incessant need to always be doing something. There wasn't a moment to spare or rest idly when you're setting out to prove to the world that you aren't the woman everyone believes you to be. My life had become manic because I was terrified to be alone with my own thoughts. I was scared to hear all the chatter, both in my own head and from the outside world. It was time to finally ask myself, *What makes Holly run?*

For years, I'd made excuses . . . dodged and weaved.

By opening up in this small way, I was starting to realize that, in order to rid myself of my dark past, I needed to start by accepting it for what it was. I knew that wouldn't happen overnight, but I had to try.

I had made a decision that had long-lasting consequences. I had lived a lifestyle that some people would never approve of. And that was okay. I was okay.

"That sucks that it wasn't all good times," Lindsay offered, "but it made you into who you are today. I mean, you had to learn whatever lessons you did for a reason."

"Wow, did you just gather a bunch of inspirational quotes from Facebook?" Hannah deadpanned. Lindsay launched a magazine at her and Hannah laughed as she dodged it. "I'm just kidding, nutball!" she said through her laughter. "Seriously, though, as corny as you sound, it's true," she offered soberly, looking over at me.

I had to agree. I don't know what my life would have been like otherwise. Perhaps I would have finally lucked out in one of my auditions or maybe I would have gone to work behind the scenes, or gone back to school. Maybe I would have met someone and had a family, or maybe I would be sitting in this same room with these same girls.

The only thing I can say for certain was this . . . I *liked* the person I had become. And that was a good thing. Sure, I had my occasional doubts, like anyone else, but I knew now the path that was before me. And that was acceptance.

I had to accept that I kept quiet about my life at the mansion because I was ashamed. I kept quiet because I wanted people to believe the fantasy version because for so long *I* wanted to believe the fantasy. It was a far safer history than the truth.

But maybe now I finally was ready to face all of this head-on. Maybe this realization wouldn't be fleeting and I could finally do something about it.

"Come on, I want to hear more about those crazy bitches," Hannah said.

"Okay, I'll tell you more," I decided as I smiled, checking the time on my phone and making the final adjustments on my long Rapunzel wig. "But right now we've got a party to host."

Chapter 14

"I have been very kindly treated in your lovely City, and everyone has been good to me. I cannot tell you how grateful I am."

—L. Frank Baum, *The Wonderful Wizard of Oz*

I wasn't in Las Vegas anymore.

The warm winter air rolled across my face as my convertible twisted up the narrow canyon streets. Hollywoodland is a historic neighborhood just north of Sunset, tucked into the Hollywood Hills. The neighborhood's entrance is flanked by two large granite stone columns that were intended to act as a gateway to the Beachwood Canyon community that its developers called "Hollywoodland." (The larger, surrounding area itself was named in 1887 by Harvey and Daeida Wilcox, who owned the property.) The neighborhood was originally conceived as an exclusive gated residential area complete with a market, health club, and horse ranch; one of the amenities to living there was the ability to call the ranch at any time and have a horse delivered to your door.

Once visitors are in the neighborhood, the first house they see is a whimsical little European cottage that looks like it was plucked straight from the pages of a fairy tale with a white wooden sign hanging over the entryway with the words "Hollywoodland Realty Co." written in pale blue. When the original developers were attempting to attract buyers to the new community, they wanted to do something to get people's attention and came up with the idea of erecting a 45-foot-high sign across the ridgeline that read HOLLYWOODLAND, which would light up at night.

Every street in the neighborhood was magical, each slightly different from the one before. At its conception, the homes within the community consisted of a collection of four styles: Mediterranean, Spanish, English Tudor, and French Normandy. Some were grand estates and others were quaint little cottages. When the Great Depression hit, building slowed to a standstill and plans to install the entry gate came to a halt. The lights that shone brightly from the sign faded to black, and later, in 1949, "land" was removed and the giant white sign simply read "Hollywood."

I first visited Beachwood Canyon years earlier and was immediately enchanted by the magical village hidden in plain sight away from the crazy city. The homes were so picturesque and charming that I couldn't help but smile. Despite being just a few minutes from the perpetually busy Hollywood Boulevard, the neighborhood felt like a woodsy retreat. It captured my imagination.

In many ways Las Vegas had become home, but L.A.'s siren song had grown louder and louder, particularly over the last few months. The holidays always went by in a blur, and this past season shouldn't have been any different, but something about it was . . . because *I* was different. The year 2011 had been a turning point for me—and as it was coming to a close, I decided that something had to give. Over the past few years, my life had become an amusement park of attractions and distractions. And even though it had been a wild ride that had made for some of my favorite memories, I had achieved what I had set out to do. It was time to get off that particular Ferris wheel.

It had never been my plan to stay in *Peepshow* forever. In fact, I decided over the holidays that I wouldn't be extending my contract past 2012. It wasn't a decision I came to lightly. For the past three years, I lived and breathed *Peepshow*, so the idea of leaving the show at the end of the coming year was both exciting and terrifying. Becoming a successful stage performer had been one of my biggest aspirations, but it wasn't my only one. As far as I was aware, I had already headlined a show for a longer continuous period of time than any burlesque performer had before in Las Vegas. I needed to move on to what was next. When Ray had asked me, "What's next for you after *Peepshow*?" the question freaked me out. It made me suddenly feel like a clueless kid who didn't know what she wanted to be when she grew up. But what I had come to realize was that whatever I did want to do, I knew I wanted to do it in L.A. (at least part of the time). I missed the city. It was the type of place where a hidden community could stand frozen in time, as the visitors and passersby just a few miles below buzzed around, blissfully unaware of its presence. L.A. doesn't change at the rapid pace Las Vegas does, but my perception of it had. It was still ruthless, dismissive, and impossibly wonderful, but I no longer saw visions of my Playboy years everywhere I went. I had grown past that life and could now see the city with new eyes again.

Ever since my first visit to Hollywoodland, when I was filming *The Girls Next Door*, I dreamed of one day having my own home there, but back then that was more of a fantasy and not a goal. My self-esteem was low, and "goals" were things I thought I could never achieve on my own. Needless to say, since I had been on my own the past few years, my attitude had changed drastically.

Over the past few months, I started thinking about buying a home in Los Angeles and began casually perusing the real estate listings. Months after I started looking, a gorgeous turreted French Normandy popped up on the market. It looked like the kind of home Snow White might live in, equal parts miniature castle and witch's cottage. The home was built in the twenties and thankfully had escaped any remodels, save for a kitchen update. It was exactly what I dreamed of, and I made an offer after seeing it once; this was going to be my house. It was just too perfect. The keys and garage door openers had been delivered to me in Las Vegas a week earlier; I could barely wait for the following Wednesday so I could spend my day off in L.A. . . . in my new home!

I made no plans for the day; I just wanted to hang out in my little Hollywood retreat and enjoy what I considered a sort of homecoming . . . by myself. And the craziest thing about it? I was actually looking forward to spending time alone. I had spent years trying to muffle all the chatter and outside noise by surrounding myself with even louder chatter and bigger noise. When I finally recognized this, I felt at peace.

When my car turned onto my new street, my little witch's castle came into view. Sitting up on a crest behind it were the enormous white letters of the Hollywood sign jumping out from behind a forest of trees. However, given the proximity of the house to the landmark sign, it was partially obscured by the landscape, and I could make out only the first five letters: HOLLY.

I smiled to myself, knowing with certainty that this was *exactly* where I needed to be. If this wasn't a sign (literally!) that I had made the right decision, I don't know what was. I parked my car in the cul-de-sac next to the house and looked toward the steep seventy-something-step climb up to my new home sitting atop its own little hill. *At least I'll stay in shape living here,* I thought. There was something that felt so safe about this place. I was so tucked away, but all I had to do was look behind me, past a lush, blooming lemon tree, to see the sparkling lights of Hollywood and downtown L.A. below.

I pulled my keys from my bag and opened the heavy wooden door. When you first step foot inside the home, you're met with a charming circular entryway with stone and wood patterned floors, another heavy, carved wooden door for the coat closet and wrought-iron banisters lining more steps: three to get down into the living room below, five to get up to the dining room, kitchen, and what was, once upon a time, the servant's quarters. Another full set of stairs led up to three bedrooms on the second floor. The walls were all plaster, the kind that looks like frosting, swirled and uneven like the roof of a gingerbread house. There was a tiny empty cupboard in the entry that once housed the original phone from the twenties. The bells that used to function as the ringer were still attached to the wall.

The stairs leading down to the basement laundry room were so narrow, I almost lost my footing trying to navigate them. I pictured the tiny (size six or smaller) feet of a flapper skipping down them without a care.

I strolled through the wood-beamed kitchen, still dominated by a 1940s oven. Beyond the kitchen lay the main patio. It was made of bricks and covered in gorgeous potted plants and sun-bleached wooden furniture that came with the home. I took a seat in one of the patio chairs and looked over my shoulder to spot two deer casually resting in the back of my yard. There were no fences on my property; the rugged, steep hills were enough to keep anyone from wanting to casually wander into my yard. Fortunately, the deer didn't care and were regular visitors (along with a coyote and a raccoon now and then).

I was struck by the stillness and how nice it was. I could hear my neighbor at the bottom of the hill playing a trumpet, which echoed through the canyon, bouncing off the hills and trees, like the soundtrack to a noir film. For the first time in a long time I wasn't rushing to get to the next promotional event, panicking that my cell reception was sketchy, freaking out because a crush was ignoring me, or worrying because I hadn't posted anything on Instagram that day.

Instead, I sat enjoying my beautiful new view and was reminded of a recent trip to church with Angel and of the sermon we heard. I can't tell you about which Bible passage the pastor was speaking, but I can tell you it left quite an impression on me. He spoke about wanting new things in life, and about how when you want new things, you have to be prepared to give up other things, even if it is just your own free time. We have only so much room in our lives, and inevitably something has to give. Up until that point in my life I was packing my schedule to the brim and still filling my list of goals with more and more things I wanted to do. Sure, I was making up for lost time, but when was enough going to be enough?

I looked back over the last few years with great fondness. I had done what I needed to do: I rescued myself from my own rock bottom and built a new life. I worked hard, played hard, and enjoyed the hell out of it. While most of the experiences were wonderful, I had my challenges as well, and I needed those because the bad or uncomfortable times are what spurred me to grow; encouraged me to challenge myself, make changes, and look for better.

In Hollywood, a story isn't finished until it's wrapped up in a perfect little bow. The movie version of this story would have me ending with a prince charming, a fairy-tale wedding, and eventually, a baby. Though that would all happen for me, I just didn't know it at the time.

But in this moment, I thought about the journey to get myself here . . . to my picturesque fairy-tale cottage in my little corner of the world. I thought about everything I learned along the way, all the people that I had met and learned from, and the person I had become. When I left L.A., I was a lost girl in a storm of confusion, but now I was returning a different person. I was still me, of course, but I was a happier me. I was done caring about what anyone else thought of the life I chose to live.

I didn't have all the answers, and I didn't know yet what my future had in store. I knew only that wherever the road would take me, I would be okay, because I had found peace and finally made amends with the one person I never thought I'd be able to forgive: myself.

Still sitting in the chair, I looked through the trees and down into the city buzzing below, a city filled with excitement and hope. I was so grateful that this adorable place was where I would get to live.

I put my feet up on the table, crunching a few of the dried leaves that covered it. The two deer perked up their ears to look at the stranger in *their* yard. You see, when you live in this town, it's not unusual for just a bit of that movie magic to rub off on your world.

"I guess what they say is true," I smiled, looking at my two doe-eyed friends. "There really is no place like home."

ACKNOWLEDGMENTS

To my husband, Pasquale, and my daughter, Rainbow, for all your love and support.

To the always amazing Leslie Bruce. Thank you for your hard work, insight, wisdom, and talent, and of course, for all the good times!

To everyone at HarperCollins, thank you for the amazing opportunity. To Denise Oswald, for once again being such an amazing editor and helping me shape this story into what I wanted it to be. To Emma Janaskie, Trina Hunn, Joseph Papa, Kendra Newton, Michael Barrs, and Mumtaz Mustafa, for all your hard work and dedication.

To Matthew Elblonk, for your tireless support, for all your hard work in making this book happen, and for seeing it through to the end.

To Max Stubblefield, for all your hard work and support and for making this book possible.

To Sue Madore, for all your hard work and amazing ideas!

To Darin Frank and Jason Richman.

To Robert Earl, Amy Sadowski, and the staff at Planet Hollywood for providing me with an amazing home and an abundance of wonderful memories during my first few years in Vegas.

To Jerry Mitchell, Scott Zeiger, Brian Becker, Jayna Naegle, Nick

Kenkel, Kristin Johnson, and the entire cast and crew of *Peepshow*. What an amazing experience!

To Josh Strickland, Angel Porrino, Laura Croft, Claire Sinclair, Bridget Marquardt, Nick Carpenter, Stacy Burke, Jason Verona, Steve Flynn, Vic, MJ, Becca, Sal, Katie, Sergio, Ross, Breslin, Tracy, and everyone who worked on *Holly's World* for documenting and sharing some of the adventures included in this book.

To Lisa G., Steve Weiser, Carmine Scialfo, and the crew at *Extra*.

To Ryan Astamendi for the wonderful cover photo, and to Arianna Garcia and Francisco Pinto for the lovely makeup and hair.

To Gina, Virginie, Nadira, and Aminata for all your help while I was busy writing this book.

To my family and friends and Liberace's ghost.

To the city of Las Vegas. What a wonderful place to find oneself.

ABOUT THE AUTHOR

Holly Madison is the author of the #1 *New York Times* bestselling memoir *Down the Rabbit Hole.* She spent five seasons on the #1 rated E! hit reality show *The Girls Next Door* before starring in her own hit E! series, *Holly's World.* Holly divides her time between Los Angeles and Las Vegas with her husband and daughter.